C000212887

Celebrating Life

'With insight and eloquence, Graham Buxton offers a coherent and compelling case for the recovery of the original sacramental relation between creation and Creator, between human culture and divine creativity. Where Christianity has allowed dualism to divide the Kingdom of God from the kingdom of the world, Buxton argues for the recovery of an authentic biblical holism where Christ shines through even the broken edges of creation. This is incarnational theology at its best!'
Ray S. Anderson, Senior Professor of Theology and Ministry, Fuller Theological Seminary, California

'Too often the Christian view of culture has been dominated too much by Plato rather than Paul. In this impressive book Graham Buxton explores an authentic biblical engagement with the world on the wide canvas of literature, art and science, politics and work. It is a book where you will encounter the slow food movement, Harry Potter, Smashing Pumpkins and Richard Dawkins – but you will also find theological depth and lessons for ministry. *Celebrating Life* is a passionate plea for every disciple to live the Jesus way in the contemporary world.'
David Wilkinson, Principal of St John's College, Durham University.

'At last, a book on mission that takes the world as seriously as it takes the church. Buxton offers not just a clarion call to involvement in the world but a forensic analysis as to how we might engage in such a task. He does so with both scholarship in relation to the past and a lively imagination in terms of the contemporary world that surrounds us. There are not many books that I am asked to read and give a commendation for that I also think to myself, "I must get that book" – This is one of them!'
Martin Robinson, Together in Mission.

'An elegantly written and very rewarding book that skilfully deconstructs many of the outmoded dualisms that beset the mindsets of both Christendom and modernity. A stimulating contribution to an equally stimulating series.'
Colin Greene, Professor of Theological and Cultural Studies, Mars Hill Graduate School, Seattle.

Celebrating Life
Beyond the Sacred–Secular Divide

Graham Buxton

LONDON ● COLORADO SPRINGS ● HYDERABAD

Copyright © 2007 Graham Buxton

13 12 11 10 09 08 07   7 6 5 4 3 2 1

First published 2007 by Authentic Media
9 Holdom Avenue, Bletchley, Milton Keynes, Bucks, MK1 1QR, UK
1820 Jet Stream Drive, Colorado Springs, CO 80921, USA
OM Authentic Media, Medchal Road, Jeedimetla Village, Secunderabad 500
055, A.P., India
www.authenticmedia.co.uk

Authentic Media is a division of IBS-STL U.K., a company limited by
guarantee (registered charity no. 270162)

The right of Graham Buxton to be identified as the Author of this Work has
been asserted by him in accordance with the Copyright, Designs and Patents
Act 1988.

All rights reserved. No part of this publication may be reproduced,
stored in a retrieval system, or transmitted in any form or
by any means, electronic, mechanical, photocopying, recording or
otherwise, without the prior permission of the publisher or a licence
permitting restricted copying. In the UK such licences are issued by the
Copyright Licensing Agency.
90 Tottenham Court Road, London, W1P 9HE

British Library Cataloguing in Publication Data

A catalogue record for this book is available from the British Library

ISBN-13: 978-1-84227-507-8
ISBN-10: 1-84227-507-0

Adbusters flag reproduced by permission of Adbuster Reprints
reprints@adbusters.org

'Digging' from Death of a Naturalist by Seamus Heaney, published by
Faber and Faber Ltd.

Girl with a Pearl Earring reproduced by permission of the
Royal Picture Gallery Mauritshuis, The Hague

Scream reproduced by permission of Australasia Copyright Collecting
Society for Visual Artists. Licence@viscoly.com

Tretmühle woodcut image © Galerie Habdank. TRETMÜHLE,
1973 Walter Habdank.

Design by James Kessel for Scratch the Sky Ltd. (www.scratchthesky.com)
Print Management by Adare Carwin
Printed and bound in Great Britain by J.H. Haynes & Co., Sparkford

Contents

Faith in an Emerging Culture
Series Preface

It is common knowledge that Western culture has undergone major changes and we now find ourselves in an increasingly postmodern (or post-postmodern?), post Christendom, post industrial, post-just-about-anything-you-like world. The church now sits on the margins of western culture with a faith 'package deal' to offer the world that is perceived as out of date and irrelevant. How can we recontextualize the old, old story of the gospel in the new, new world of postmodernity? How can we fulfill our missional calling in a world that cannot any longer understand or relate to what we are saying? 'Faith in an Emerging Culture' seeks to imaginatively rethink Christian theology and practice in postmodern ways. It does not shrink from being explorative, provocative and controversial but is at the same time committed to remaining within the bounds of orthodox Christian faith and practice. Most readers will find things to agree with and things which will irritate them but we hope at very least to provoke fresh thought and theological/spiritual renewal.

Introduction and Acknowledgements

This is a book about discovering the fullness of our humanity. Scattered throughout the text is the word 'celebration,' which has everything to do with affirming the goodness of God's creation and of human life, including the myriad different ways in which human beings express that life in contemporary society, whether in poetry and politics, in movies and management, or in sculpture and science. This affirmation is not to be confined to a mental assent, a nod in the direction of contemporary culture, but involves a genuine engagement with others, so that the traffic between gospel and culture is not one-way but two-way. Christians have much to learn from those who live outside the borders of the church. Sadly, however, the lives of many are characterized by what has commonly been referred to as the 'sacred–secular divide syndrome,' in which a wedge is placed between the church and the world. The result is that the Christian life is often portrayed as being *above* the world, rather than *within* the world, an unholy and unwholesome dualism that not only robs Christians of the abundance of life that God has given to them (see John 10:10), but also causes others who might otherwise be attracted to Christianity to switch off completely.

While celebration is the central focus of this book, the reader will notice two other important themes. The first is the acknowledgement that a robust participation in God's world may lead some to compromise their faith, an ever-present reality within

Christian circles – this is presented in a number of places as the danger of assimilation. This calls for wisdom and discernment so that the church's prophetic cutting edge is not blunted. The second is the recognition of suffering and oppression in human society – celebration loses its meaning if it serves to distance Christians from the reality of struggle and pain. This calls for a redemptive concern coupled with the courage to get involved. To be a celebrating church is to be a prophetic church.

The opening two chapters serve as an introduction to the concept of the sacred–secular divide syndrome, in which Christians are exhorted to actively reconnect with culture and creation. This reconnection is then fleshed out in five chapters that look at literature, the creative arts (including music and movies), science, politics, and the world of business. Space unfortunately precludes a more extensive span of contemporary culture. The final chapter presents nine 'theses' covering three main areas – the Trinity and creation, contextual incarnation, and the nature of redemptive grace – giving important theological shape to the overriding theme of the celebration of life. The ultimate aim of the book is to help those who are trapped in a narrow understanding of the Christian faith, one that has been shaped by dualistic thinking, to relocate out of a less-than-joyful Christian life into one that resonates with the dance of God in the world, a theme that I first wrote about in my earlier book *Dancing in the Dark*.

Many people have helped me in the writing of this book. I would like to express my gratitude to numerous groups of students at Tabor College, Adelaide, and Fuller Theological Seminary in Pasadena, Los Angeles, who have sharpened my thinking as I explored some of these ideas with them. David Wilkinson helped in some of the rewriting of the first two chapters, and I would like to acknowledge his contribution in the early stages of the book. I am grateful to a number of colleagues at Tabor who read earlier drafts of various chapters, especially Mark Worthing and Brian Trainor. I would like to single out one of my doctoral students, Brad Bessell, with whom I enjoyed discussing some of my ideas, and who gave me new insights into the 'heavy metal' scene! On the publication and production side, Robin Parry, Paternoster's Editorial Director, has been a continual source of encouragement, and the team at Paternoster has been as helpful and supportive as ever.

My wife, Gill, and immediate family – including especially my grandchildren, through whom I have seen the world in fresh and delightful ways! – have been an inspiration to me in the development of the ideas in this book. I dedicate this book to them with my love, and with my prayer that their lives will be a shining witness to the God who calls us all to enter into the joy of life and living in the goodness of his creation.

Graham Buxton
Adelaide, January 2007

1

What Has the Gospel To Do with Culture?

A brief exploration of the concept of dualism from the perspectives of philosophy, history, theology, and culture

In recent years one of the most frequently debated topics of conversation in Christian circles has been the church's perceived failure to relate effectively to contemporary culture. Themes like 'engaging with our culture,' 'participating in the world,' 'relevance,' 'incarnational ministry,' 'connecting with culture,' 'missional church,' 'emerging church' and a host of other synonymous expressions abound in contemporary Christian literature. A number of books have specifically addressed the need for the Christian church to engage more authentically with today's culture, a culture that has been tagged 'postmodern,' often to the exclusion of any other label. Conferences and seminars overwhelm the Christian public, urging believers not only to become like the 'men of Issachar,' who 'understood the times' in which they lived,[1] but to *get involved* in society as salt and light, seeking to make a difference.

All this is well and good, and we are surely right to applaud attempts to get Christians out of church buildings and into the structures of contemporary society. It is the purpose of this book to suggest why this is important and to focus on particular areas where the task is greatest. At the same time, however, we must be careful that we do not lose what is good and rich in the tradition of the Christian church in our desire to immerse ourselves in the culture of the world. For there is the ever-present danger that as the Christian community explores ways in which it can become more involved in the world, assimilation creeps in and before we know what is happening we are beginning to live more as the world does in our laudable desire to identify with those who do not yet know what it means to live in the light and truth of God's love. This is a corrective that needs to be recognized by all who are concerned to see a greater rapprochement between gospel and culture today.

A well-documented example of the ease with which assimilation can infect the church is the notorious Nine O'clock Service, variously hailed in its time as a 'Damascus Road experience,' 'a highly disciplined congregational community,' and 'a sign of hope.' The Nine O'clock Service (NOS) was established in the mid-1980s under the covering of a thriving Anglican church in Sheffield, England, with ostensibly noble aims: to create a community of like-minded young Christians offering an alternative worship experience for those who were uncomfortable with conventional church services. Its theological beginnings were noncontroversial, grounded in spiritual discipline, prayer and a Wimber-inspired charismatic experience. Early features of the NOS were both exciting and confrontational, ranging from a contemporary music style that incorporated the 'acid house' style of the late 1980s, the incorporation of dance and multimedia in the services, and a Communion service that included Latin chants, incense and a more contemplative worship approach.

A significant and culturally relevant highlight of the worship at NOS was the 'Planetary Mass,' designed to increase awareness of ecological concerns. It was a visually exciting phenomenon, with a highly relevant message: it was time to restore the sense of the sacred to our technologically driven age and to get back in touch with nature. Another of the goals of the fast-growing young community was to challenge the mass consumption 'spirit of the age,' responding to the needs of those overwhelmed by materialism and the injustices of a greedy and self-serving society. It was heady stuff and, with large numbers flocking to NOS, the postmodern experiment was being hailed as a huge success. But cracks were beginning to appear in the structures, exposing deep flaws that contributed to its sensational downfall. The leadership had espoused a fluid and more theologically suspect approach to creation spirituality, drawing from the work of the American writer Matthew Fox, whose core beliefs are noticeably divergent from mainstream Christian doctrine.[2] In addition to these theological concerns, there were growing tensions as the NOS leadership developed a more authoritarian style. Church members were manipulated and abused – spiritually, emotionally, and sexually – especially following the relocation of NOS, and by 1995 the whole experiment had collapsed in a blaze of negative publicity.

Other examples could have been given of the way in which those with exemplary aims begin well but finish badly. The history of televangelism, for example, is littered with the stories of those who have been corrupted by sexual and financial scandal. Many others, of course, have stayed remarkably untainted by such disgraces, and Billy Graham stands out as one fine example of a godly man who walks the corridors of power without being corrupted by that power. The lesson we need to learn here is that Christians need to be accountable to one another (as Billy Graham himself has been throughout his Christian ministry) as they engage incarnationally in the world. Assimilation is a clear and present danger for all who seek to be a channel of influence for Christ in the world. While experimentation is good and should be encouraged, those who are anxious to carve out a new way of promoting the gospel cannot cut themselves off from the wise counsel of others or the healthy traditions of the past.

Life in separate compartments

This book, however, takes a more positive perspective as it addresses the age-old question first posed by the third-century Christian apologist Tertullian, 'What indeed has Athens to do with Jerusalem?' Tertullian was particularly concerned about the influence of the intellectual climate of the Greek academy on the Christian church as it sought to live out the gospel in the pagan world of his day. He was zealous in his defence of Christianity, and in his writings he roundly refuted heresy and proclaimed the truths of the gospel with great passion and conviction. In his desire to protect Christianity from both pagan influences and a watered-down version of the real thing, he had a profound influence upon later church fathers and theologians. We shall consider the historical context more fully later on in this chapter, but we may note here that Tertullian's words about Athens and Jerusalem can be broadened to refer not just to the intellectual and philosophical debates of his day, but also more widely to the relationship between contemporary culture and the Christian faith. What indeed do contemporary culture and the Christian church have in common? How dangerous is the cultural climate to the Christian gospel?

There are those who demand that the traffic should be one-way . . . even to the point of viewing the church as a 'safe haven' from the corruptions of the world, a view that derives in large part from the way Tertullian's question has been interpreted over the years by the church. It is a perspective that drives a wedge between the church and the world so firmly that little or no good can be seen in the world, which is perceived as being in the grip of evil and in need of redemption in every corner. One young man believed that he should get rid of all his non-Christian CDs shortly after he had become a Christian – he would be more than happy to have them in his collection now, but at the time he was encouraged to throw them all away, a decision he now regrets. Another actually went to the top of a large hill and threw his collection of 500 CDs over the top – rich pickings for any passers-by! These are not unusual stories in some sections of the Christian church. Now it may be that some CDs are sufficiently objectionable in their lyrics to deserve such treatment, but the point is that these two young men both experienced a sense of guilt that they were somehow hanging on to the things of the world by retaining their CDs.

The syndrome we are describing here is the 'sacred–secular divide,' and it has plagued the church throughout its life. Simply put, life is divided into two compartments, the holy and the unholy, or the sacred and the profane: for one compartment – obviously the first! – read 'church,' and for the other read the 'world.' It was said (somewhat unjustly) of the great scientist Michael Faraday that his life in the lab was a different world to his life as a lay preacher on a Sunday. One way in which this syndrome has been expressed over the years is in the distinction between clergy and lay in the life of the church. I am an ordained Anglican clergyman; as I prepared for training, I experienced family and friends voicing their views about the fact that I was now 'going into the church,' as if previously I was somehow 'out' of the church! At the same time some of my friends despaired that I was leaving the 'real' world to enter some kind of spiritual asylum. Yet which vocation is higher? The Christian artist who seeks to convey his faith through his art or the Christian minister who leads her congregation week by week? As we shall see throughout this book, and as is apparent in any careful survey of the relationship between the church and the world today, this sort of question applies to many different areas of life.

For example, there are some Christians who are deeply suspicious of those who are engaged in scientific research, convinced that there is an unbridgeable gap between Christian and scientific worldviews. For some, the debate is most heated in the creation–evolution controversy, fueled by those who insist on seeing the issue in terms of creation *or* evolution. Notice the divide: one or the other. Right is on one side, wrong on the other.

It was not so long ago that the movie-theatre and the dance floor were seen as being in the grip of 'the Evil One,' and some Christian groups prohibited their flock from darkening the doors of these demonic palaces! Again, the distinction is between holy versus unholy. We may live in more enlightened times today, but tensions remain among Christians about how enlightened we should allow ourselves to be as far as the entertainment world goes. Many centuries ago Plato voiced three objections to literature – that it is 'fictional and deficient in truth, that it leads to immorality, and that it is not useful and therefore a waste of time.'[3] On these grounds, he claimed, poetry and fictional literature were to be avoided at all costs by the church. As we shall see later, Plato's division between 'higher' and 'lower' reality critically influenced the way the church distinguished between the 'sacred' and the 'secular' in life, with regard not only to the creative arts generally, but to all of life.

6 *Celebrating Life*

Other areas are addressed in this book, such as Christianity
and the important social sectors of politics and business.
Schooled in management, I began my Christian life believing
that there was a yawning gap between Christianity and the way
the world goes about its business of life and living. This view
can lead to the dismissal of everything that the world has to
offer in terms of wisdom and experience, to the point that an
unreal dualism begins to shape the way life in the commercial
world is perceived: businessmen live according to secular
principles, and God's people live according to spiritual, or
sacred, principles. And so the divide between sacred and secular is reinforced in our minds, contributing to an unhealthy and,
at times, narrow superspirituality.

The word 'dualism' has now entered the discussion, and so
we need to expand our thinking as we consider its meaning,
both in the history of philosophy and in its cultural expressions.
In their book, *The Transforming Vision*, Walsh and Middleton
define dualism as 'a split-vision world view.'[4] As we shall see
later in this chapter, dualism has its origins in Greek philosophy,
with its sharp distinction between the body and the soul. The
early church affirmed the goodness of creation, but continually
stumbled over the Greek dualistic worldview, resulting in an
unhealthy and unbiblical separation between spirit and matter.

Michael Wittmer helpfully points out that Christians are, in
fact, metaphysical dualists, but only in the sense that they
believe in a *horizontal* distinction between God and his creation.
There is an ontological chasm between the infinite Creator and
his finite creation. However, many draw their line in the wrong
place, living 'as if there is a vertical line separating two
contrasting parts of God's creation.'[5] The result is a metaphysical dualism between spirit and matter, a worldview also
associated with the seventeenth-century French philosopher
René Descartes, who formulated his theory of mind–body
dualism, or two distinct principles of reality in the universe.

The consequence of this way of thinking is to split reality into
two compartments – the holy and the profane, sacred and
secular – distinct and in opposition to each other. As we have
already stated, it is a view that is all too common within the
Christian community, with a number of important implications.

Firstly, it often leads to a fragmentation that dismisses what happens 'outside the church' as somehow unrelated to God and his kingdom: it is the all-too-common 'ostrich' mentality. Secondly, it may lead to a triumphalism which ignores or neglects what is happening 'in the world,' with the result that the mission of the church is frustrated: Christians who think like this simply do not see the need to get involved in the world.

A third potential consequence of the compartmentalization implicit in dualistic thinking is an approach to mission which seeks to bring 'those out there' into the safe haven of the church, reinforcing the split vision between the 'in' and the 'out.' Frost and Hirsch define this as the 'attractional' flaw in the Christendom-mode church. Without in any way dismissing the importance of the church being attractive to unbelievers, they argue that too much energy and time is devoted to getting its internal features right in order to draw people out from their own context and into the programs and public meetings of the church.[6] Throughout their book, the two authors explore the implications not only of the attractional flaw in the DNA of the church, but also of two other flaws, which they label dualistic and hierarchical. Arguing that these three flaws are deeply embedded features throughout the universal church, they offer an alternative missional ecclesiology that embraces an incarnational orientation, a messianic spirituality, and an apostolic form of leadership, so reversing the three 'mistakes' of the Christendom-mode church.

A fourth consequence of dualism is that it creates the false impression that all is 'light' in the church, and all is 'darkness' in the world, so it is best to steer clear of the world and its perverse influences. This view is, as Tom Wright states, 'essentially immature, inviting Christians to embrace an oversimplified world, all black and white with no shades of gray.'[7]

Finally, dualism fails to appreciate the inherent goodness in all that God had created, leading to (as well as arising from) mistaken and false ideas not only about the nature of God, but also about the nature of creation and salvation. Rikki Watts asks the question, 'What does it mean to be saved?' . . . to which he replies that you cannot really talk about salvation until you talk about creation, because to be saved is to live out the love of God concretely with real people in this life. So, 'you can't get away from physicality.'⁸ This has affected the way Christians have viewed questions of the care of the environment, the nature of being human and a future hope. Too often dualism has suggested that at death Christian 'souls' will be liberated from this earthly existence to the safe haven of a type of ghostly heaven.

Tertullian's question about Athens and Jerusalem reflects a pervasive dualism that is characteristic of many periods of Western culture. As we have already stated, the Christian church has not been immune from this dualistic paradigm of reality – and life – and has in fact contributed in large part to its continued presence as a controlling paradigm in the thought-forms of both Christian and non-Christian alike. However, recent postmodern insights have been fertile in suggesting a more holistic theology of the church's engagement with, and participation in, contemporary society. This perspective affirms that God has created a good world, in which he is intimately and necessarily involved, and that his presence is to be celebrated in every area where men and women are active in social, political, cultural and educational discourse and behavior. Sadly, the church has too often retreated from the world, adopting either a 'siege mentality' or an unwholesome triumphalism, both of which have their roots in dualistic thinking.

Of course, as Christians rightly insist, there is a distinction to be made between the kingdom of God and the kingdom of this world. However, at times it is hard to distinguish Christians from everyone else, which was not the case with the early disciples of Jesus, who turned the world they knew upside down. As Christians we are not meant to blend into society, unnoticed and indistinct from everyone else; we are called to be salt and light, making a difference in the world. The following true story from Zimbabwe illustrates this well. While transporting psychiatric patients from Harare to Bulawayo, the bus driver stopped at a roadside shebeen for a few beers. When he got back to his vehicle, he found it empty, with the twenty patients nowhere to be seen. Realizing the trouble he was in if the truth were uncovered, he halted his bus at the next bus stop and offered lifts to those in the queue. Letting twenty people board, he then shut the doors and drove straight to the Bulawayo psychiatric hospital, where he hastily handed over his 'charges,' warning the nurses that they were particularly excitable. Staff removed the furious passengers to wards; it was three days later that suspicions were aroused by the consistency of stories from the twenty. As for the real patients: nothing more has been heard of them and they have apparently blended comfortably back into Zimbabwean society!

So there is a *duality* to be acknowledged. Jesus said: 'Whoever follows me will never walk in darkness, but will have the light of life' (John 8:12). There is light and darkness, right and wrong, good and evil. But what has happened – and we need to examine the historical and philosophical foundations for such an interpretation – is that all that is light, right, and good has been identified with one side of 'reality' (= the church) and all that is dark, wrong, and evil with the other side of 'reality' (= the 'world'). The result is that many Christians have adopted a 'siege mentality,' hauling up the drawbridge so that there is little real intercourse between the church and the world. Instead of *celebrating* all that is good in the world, some Christians view the secular world as unspiritual, even to be avoided.

Two-way traffic

The realization that there *is* a distinction between the kingdom of God and the kingdom of darkness is, however, important. Rather than *separating* Christians from the world, such a distinction should encourage the church to demonstrate to others the freedom of the gospel. Sadly, many Christians display a lifestyle that reflects standards that are far from those of the gospel. To be a Christian is to be involved in the world, not separate from it, but involved as a distinctively Christian person. But it is also to recognize that there is much in the world that is good and holy and beautiful, which Christians can appreciate and from which they can learn. In other words, the traffic between church and world is *two-way*, not one-way. We need to recognize both the freedom of the gospel as gift to all people, manifested and transmitted through the church, and the joy of life and living which is also God's gift to all people (see John 10:10), present and available in many dimensions of what has too often been disparaged as 'secular life.' Consider the following excerpt from George Eliot's *Adam Bede*. Five men are busy in a workshop, and one of them, Adam Bede, addresses his brother Seth:

> Nay, Seth, lad; I am not for laughing at no man's religion. Let 'em follow their consciences, that's all. Only I think it 'ud be better if their consciences 'ud let 'em stay quiet i' the church – there's a deal to be learnt there. And there's such a thing as being over-speritial; we must have something beside Gospel i' this world. Look at the canals, an' th' aqueducs, an' th' coal-pit engines, and Arkwright's mills there at Cromford; a man must learn summat beside Gospel to make them things, I reckon. But t' hear some o' them preachers, you'd think as a man must be doing nothing all 's life but shutting 's eyes and looking what's a-going on inside him. I know a man must have the love o' God in his soul, and the Bible's God's word. But what does the Bible say? Why, it says as God put his sperrit into the workman as built the tabernacle, to make him do all the carved work and things as wanted a nice hand. And this is my way o' looking at it: there is the sperrit o' God in all things and at all times – week-day as well as Sunday – and i' the great works and inventions, and i' the figuring and the mechanics. And God helps us with our head-pieces and our hands as well as with our souls; and if a man does bits o' jobs out o' working hours – builds a oven for 's wife to save her from going to the bakehouse, or scrats at his bit o' garden and makes two potatoes grow instead o' one, he's doing more good, and he's just as near to God, as if he was running after some preacher and a-praying and a-groaning.[9]

More serious are the words of Archbishop Oscar Romero, shortly before his violent death for being 'too politically involved' among the poor of Latin America: '[I have been learning] a beautiful and harsh truth, that the Christian faith does not separate us from the world but immerses us in it; that the church, therefore, is not a fortress set apart from the city, but a follower of the Jesus who loved, worked, struggled, and died in the midst of the city.'[10]

In his book *Spirituality and Liberation*, Robert McAfee Brown is adamant that a life of personal spirituality and a life devoted to political liberation are not to be divorced from each other: they are in fact very much intertwined. To be spiritual is to be liberationist, and vice versa. He offers some variations on the theme of the 'Great Fallacy,' the fallacy that life is divided into two areas or compartments . . . and if we know what's good for us, we'll keep it that way! For example:

> IRATE PROTESTANT LAYPERSON: Pastor, you've got no right to bring the election into the pulpit. It's not your job to deal with political issues. Just remember, religion and politics don't mix.
>
> CALM PARISHIONER: We all had a truly spiritual experience being off in the woods on retreat, far away from all the mess of the world we live in most of the time. For the first time in months, I felt really close to God.
>
> TROUBLED TEENAGER: I've got problems. What do I do about drugs? Is sex okay? How am I going to get a job when I get out of high school? I'm tired of getting dragged to church to sing boring hymns and pray to God.[11]

Brown offers a sample list of opposites that we encounter in the real world, in no particular order.[12]

sacred vs. secular
prayer vs. politics
faith vs. works
withdrawal vs. engagement
church vs. world
eternity vs. time
theory vs. practice
religion vs. ethics
soul vs. body
personal vs. social
spirit vs. flesh
holy vs. profane
heaven vs. earth

otherworldly vs. this-worldly
divine vs. human
meditation vs. agitation
mysticism vs. humanism
saint vs. sinner
spiritual vs. material
contemplation vs. action
God vs. humanity
inner vs. outer
love vs. justice
creeds vs. deeds
priest vs. prophet
evangelism vs. social action

abstinence vs. sex	liturgy vs. legislation
immortality vs. resurrection	Jesus the Christ vs. Jesus of
Greek vs. Hebrew	Nazareth
'verticalism' vs. 'horizontalism'	theonomy vs. autonomy
transcendence vs. immanence	spirituality vs. liberation

The point is that whatever words we use, we keep on dividing life up into two realms. *We have a dualistic mentality.*

Background to dualism

In order to understand the background to the idea of dualism, which has given rise to the sacred–secular divide discernible in contemporary culture, we need to delve into Hellenistic philosophical thinking, with particular emphasis on Plato. In an extensive series of volumes on dualism, Fontaine argues that dualism exists 'where there are two systems or concepts or principles or groups of people or even worlds that are utterly opposed and cannot be reduced to each other . . . One of the two is always thought to be of a much higher quality than the other, so much so that one pole is always seen as distinctly inferior, fit to be neglected, repudiated, or even destroyed.'[13]

Many assume that the concept of dualism has its beginnings in the ideology of the Persian philosopher Zoroaster. Fontaine disputes this, insisting that dualism as such cannot be traced to a historical origin. For him, it has always existed: it is not so much a historical phenomenon as an *anthropological* one:

It occurs in every conceivable field of life, in religion and philosophy, in history and politics, in literature and art, in social relationships and in personal life. Wherever we are looking, we see people grappling with or suffering from or trying to accommodate themselves to unbridgeable oppositions. We are in the presence of a general human phenomenon; since it fundamentally forms part of our human make-up, we are entitled to call it anthropological. The origin of dualism is not to be found in history or mythology, in philosophy or religion (not even in the dualistic Iranian religion), but in the human condition.[14]

The term 'dualism' was actually coined at the beginning of the eighteenth century in the writings of Thomas Hyde, a professor of Hebrew at Oxford University. He, like many others, referred to the ancient Persians, especially their notion of two principles, one *eternal* and one *created*. But the term can be most easily understood with reference to the metaphysical ideas of Plato, the great Greek philosopher who was born into an upper-class family in Athens in 427 BC. During the early years of his life he became very much aware of the reality of political and civil strife in Greece, particularly between the two important cities of Athens and Sparta, and also within the cities themselves. He reacted strongly against the tyrannical rule of Athens over her subjects, and he eventually saw the decline of the Athenian Empire.

Plato was also deeply troubled by the moral relativism prevailing in Greece, summed up in Protagoras' famous statement: 'A man is a measure of all things: of what is, that it is, and of what is not, that it is not.' The idea of 'each man for himself' hardly encouraged people to live together in harmony and unity! So both politically and personally life in Greece was not something to be admired, leading the philosophers of the day, especially Socrates – Plato's mentor – to ask: How then do we know what is 'Good'? How can we achieve the highest good, or *summum bonum*? What are the virtues that will enable people to live together without strife?

Plato was not an activist – he was a thinker. One of his major goals in his philosophical thinking was to try and articulate a system, or theory, which would contribute to the achievement of good government, which is the primary thrust of *The Republic*.[15] But to do that he had to come to grips with the nature of reality and truth, which is the essence of metaphysics. This was, for Plato, the highest form of inquiry, higher even than ideas about God. Plato's own ideas about God were confusing – sometimes he seemed to be monotheistic, at other times polytheistic, even pantheistic. What really interested him was the nature of ultimate reality that was, as for Greek philosophy generally, *impersonal* rather than personal. The idea was that beyond and above the idea of God was this notion of pure 'perfection' that was far removed from the reality of the known physical world.

In the sixth century BC, the philosopher Thales, who lived on the eastern shore of the Aegean Sea, suggested that all reality consisted of water. What he was trying to do was to identify the one unifying metaphysical principle that held everything together. The modern philosopher R. M. Hare writes: 'We find in these early thinkers the beginnings of the urge to reconcile the 'One' and the 'Many', which is a recurring theme throughout Greek philosophy, above all in Plato. There confronts us a multitude of phenomena in the world as it presents itself to our senses; cannot some unifying principle be found to bring order into this chaos?'[16]

In other words, is there some constant, unchanging principle, above and beyond the material world, which gives some sort of order and meaning to the changing restlessness of the known world around us? Here we have to probe a little more deeply into the background to Plato's thought. Two philosophers who influenced Plato greatly in his search for a solution to this problem were Parmenides and Heraclitus. Parmenides taught a *universal unity of being*: Being alone exists, eternal and unchangeable. As you look around, you may see everything changing and in a state of flux, but that is not as it really is, for that is only as it *appears*. On the other side, we have Heraclitus, the 'philosopher of *eternal change*,' which he expressed in analogical terms as the continuous flow of a river which always renews itself. So, on the one side, we have a philosophical system that is grounded in the unity of *being*, and on the other side a system that focuses on a multitude of phenomena in a state of *becoming*. It is the known as the classic dualism between the 'One' and the 'Many.'

To the logical philosophy of Parmenides, Plato added strains of mystical thought drawn from Pythagoras and from the 'mystery religion' known as Orphism, which was current in Greece at the time. This mystical strain was dualistic in presenting a separation between mind/soul and body, and would therefore have been influential in Plato's attempt to resolve the tension between the idea of reality as unchangeably one and the eclectic, many-sided changing world of appearances. The point is that Plato accepted this idea of a split world, and much of his philosophical energy was devoted to achieving some sort of synthesis between these two worlds, the 'One' and the 'Many,' between the constant and the changing, between being and becoming. 'He found it . . . by postulating two worlds, a world of sense, always in flux, and a unified world of Ideas, not available to our senses but only to thought, which alone are fully knowable.'[17] In *The Republic* these two worlds are defined in terms of the higher world of knowledge, on the one hand, and the lower world of opinion on the other. In Plato's thinking, the dimension of knowledge is subdivided into pure thought or intelligence and mathematical reasoning, which alone are capable of apprehending the intelligible world of Forms; and the dimension of opinion is subdivided into belief and illusion, which reflect the nature of the physical world in which we live.[18]

In order to explain this, Plato presents us with his famous *simile of the cave*. The simile may be summarized simply as follows. Imagine a cave, running a long way underground, in which there are prisoners, who have been bound since they were children in such a way that they can look only directly ahead at a wall in front of them. Behind them a fire casts shadows of objects that are paraded behind them – and invisible to them because they cannot turn their heads. For these bound people, reality is represented by the shadows on the wall rather than the actual objects themselves.[19]

Ian Bruce helpfully summarizes what has come to be known as Plato's 'Theory of Forms' as follows.[20]

The theory basically postulates the existence of a level of reality or 'world' inhabited by the ideal or archetypal forms of all things and concepts. Thus a form exists for objects like tables and rocks, and for concepts such as beauty and justice . . . The forms are eternal and changeless, but enter into a partnership with changeable matter, to produce the objects and examples of concepts, we perceive in the temporal world. These are always in a state of becoming, and may participate in a succession of forms. The ever-changing temporal world can thus, only be the source of opinion. Plato likens the opinions derived from our senses, to the perception of shadows of real objects, cast upon the wall of a cave.[21] True knowledge however, is the perception of the archetypal forms themselves, which are real, eternal, and

unchanging. Whilst the forms are invisible to the eye, our souls
have participated in the eternal world of forms prior to being
incarnate in a physical body, and retain a memory of them . . . All
learning, Plato maintains, is but recollection of what our soul
already knows.

At the human or anthropological level, the dualism between
body and soul is fundamental to Plato's philosophy. Essentially
the soul or mind belongs to the higher pure realm, and the body
belongs to the lower realm of nature. We see here the
development of the sacred–secular divide that was to pervade
much of Western thought post-Plato.

But what of the *religious* dimensions in Plato's philosophical
thinking? Firstly, Plato's 'Good' is located within his higher
realm of Ideas or Forms. Some people think that he equates the
'Good' with deity, but Plato is not at all clear in his definition of
God. Perhaps God is the 'Demiurge,' who moulded pre-existent
matter into the world as we know it – a being totally dependent
upon the 'Good,' which is itself utterly self-sufficient and
perfect. However, some have suggested that Demiurge cannot
really be identified with God as such, since he is inferior to
Ideas. For Plato, Demiurge is eternal alongside both the 'Good'
and physical matter. In summary, Plato's religious understanding is ambiguous and confusing!

Sanders suggests that Plato 'distinguished between a personal God (the Demiurge) and an impersonal principle (the
Good) and then elevated the principle above the personal in the
order of being.'[22] This would certainly be in keeping with the
rational elements of Greek philosophy. Whatever our understanding here, the important point to derive from all this is that
Plato's system of philosophy led to a way of thinking which
interpreted creaturely life in the lower world as inferior and
evil; Greek philosophers talked about the body as the 'prison
house of the soul,' and in *Phaedo* Plato viewed the body as that
which defiles the soul and impedes the soul's knowledge of the
divine. The higher world (the world of Ideas) was perfect, pure,
and the goal of human attainment.

It is worth noting here that Greek philosophy emphasized
the superiority of *unchanging, timeless, unfeeling* reality.

Changeableness, temporality, and emotion were considered to be the characteristic features – negative ones, too – of the lower physical world, the world of creatures, of you and me. Plato's idea of God – whatever that was – corresponded to the superior, higher world with the inevitable implications of a God who is unchanging, timeless, and unfeeling. To argue for any other sort of God was – for the Greeks, and for others in subsequent centuries, including many influential Christian thinkers – to argue for a God who is no longer perfect, and therefore no longer God.

What the early church thought

The *biblical* presentation of reality is totally at odds with the Greek ideas associated with Plato; indeed the Hebrew worldview is much more robust and holistic than anything that the Greeks had to offer us. Nancy Scott reminds us that the Hebrew mindset was quite different from the Greek mindset:

> The Hebrew view of the world was grounded in the earthy, material reality in which they lived, and yet it was overshadowed at every point with spiritual truth. In contrast to the Greek view that the highest human experience was knowledge, to a Hebrew scholar like Paul, moral beauty and righteousness was the highest human experience. There was no need to separate experience into spiritual and material, as everything they did or thought, from their perspective, included both. The process of broken humans being transformed into the glory of holiness, to which we would ultimately be completely conformed in the Kingdom, was the hope of Paul's gospel.[23]

The implications of this Pauline perspective are profound:

> Perhaps we can reclaim in the arts and sciences the beauty of creative expression for which God created us. We can cease to frame everything as either/or, and enjoy the many gifts God has given us in our earthly, material world. Perhaps we will value more firmly the creation itself, and become better stewards of the

natural resources God has given. We can better see that the material world is imbued with the splendour and majesty of its Creator, and we can rejoice in His presence in all these things. But most of all, perhaps we can have a voice to communicate the relevance of the gospel to this dying generation.[24]

The Jews have always maintained a robust affirmation of the created world. Indeed, as Walter Brueggemann has argued, the Old Testament has as a central theme the importance to God of the land. McAfee Brown comments: 'The affirmation of God as Creator is a late development in Jewish reflection about God, but it is an affirmation that has persisted, centrally and powerfully, ever since.'[25]

But this is not how the Christian church viewed reality over the centuries. The primary culprit is Augustine, notwithstanding all the good and noble things that he contributed to Christian theology. A number of important historical figures may be identified with regard to the impact of Greek thinking on the Christian church.[26] Aristotle, for example, was concerned not so much with the nature of God, but with the idea of change and movement. This led him to propose a First Cause of all motion, what he called the 'unmoved mover' who sets all things into motion. Such a 'mover' must by definition be itself unmoved if it is to be the perfect 'first cause.' Consistent with Greek thinking, such an 'unmoved mover' was unchanging and unchangeable, a pure contemplative being, apathetic towards the world.

The great Jewish thinker Philo tried to reconcile biblical teaching with Greek philosophical ideas. He adopted a hierarchical cosmology with three levels: the unknowable, transcendent God at the top; then a knowable realm, full of knowable intermediaries; and at the bottom the knowable realm of matter. While not as speculative as Plato in his ontological scheme, Philo's legacy was still strongly philosophical, even though he accepted that God could have an effect upon his creation, a creation which he actually brought into being (as distinct from Plato's belief in matter as eternal).

Tertullian, as we saw at the beginning of this chapter, sought to break the hold of Greek philosophy on the development of

Christian theology, especially in his insistence that God was not an abstract deity, distant from his creation, but one who interacted with his world. Christianity was, for him, 'basically a counter-cultural movement, which refused to allow itself to be contaminated in any way by the mental or moral environment in which it took root.'[27] Yet, as Sanders observes, he struggled with the idea of a God who suffers. Origen taught the immutability of God and, in contrast to Tertullian, partially accommodated to the Hellenistic worldview. His view of the incarnation reflected others before him: only the human side of Jesus suffered; his divinity remained untouched. Other biblical references to the Passion of God are explained by Origen as anthropomorphisms and were not to be taken literally.

So the early church's understanding of the relationship between God and creation was, in Sanders' words, 'a mixed bag of Greek metaphysics and biblical faith.' While early church prayers and liturgies expressed the relationship between God and his people, more abstract notions of God began to inform the thinking of the Christian church. It is here that we need to turn to Augustine (AD 354–430) who became interested in Neoplatonism (under the influence of Plotinus (AD 204–70) and then followed Manicheism for nine years.[28] However, Augustine began to distrust their claim to access Absolute Truth by rational means and in AD 384 went to Rome where he came under the influence of Bishop Ambrose (AD 339–97). It was here that Augustine accepted the Christian faith (and church) as that for which he had been searching.

Augustine held that inner reflection/contemplation was greater than pursuing sensual gain. In fact, his ascetic denial of his sensual instincts may have come largely as result of his conversion experience and regret at his past life (he was an incorrigible womanizer, and fathered a child out of marriage). Yet ascetic denial would also continue to recur in his thinking and form a major part of his theological worldview. After his common-law wife's death he returned to Africa in AD 388 where he was coerced into eventually becoming Bishop of Hippo. Augustine's 'otherworldly' focus prioritized the spiritual over the physical: in *The City of God* he spoke of the rational soul 'inhabiting' the body.[29] By primarily focusing on the

spiritual realm he reinforced in the Christian church a negative
view of human sexuality and an unhealthy contempt for the
body.

Following Augustine, the shape of Christian theology was
typically characterized by a worldview which put a wedge
between the spiritual and the physical, and the Christian church
was set on a course which posited the church *over and above* the
world. The church as an ecclesiastical institution was seen as the
repository of grace, and all of nature was excluded from the
realm of grace. The picture we have here is that of grace *versus*
nature: 'The spiritual realm of ecclesiastical affairs was regarded
as superior to the natural world and was thus more highly valued.
This elevation of one dimension of creaturely life at the neglect
and expense of the other was, in effect, a form of idolatry.'[30]

Options for the church

This wedge between nature and grace was critical because it
opened up the way for the secular, natural realm to assume
dominance in Western culture in the periods of the Renaissance
and the Enlightenment. Pit grace *against* nature, and sooner or
later nature was going to climb into the driving seat. In other
words, the dualism that pervaded the life of the church 'opened
the door to the triumph of secularism as the guiding spirit of
Western culture.'[31] The tables were turned. This had implications for the way the created world was viewed. Instead of the
world, and created matter, being relegated to an inferior role in
the order of reality (as in earlier Platonic dualistic thinking), the
growth in humanism and the scientific worldview gave creation
a place centre-stage. The world was no longer something to be
avoided but to be embraced. Creation was seen as something
significant, but – and this, of course, is the legacy of modernity
– its significance was grounded in its being viewed as a world
to be mastered and exploited rather than appreciated as God's
good creation. This left the church out on a limb. Humanism
pushed the church out on the margins, where it was left,
hopefully, to disappear from the scene of life . . . an irrelevancy
in a world that had now come of age.

But, as Tom Wright asks, 'Is the church to sit on the margins of the world, offering a salvation that is an escape, which seems to leave the world to go its own way?'[32] Is that the biblical view? There are some who think precisely this, arguing that the church offers a safe haven from the corruptions of the world. This, of course, buys heavily into the dualistic paradigm we have been talking about. Wright offers another scenario. If we *do* feel that we, as Christians, have something to say, how are we to say it? 'Are we to leap with both feet into the political pit of snakes, issuing denunciations to the left and (more likely) right, and getting ourselves a bad name for mingling religion and politics . . .?'[33] Wright's response is helpful. Rather than going down the road of personal piety (the way of escape) or political activism, our approach must be based on a realistic understanding of the way the world really is.

Wright suggests that there are two options that most people follow. Either they go down the dualist path, 'cutting the world in half,' or they try to put everything back together again, and become monists. We have already looked at some of the problems associated with dualism. What about monism? That way, too, is unbiblical. The monist either sees the world as one big materialistic 'machine' to be analyzed and dissected scientifically, or treats the cosmos as one great integrated mystery, identified with God himself. No dualism here, separating the spiritual and the physical, because all is one in the new pantheistic worldview. The Bible, however, presents us not only with a view of creation that is far richer and far more wonderful and mysterious than merely the sum of its parts, but also with a theology of creation that makes a clear distinction between God and the created order. There is plainly no room for monism here.

So what path are we to follow? Wright's answer is radical. The church needs to repent of the narrow dualism that avoids any form of genuine contact with the world, a suffocating dualism that treats God's creation as intrinsically contaminating rather than intrinsically wholesome and good; and it needs to repent of a monism that fails to clearly differentiate between God and his world, and between good and evil.

The problem that the church has fallen into over the centuries, as we have seen, is that it has too easily and uncritically identified evil with the natural, material world. This is the Augustinian, Neoplatonic legacy. If the world is as bad as some say it is, then the sooner we get back to the good old dualist days, the better! This return to dualism could be one of two varieties: on the one hand, we may adopt a dry, dusty form of dualism, preaching good old evangelistic sermons, and avoiding any contaminating contact with such topics as politics or sex. The overriding concern in this form of dualism is to ensure that everything done is kept under control within clear and narrow guidelines. As an alternative to this over-cerebral, intellectual and wordy 'dry' dualism, Tom Wright offers what he calls 'wet' dualism (borrowing some terminology from *The Pilgrim's Regress* by C. S. Lewis), which presents us with an over-simplified black-and-white sort of world. In this world the *true* church consists of the children of light, and the rest of the world lies in thick darkness, in which demons abound and are in an incessant war with angels![34]

And if dualism is not a very good option, then monism doesn't offer anything much better. In monism, God and the world get all confused to the point where the difference between good and evil is denied. This is the 'if you can't beat them, join them' approach! It is the way of *assimilation*. Now that is the danger into which many Christians fall; if we agree that cutting ourselves off from the world is not the right way to go, then let's swing the pendulum in the other direction and go out and enjoy all that God's good creation has to offer us. Let's celebrate!

Where is the danger? Well, the danger is that you fail to offer any theological critique: '[the church] is so concerned to be *like* the world that it ends up having nothing to say *to* the world. It is so concerned, to put it charitably, not to offend the noble pagan, that it refuses to call evil by its proper name and finishes by declaring that evil is simply a variant form of goodness.'[35]

So we need to beware the twin dangers of *dualism* and *assimilation*. In our ministry in the world, as we seek to understand the times in which we live – like the men of Issachar in 1 Chronicles 12:32 – we need to be careful that we do not too readily succumb to the seductive temptations of the world and jump out of the frying pan of dualism into the fires of assimilation. As we noted at the beginning of this chapter, we will need to recognize this temptation as we concentrate throughout this book on the pressing need to dismantle the sacred–secular divide that permeates much Christian thinking today.

2

Connecting with Culture and Creation

*An appeal for a positive, yet discerning, attitude
towards culture and creation*

In Chapter 1, we focused on the pervasive influence of dualism
in society today. The phenomenon is given its most recognizable
expression in the term 'sacred–secular divide,' which distinguishes sharply between the Christian church and contemporary
culture, to such an extent that some people – whether or not
they have Christian convictions – believe that it is best to keep
them as far apart from each other as possible. Of course, in
practice, that is hardly possible, especially if we are mindful of
Jesus' calling for his followers to be the light of the world (Matt.
5:14). But, as we have seen, the concept is sufficiently entrenched
in some segments of the church for us to give it serious
consideration. In order to do so, we need to understand what is
meant by the idea of culture.

Hoebel defines culture as 'the integrated system of learned
behaviour patterns which are characteristic of the members of a
society and which are not the result of biological inheritance.'[36]
So culture is a *social* concept, reflecting patterns and rules that
arrive through consensus over a period of time. Walsh and
Middleton argue that when we look at culture, we are looking
at the pieces of a puzzle, reflecting the full range of human
activity: 'We can see the functioning of assorted institutions, like
the family, government, schools, cultic institutions (churches,
temples, synagogues and so on) and businesses. We can observe
different modes of recreation, different sports, transportation

and eating habits. Each culture develops a unique artistic and musical life. All these cultural activities are pieces of a puzzle.'[37] However, not only is culture the product of human beings . . . human beings are the product of culture. Each of us develops throughout life within the context of our own culture. We make decisions that, more often than not, reflect the norms of our culture, and dress, speak, and eat according to cultural expectations and norms that have been established over many years. Rodney Clapp argues that, for this reason, we are all sectarians, because 'whatever we may consider the core of our identity, all of us learn that identity through the language and practices of one or another culture.'[38] These cultural norms are strengthened in the media, particularly through television, film, video, and popular journals and magazines, all of which not only convey powerful messages that reflect the prevailing culture, but also – by their very power – help to influence and therefore *shape* contemporary culture.

This means that culture may at times reflect patterns of belief and behavior that are positive and good and that correspond to Christian standards of truth and ethical living, while simultaneously propagating ideas that may be very far from these ideals. For example, today's teen magazines and TV 'soaps' drill home to young girls the creed that you need to be thin to be beautiful. These messages are presented not as a response to the growing problem we have with obesity in Western society, but as part of a corporate-driven bombardment to sell cosmetics and clothes, with the aim of stimulating purchases of new products to keep corporate shareholders happy. The consequent 'religion of shopping' has become so

pervasive that a counter movement known as 'culture jamming' – inspired by the Vancouver-based magazine *Adbusters* – aims to be for today's generation what civil rights, feminism and environmental rights activism were for previous generations. One classic example was a campaign a few years ago that featured the American flag, the stars and stripes, in which the stars were replaced by rows of miniature corporate logos, symbolizing all that the 'culture jammers' felt was wrong with America!

Of course, it is all too easy to present a totally negative picture of contemporary culture, but it is as well to be clear in our minds about the dangers of assimilation as we tackle the prevalence of the sacred–secular divide syndrome in society today. The key word here is discernment. As we deliberately, enthusiastically, and (in the light of the gospel command to be 'lights of the world') faithfully get involved in God's world, celebrating his goodness in creation, we need great wisdom, particularly when some church members display lifestyles and values that are indistinguishable from those who live around them. As we saw in Chapter 1, there is a duality to be acknowledged even as we seek to expose the pervasiveness of dualism. The seductions of this world are subtle and dangerous, as the prophet Isaiah acknowledged many years ago:

Woe to those who call evil good and good evil,
who put darkness for light and light for darkness,
who put bitter for sweet and sweet for bitter.
Woe to those who are wise in their own eyes
And clever in their own sight.[39]

As we explore the different ways in which dualism has penetrated the relationship between Christianity and various elements of contemporary society, the importance of discernment will emerge as a critical faculty in order to ensure that the gospel of Christ is not compromised in the commendable desire for relevance. Two words that are helpful in describing a proper understanding of Christian ministry are *faithfulness* and *relevance*: these are the two essential requirements that govern the ministry of the church, whether in far-flung corners of the globe or in the immediate neighborhood. Our ministry needs to reflect the ministry of Christ in the world: 'As the Father has sent me, I am sending you,' said Jesus to his disciples, as he breathed on them the empowering Holy Spirit (John 20:21). We dare not lose our center in the unchanging Word of God. However, at the same time, we dare not lose touch with the world that Christ came to save.[40]

Since arguing in recent years for a perspective that embraces both faithfulness and relevance, I have come to think that relevance may in fact be too weak a stance in the church's relationship with culture. Relevance suggests a reactive posture that is not at all in keeping with the more proactive injunctions implicit in the gospel command to be salt and light in the world. With this in mind, it may be more appropriate to speak of the church as a *prophetic* voice in the world, communicating a vision of the kingdom of God that challenges the norms and patterns of behavior that characterize contemporary society.

The relationship between Christ and culture

Throughout the ages Christians have understood the relationship between Christianity and culture in different ways. This understanding shapes the earthly life of Christians, and plays a fundamental role in relationships among Christians, and between Christians and non-Christians. In a series of lectures given in the United States in 1949 on Christian social ethics,[41] H. Richard Niebuhr described the relationship between Christianity and civilization as an 'enduring problem' that has reared its head through all the Christian centuries, from Jesus' day right through to modern times. In his ministry on earth, Jesus called people to repent of their self-centred ways and to embrace the kingdom of God, personified in himself. As the Word made flesh, he was uncompromising in his radical pronouncements. Many people felt uncomfortable in his presence. Yet, equally, others felt wonderfully comforted, accepted, and restored because he gave of himself to them. As the Word made flesh, he entered into the pain and reality of ordinary human experiences, mixing with outcasts, prostitutes, and all manner of needy people: in doing so, he continually crossed the accepted boundaries of his day.

The 'enduring problem' of the Christ–culture relationship, argued Niebuhr, has continued to surface throughout the following two thousand years: not only Jews 'but also Greeks and

Romans, medievalists and moderns, Westerners and Orientals have rejected Christ because they saw in him a threat to their culture.'[42] Of course, as Niebuhr himself points out, there are also those who, throughout the ages, feel no great tension between church and world, so interpreting Christ in cultural terms. In fact, Niebuhr identified five approaches to the relationship between Christianity and culture in a typology that has become widely used in missiology.

In recent years there has been some criticism of Niebuhr because of his failure to emphasize the more important question of how Christ relates not to culture but to *humanity* in every culture. He has been criticized for a monolithic treatment of culture that is insufficiently nuanced with regard to the complexities of cultural dynamics, such as race, gender, and ideology; others complain that the assumptions that underscore his typology are the product of modernity.[43] Nonetheless, Niebuhr's analysis is still helpful in presenting us with an initial diagnostic framework, even though we might agree with his critics that his approach fails to anticipate a post-Christendom society. His classification scheme distinguishes between Christ Against Culture, the Christ of Culture, and three different forms of what he calls the 'church of the centre':

Christ Above Culture
Christ and Culture in Paradox
Christ the Transformer of Culture.

'Christ Against Culture' reflects the dualistic paradigm that we have already been addressing. In this category, Christians see the world outside the church as hopelessly corrupted by sin. God calls Christians to 'come ye out from among them' in order to form 'communities of holiness.' The Amish communities are typical expressions of this approach, and Mennonites, Christian Brethren, Pentecostals, and most types of fundamentalists have included individuals and congregations that fit this model.

Niebuhr picks out the great nineteenth-century Russian author Leo Tolstoy – the writer of such classics as *War and Peace* and *Anna Karenina* – as one man whose rejection of culture typifies this position. In *A Confession*, his own introspective autobiography, Tolstoy expresses a self-loathing disgust at his way of life, especially during his early adulthood, in which murder, fornication, lying, drunkenness, and violence characterized his behavior. It is little wonder that, like Augustine many centuries before him, Tolstoy turned his back on the world following a radical conversion. However, unlike Augustine, Tolstoy believed that evil was resident less in human nature than in the institutions of culture itself, including the organization of the church. Tolstoy's crusade against the state – viewed as the enemy of Christian faith – embraced political and economic institutions, philosophy, science, and the arts. Unfortunately, Tolstoy's Christianity was legalistic in the extreme, and bore little relation to the grace-filled personal faith that lies at the heart of the gospel. The truth is that the 'Christ Against Culture' position embraces not only those who are, as Niebuhr quaintly puts it, 'half-baked and muddle-headed,' but also those who have a genuine single-hearted sincerity of faith, even to the point of martyrdom.

At the other end of Niebuhr's typology is his 'Christ of Culture' category in which the absolute conflict of one against the other gives way to a harmony between them. Christians in this mode seek to discern and then champion the highest moral and spiritual common ground between the teachings of Christianity and the noblest values of culture. For example, in one extreme expression of early Gentile Christianity, Christian Gnosticism sought to lift the gospel out of its enslavement to belief into the more enlightened realm of knowledge. In the medieval era, the moral theology of the French theologian Peter Abelard eschewed all conflict between Christ and culture, offering essentially what amounts to kindly and liberal guidance for good people, rather than the radical discipleship of the Sermon on the Mount. The result is a form of 'cultural Christianity,' epitomized in modern times in the close national association between 'God and country.' This type of relationship, however, while always in danger of capitulating to contemporary cultural norms, rightly emphasizes the notion of common grace. Perhaps the main problem, though, as Niebuhr has pointed out, is that 'it is not possible honestly to confess that Jesus is the Christ of culture unless one can confess much more than this.'[44]

The rise of the 'Religious Right' in American politics, associated with the Republican Party and the much-publicized confession of President George W. Bush as a born-again Christian, may be seen as one expression of the 'Christ of Culture' category, though there are some within their ranks who are more 'conversionist' than others. The Republican Party of Texas, for example, affirms that the United States is a 'Christian nation.' In such a context, moral values have become synonymous with Christian values.

The 'Christ Above Culture' view is more of a 'both-and' than an 'either-or' perspective, though both dimensions are evident in Neibuhr's statement that the person holding this position 'seems to provide for a willing and intelligent cooperation of Christians with non-believers in carrying on the work of the world, while yet maintaining the distinctiveness of Christian faith and life.'[45] The great medieval theologian Thomas Aquinas would be a good representative of this 'synthesist' tendency, but it is evident among many mainstream Christians today. While not a typical evangelical perspective (because of its failure to recognize the extent to which sin has permeated the human race), it does however find adherents among contemporary evangelicals who want to affirm the importance, indeed primacy, of grace, yet who also want to keep their feet firmly in the ground of nature. A good example of this position can be found among Christians who are active in the contemporary science–faith dialogue, like Sir John Polkinghorne, the distinguished theoretical physicist, who resigned his chair in physics in 1979 to train for the Anglican priesthood. Sir John is known throughout the world for his contributions to the rapprochement between science and religion, a theme to be taken up in a later chapter of this book.

In 'Christ and Culture in Paradox,' which Niebuhr calls 'paradoxical dualism,' God is understood as one who works within the structures of society in order to maintain order and stability. The result is that Christians live within a strong *tension* between the authority of Christ and the claims of culture. They believe that God has ordained worldly institutions, and that they must work within those institutions as best they can. But the kingdom of God is manifestly 'now' as well as 'not yet,' which creates a powerful conflict as Christians seek to live faithfully within culture. This position acknowledges the genuine struggle of living in the world, and accordingly it is replete with paradox. Christ's power over sin is well understood, but so too is the power of sin itself. Obedience to secular institutions has to be balanced with obedience to Christ. Such paradoxical reality is anathema to those evangelicals who prefer the clarity of binary opposition, and there are many such pairs in the Bible: light versus darkness, good versus evil, the kingdom of God versus the kingdom of Satan, the church versus the world, the flesh versus the Spirit. Yet the Scriptures speak of the kingdom itself as a 'mixed field' (Matt. 13:24–30), full of wheat and tares, and of the Christian life as being in the world but not of it. To summarize, Christians are inescapably involved in a world that has been tainted by human sin; they cannot, nor should they seek to, disengage from culture, even as they acknowledge its corruption. They live in the world as a redemptive presence.

Niebuhr's final category within his 'church of the centre' triad is 'Christ the Transformer of Culture.' This is the classic 'conversionist' model, associated with Augustine, Calvin, and Jonathan Edwards, in which Christians are privileged to play an active role in culture. Christ is at work in the world, converting people *within* their cultural environments, not outside them. So culture is recognized as a positive reality, stemming from a more affirmative appraisal of creation. Conversionists therefore have a more positive and hopeful attitude towards culture than do dualists, for whom culture is a closed door. If redemption is the grand theological clarion cry of the dualist, the conversionist has a great interest in creation. Creation is in itself not *irredeemably* corrupt, but capable of conversion. For Niebuhr, the 'the conversionist is less concerned with . . . preparation for what will be given in a final redemption, than with the divine possibility of a present renewal.'[46]

Authentic contextualization

Niebuhr's typology is a helpful framework within which to appreciate the different perspectives taken by people throughout the ages in their understanding of the relationship between the Christian church and contemporary culture. In a recent book, John Drane reflects on the impact of the accelerating cultural change that has taken place over the past twenty years, a change that has generated massive uncertainty.[47] He traces the political and economic shifts throughout Europe, America and Australasia (since the time of his writing, terrorism has become the number one global concern following the horrific events of 9/11); the shift in the centre of gravity of Christian faith, from Europe to the two-thirds world; and the growing disenchantment with modernity and its confident 'Mr Fix-it' promise of progress through the benefits of science and technology. Seeing the Western Christian tradition as part of the problem, on the grounds that it is 'perceived as a part of the old cultural establishment that seems to have created our present predicament,'[48] Drane concludes that the church 'has generally allowed itself to be used as a channel for secular culture, rather than critiquing prevailing assumptions by reference to gospel values.'[49]

What is needed in the church is honest, critical, contextual inquiry, not culture-denying but culturally aware. Jesus, the incarnate Word of God, and Paul – like Jesus, the *apostolos* of God – worked *within* their cultural milieus, understanding, interpreting, relating to them: yet they necessarily called people *beyond* their cultural horizons. Writing from within his own North American context, the Canadian theologian Douglas John Hall laments the church's failure to proclaim a theology of the cross in the midst of the triviality in which North Americans are trapped. The church has certainly welcomed relevance, but at the price of faithfulness to the gospel. His answer is to invite theology – and here we might add ministry too – to sharpen itself and become more explicit. The link between gospel and culture is then clearly stated in terms of contextualization:

A truly contextual theology will be a critical theology: for it can serve the biblical God in its social contxt only by naming the inadequacy and the dangers of the illusion its society tries still to cling to. Its task is not to buttress that illusion but to explore the depths of truth present in our real disillusionment, so that the new metaphysic of hope which may come to be shall be constructed out of God's Word, and not only out of our own desperate need.[50]

Drane's analysis of the state of the Western church today most closely approximates Niebuhr's 'Christ of Culture' category, and it is clear that there are searching questions the Christian church needs to ask of itself if it is to celebrate the good news of Jesus Christ in a world that is itself searching for answers to the alienation, confusion, and brokenness that permeate human lives and social structures. Pointing us to a way forward, Drane reminds us that God is at work in his world and always has been; it is time, therefore, for the church to take the incarnation seriously on the grounds not that we are different from other people, but precisely the opposite . . . because we are *no* different from them. In this, he is directing us to the 'church of the centre,' in which all three of Niebuhr's models may find a sympathetic hearing.

Reconnecting with creation

Of significance for us too is the recognition that in order to make sense of our world Christians need to reconnect with creation. This is the first of four themes explored by the English poet and leadership consultant Gerard Kelly in an article on the sacred–secular divide.[51] Each of his suggestions has been road-tested in his own experience, so they are not abstract ideas, but concrete suggestions for the church of today. We need to rediscover the claims of God over the wideness of the world he has made, argues Kelly, but he errs in suggesting that before he was the God of Sinai or of Calvary, our God was the God of Eden. God's relationship with the world begins in the fact not that he made it as Creator but that he made it as *Father*. Trinitarian theology requires us to say that before God was Creator he is Father.

The Apostles' Creed opens with these words: 'I believe in God the Father Almighty, Maker of heaven and earth.' In the Nicene Creed, the confession is a little fuller: 'I believe in one God the Father Almighty, Maker of heaven and earth, And of all things visible and invisible.' Notice the order expressed there: first Father, then Creator. That order of priority is important, though perhaps we have never noticed it before when reciting the creeds. In fact, we might say that God is Creator because he is, first of all, Father. The great Scottish theologian, Thomas Torrance, once wrote these words: 'the creation of the world out of nothing is something *new even for God*. God was always Father, but he *became* Creator.'[52] The significance of these words is enormous: God created as an expression of his inner being, his inner life as the triune God of grace. In divine freedom and love he brought into being, out of nothing – *ex nihilo* – something beautiful, extraordinary, relational, and altogether wonderful . . . like himself. Psalm 8 is what one commentator has called 'an unsurpassed example of what a hymn should be, celebrating as it does the glory and grace of God, rehearsing who he is and what he has done, and relating us and our world to him.'[53]

When we look at the wonder of God's creation, we often find ourselves drawn to the majesty of the one who brought it all into being. This is not to say that we will go on to understand God as *Father*, and so enter into a personal relationship with him. It is one thing to proclaim God as Creator – it is quite another to worship him as Father . . . *but the two are related*. Only by revelation, as Karl Barth has rightly insisted, can we truly know God as Father. To call God Father is to declare that he is a relational God – he is the Father of the Son. And so we are into Trinitarian language – God is Father, Son and Holy Spirit . . . he always has been, and always will be. But because God as Father is also the Creator God, we should expect to see traces of God's fatherhood in his creation. It is precisely for this reason that we should 'connect with creation.'

It is only when we begin to understand how much God loves his creation, and how much he is therefore totally involved in what he has made, that we will really understand our involvement with him in all that he is doing in the world. All pastoral ministry is therefore a participation in the ministry of God in the world. Entry into the life of the Trinity means entry into the life of a God who is involved in every part of creation, a God who invites us to celebrate the joy of life and seek renewal in all the areas of brokenness around us. In fact, we could go further, and insist that salvation is not just about being caught up into a glorious new life in God – though it certainly is that! It also means that we are called to participate in rich and fulfilling ways in all of creation, sharing in the life of God's universe.

The gospel is not a question of God giving you and me a new life, as if that life existed *apart from him*, parceled and distributed to those who respond to him in faith. That is not the gospel at all: that view presents us with a deistic perspective – God out there giving something to us so that we can now live a new life. That way, our life becomes something *separate from God*. The gospel is not so much about God giving us a new life, but of us being caught up into the very life of God himself, so that humanity and Trinity – and creation – are bound together forever. To have our eyes opened by the Spirit to this truth is to experience for ourselves the real meaning of salvation. God has not created us to praise and honour him as if he, in his triune being, lacked something. Rather, he has created us that we might live in the fullness of his 'spilled-over' life in the creation that is bound up within his triune life.

So, to separate God from his creation is clearly not a helpful exercise. But an intriguing question remains, How does God as Trinity actually relate to all that he has created as physical reality? This may be rephrased in the form of another question, Is God in space, or space in God? It is worth exploring this subject for a moment, and the insights of Jürgen Moltmann are particularly valuable here. In a chapter on 'The Space of Creation' (in *God in Creation: A New Theology of Creation and the Spirit of God*[54]) Moltmann notes that ever since Augustine there have been many theological meditations on time, but very rarely do we find any on *space*. With regard to time, theology has rightly focused on the importance of history, but space has been left to the scientists.

Moltmann's starting point is to look at space from a philosophical perspective: in other words, if modern science suggests to us an 'infinite universe,' how does that connect with the idea of God himself? Could we say that God is the outermost 'frontier' of space? In earlier centuries, the idea of a closed cosmos offered a sense of security – the idea of a 'boundless emptiness' was more troubling. So Pascal: 'The eternal silence of these infinite spaces frightens me.' A good example of this is the way in which we like to fence off our land and declare to the world that this is 'my bit of England' [or whatever country we belong to]! We feel secure when we border ourselves in – we like to create our own environment within which we can feel, if not safe, at least 'at home.' We like boundaries. This leads Moltmann to suggest that space is not to be regarded as a *homogeneous* concept. In his theology of space, which is thoroughly *ecological*, every living thing has its own world in which to live, a world to which it is adapted and which suits it. Space, as created reality, is primarily *living space* for the richness and variety of different forms of life.

It has been suggested that Moltmann's theology of space as developed in his writings tends towards anthropocentricism; in other words his theology stops at the end of the biosphere, and he does not consider the rest of the universe where there is vast space and no life. However, his insights are helpful in formulating an understanding of the relationship between a finite earth and an infinite God, particularly from an ecological perspective.

If creation is treated as an object to dominate – which is sadly our experience in the modern world – then the particular environments created by God for the nourishment of unique living things are destroyed in the drive to create a homogeneous environment amenable to humanity's desire to dominate all things. The drive for uniformity (especially in our highly globalized culture) weakens and destabilizes the rich diversity of God's creation. Everything becomes 'McDonaldized' in our modern consumer-driven culture. Things are valued for their usefulness to humanity rather than for what they are *as creations of God*.

Classical incarnational theology addresses the question, Is it really possible for the finite earth to become the dwelling place of an infinite God? That, however, is asking not the wrong question, but the reverse of perhaps an even more important question, Can the infinite God be the dwelling place of a finite earth? It is far more helpful to declare, with Moltmann, that '*God is the dwelling place of the world created by him.*' The theology of creation that we are developing here sees *God as the eternal dwelling place of his creation*. God, in his triune glory, creates space within himself, making room within himself for his creation. In Moltmann's words, the created world 'exists in the space God yielded up for it through his creative resolve.'[55] Contemporary physics reminds us, of course, that we cannot separate time and space, so it is far more satisfactory to speak of God as the dwelling place and time frame of the world created by him.

As we shall see in a later chapter, new insights in contemporary physics and biology emphasize that everything in the universe is bound up with everything else – all things are what they are because they are related to everything else. In a book called *The Cosmic Dance*, the Italian theoretical chemist Guiseppe Del Re writes: 'Major conceptual advances in science now require that we recover a view of the universe in which every single thing or event is in fact related to everything else.'[56] For example, the concept of nonlocality, a pivotal concept in quantum mechanics, reflects a radical interconnectedness that points towards an underlying order in the universe. Similarly, the concept of 'emergence,' which is a term that physicists use to describe what happens when an interconnected system of relatively simple elements self-organizes to form more intelligent, more adaptive and complex higher-level behavior, points towards the interconnectedness that characterizes the universe. Moltmann likes to refer to the 'creation-community,' a community of both creatures and environments contributing to a 'web of life on earth.' His concept of 'creation-community' is grounded in an inclusive Trinity that is 'so wide open that the whole world can find room and rest and eternal life within it.'[57]

So when we consider approaches to creation and culture that depend upon a dualistic separation between God and the world, we are denying the Trinitarian nature of the God who has made space for the world within himself, and who loves this world with a passion that ultimately led to the incarnation and the cross. That is why we cannot endorse dualism if we truly believe in God as Trinity. God is not a deistic being, separate from his creation, but intimately involved in all that he has made – he is immanent as well as transcendent.

He is a God who has made all things well, who has blessed his creation, and invites us to participate with gratitude in all that he has made. In some introductory comments in G. K. Chesterton's *Orthodoxy*, the popular Christian writer Philip Yancey suggests that, rather than complaining about the sexual permissiveness and greed and violence that reflect the way many abuse God's good gifts, Christians should demonstrate to the world where good gifts actually come from. 'Evil's greatest triumph,' he writes, 'may be its success in portraying religion as an enemy of pleasure when, in fact, all the things we enjoy are the inventions of a Creator who lavished them on the world.'[58] It is precisely because he came to understand Christianity as the only reasonable explanation for the existence of pleasure in the world – 'We should thank God for beer and Burgundy by not drinking too much of them'! – that Chesterton came to faith.

Paying attention to creation

In his brief article on the sacred–secular divide cited earlier, Kelly also invites us to make 'sacred' the 'secular.' Among other things, this means offering the ordinary, or 'practising the presence of God.' Here he suggests a delightful little book by the French Jesuit priest Jean-Pierre de Caussade entitled, in the French, *L'Abandon à la Providence Divine*, translated into English as *The Sacrament of the Present Moment*.[59] In this short mystical treatise, de Caussade invites us to attend to our present circumstances as the gift of God. Unfortunately, many Christians are like 'deaf people at a concert.' As Evelyn Underhill said: 'They study the program carefully, believe every statement in it, speak respectfully of the quality of the music, but only really hear a phrase now and again. So they have no notion at all of the mighty symphony which fills the universe, to which our lives are destined to make their tiny contribution, and which is the self-expression of the Eternal God.'[60]

The 'mighty symphony' to which Underhill alludes may be interpreted as the symphony of a creation that continually speaks of the glory of God. To experience human life in all its fullness has to do with *paying attention* to this creation in such a way that we see it with new eyes, epitomized in the following well-known lines from *Aurora Leigh,* Elizabeth Barrett Browning's nineteenth-century verse-novel of contemporary early Victorian life in England:

> Earth's crammed with heaven,
> And every common bush afire with God:
> But only he who *sees,* takes off his shoes,
> The rest sit round it, and pluck blackberries.[61]

In order to make 'sacred' the 'secular,' not only do we need to see God's creation with new eyes, but we also need to take time out to 'smell the roses.' Carl Jung is once reported as saying that hurry is not of the devil . . . it is the devil! Many Christians can testify to the reality of pressure and busyness in their lives – and that is even before they get involved in church activities! James Gleick has written a book called *Faster,* subtitled *The Acceleration of Just About Everything.* One example given on the back cover exactly puts the finger on the spot, Do you hit the 'door close' button because the lift doors are taking too long to shut?! Or, How many times do we register impatience and frustration when the webpage we are seeking takes several seconds longer to download than we have come to expect? In a racy style, Gleick's critique of contemporary society – 'While you wait, you look at your watch. It's a habit'[62] – dissects our struggle to squeeze as much as we can into every 1,440 minutes of each day.

Nowhere is this more evident than in the way we eat . . . or don't eat, if we consider seriously the true meaning of the word. Instead of taking time to enjoy food, many people have forsaken the pleasure of eating in their race to get more into their days. Not only more work, but more play too! We rush from one task to the next, one appointment to the next, one leisure pursuit to the next . . . and the prime casualty in our misguided rush to complete as much as we can in each day is the sheer pleasure of eating good food. Very rarely do families sit round a table and enjoy a meal *together.* In addition to the ubiquitous McDonald's, the quintessential purveyor of 'fast food,' the microwave has made possible individual meals whenever we want them, ready to serve within a few minutes.

One notable response to this assault upon our eating-time is the international Slow Food movement, which officially began in Paris in 1989, and has now spread to many other countries around the world. The movement actually had its origins in Italy a few years earlier: the Italians, whose love of good food and wine is legendary, now represent about half the total membership. Local Slow Food centers organize food and wine events and initiatives, create moments of conviviality, raise the profile of products, and promote local artisans and wine cellars. Taking time to *taste* food is what the Slow Food movement is all about. But it has to do with more than just pleasure, although that is good enough reason for its existence and prosperity! The movement has an ecological side to it: one of its stated aims is to encourage respect for nature and the environment, giving rise to the term 'eco-gastronomes.' The pleasurable enjoyment of good food and wine cannot be disconnected from the pleasure of others.

The nineteenth-century German philosopher Ludwig Feuerbach once famously observed that 'You are what you eat.' The sacrament of the Lord's Supper, or Eucharist, has become so trivialized in many church settings – rushing unthinkingly through the sacrament – that Feuerbach's insight may actually be interpreted in a very suggestive way. Eating something actually brings us into relationship with it – its history enters our lives in a deeply participative way. The food becomes an integral part of us. Likewise, in the Eucharist, we mysteriously take Christ's body into ours, with the result that Jesus' prayer in John 17:20–23 becomes the language of mutual participation. So to eat more deliberately and thoughtfully – rather than bolting our food down before we rush off to the next important thing – is to participate in a richly holistic and communal experience. *Keep it slow, stupid!* could be the new slogan of our age!

Similar to the Slow Food movement is the trend in some countries of people moving out of high-density urban areas in order to escape from the pressures of urban living. The phrase 'sea change' has often been used to describe this phenomenon,[63] which reflects the need that some people have to experience a more fulfilling and less stressful way of life by moving to what they hope will be an idyllic rural retreat 'away from it all.' The

1970s BBC television comedy series, *The Good Life*, featuring Richard Briers and Felicity Kendal as the archetypal middle-class couple who decide to turn their suburban home into a self-sufficient farm-cum-allotment, still attracts impressive repeat audiences, a measure of the continued relevance of its subject matter.

Tom Sine recounts a life-changing experience during work on a project in rural Haiti: the people among whom he labored had a 'Gospel-rhythm' to their lives, always having time to stop and talk with passers-by:

> On many warm Haitian evenings during my sojourn we would visit the homes of friends. They would open their homes to us and serve us food and drinks. We would spend a whole evening telling stories, laughing, singing, and playing with the children to the flicker of kerosene lamps . . . I thank my Haitian friends for helping me discover a more biblical approach to my time.[64]

The bottom line is this, How on earth do we make the 'secular' sacred if we do not even have time to say thank you for the good things that God has given to us in this world? No time to say thank you, because life is too short and we need to rush on to the next thing . . .

True worship

Kelly's third proposal for combating the sacred–secular divide syndrome relates to worship. How far, he asks, do we carry the real world into our worship? Quoting Maggi Dawn, he argues that true worship is 'the crucible where real life and experience meet theology head on.' Here are some questions that relate more widely to the life of the church, suggested by Mark Greene, Executive Director of the London Institute of Contemporary Christianity:[65]

(1) Why is this a common statement? 'I teach Sunday School 45 minutes a week and they haul me up to the front and the whole church prays for me. I teach school 45 *hours* a week

and no one ever prays for me.' Would that be true for you and your job?

(2) Why have many church leaders and most Christian magazines expressed their opinion about the Harry Potter novels but completely ignored the literary content of current school English curricula?

(3) Why have 50 percent of evangelicals never heard a sermon on work?

(4) Why is this statement from a former senior leader in a large student ministry true? 'I could practically guarantee that you could go into any Christian Union in Britain and not find a single student who could give you a biblical perspective on the subject they are studying to degree level.'

(5) Why do we set a lower educational standard for the way we teach kids in our churches than the standard set in the school room?

The answer to all these questions, of course, is that in each case the secular–sacred divide is well and truly entrenched in church culture. The 'really spiritual' is divorced from the real world. The credibility gap between belief and everyday life is powerfully articulated in Robert Banks' *Redeeming the Routines*, in which the author exposes ten ways in which this gap is expressed.[66] This is the central thesis of the book we referred to earlier by Robert McAfee Brown, *Spirituality and Liberation*. Midway through the book, he reminds us of that well-known verse, Micah 6:8:

> He has showed you, O man, what is good.
> And what does the LORD require of you?
> To act justly and to love mercy
> and to walk humbly with your God.

In a precise and clear exposition, Brown argues that in this verse '[w]e do not have *three different assertions* being made, but one assertion being made in *three different ways.'* So we 'cannot talk compellingly about any one of the three phrases until we have talked about all three of them.'[67] He expresses the logic of his case persuasively in the form of three equations: to *act justly* means to love tenderly and to walk humbly with God; to *love tenderly* means to walk humbly with God and to act justly; to *walk humbly with God* means to act justly and to love tenderly. So you cannot divorce spirituality from issues of social justice and compassion and care for the needy. True worship has to do with how we live the *whole* of our lives, not just that part which we take along to church on Sundays. Worship has to do with getting involved in God's world precisely because that is where he is involved. We shall have more to say about that later. Paul reminds us in Romans 1 that our worship is reflected in the offering of our bodies as living sacrifices, holy and pleasing to God.

Discerning the Spirit

Finally, Kelly suggests that Christians need to 'opt for obedience.' It is often suggested that to be a dualist is the tough option, a far more difficult task than opting *into* the world: dualism demands self-discipline and sacrifice to stay clean and pure and 'set apart' from the world. However, the truth lies in the opposite direction: dualism is actually an easy option, a kind of 'religious cop-out.' All we have to do in dualism is to sort out the 'holy' from the 'unholy' and then live according to our rules. But, says Kelly, 'wrestling with obedience and holiness in the mud and grime of the real world is hard work: it takes energy and commitment, and more often than not leaves us bruised.' It is for this reason that we are called as Christians to discerning selective engagement in the world: 'the 'issue is not whether to participate' in other cultures, 'but how and when' to participate.'[68]

Of course, it should not surprise us that our willingness to combat prevailing dualistic paradigms can open up doors of opportunity for sharing the gospel with others. Those opportunities, however, can arise quite unpredictably. A guitarist in a Christian punk rock band (yes, they do exist!) was playing in a string of shows along the east coast of Australia. In Sydney, the band was playing at a small venue that held a couple of hundred people. After the show the guitarist grabbed a well-deserved beer and headed into the crowd for the traditional 'after-show mingle.' An enthusiastic young man approached him and they began to chat. He wrote reviews for a Christian magazine and expressed his pleasure with the show. He then went on to express his disgust with the band's second guitarist who wore a Deep Purple T-shirt on stage. How could he, a member of a Christian band, wear a secular band's T-shirt? To many this may seem a trivial issue, but it was a major stumbling block for the Christian reviewer. After an hour-long conversation the guitarist could not penetrate the reviewer's narrow dualistic mentality, so they went their separate ways.

Ironically, in a nearby café the T-shirt sparked off an evangelistic conversation between the second guitarist and a person who had walked into the café off the street, both of whom had a common admiration for the Deep Purple band. The very thing that offended one 'righteous' Christian was the means of drawing someone else into a meaningful conversation about Christ!

It can be hard work discerning what is right, and there will be occasions when Christians not only 'offend the noble pagan' by exposing sin and evil in the world, but also offend their fellow believers by living more authentically 'on the edge.' Sometimes that will mean getting alongside others with whom we share a common interest that may on the surface have absolutely nothing to do with the gospel. At other times it may be more bruising, as we participate in 'the mud and grime of the real world.' Whatever the setting, our starting point as Christians is that this is God's world, and he is at work by his Spirit, who works in many different, and often improbable, ways to restore people to God and to each other.

We also need to recognize that the Spirit typically works in deep and hidden ways in order to restore people to God. John Taylor encourages us to have a theology of mission that starts by being too inclusive rather than too narrow, suggesting that a passionate concern for the humanness of people may make a good beginning: 'As a first step we must begin to see our engagement in mission as a participation in the continuing work of creation and not simply in the redemption of that which was long ago created.'[69]

This interpretation of mission as a participation in the continuous creation of God in the world is not easily embraced by some Christians. The starting point in mission for most evangelicals, for example, tends to be exclusive rather than inclusive, and is expressed in the language of redemption–forgiveness–salvation rather than creation and wholeness. As Christians, we need both the courage to look beyond our narrow church boundaries and also the wisdom to discern where the Spirit is at work, often in the unlikeliest places and in the most improbable ways.

3

The Power of Literature To Enhance Our Humanity

A robust response to those who fail to discern the serious business of reading novels and poetry

In the movie *Dead Poets Society*, a new and idealistic English teacher called John Keating, played by Robin Williams, arrives at Welton Academy, a conventional boys' preparatory school in the United States. The teaching approach at the school is structured, predictable, and narrow: and Keating, a Welton alumnus, immediately sets about challenging the suffocating and life-denying conformity that he sees all around him. Following an amusing scene in which he encourages all the boys to rip out the pages containing the preface to a poetry text because they describe a scientific way to measure the greatness of poetry, he addresses the class:

> Now in my class you will learn to think for yourselves again. You will learn to savor words and language. No matter what anybody tells you, words and ideas can change the world. I see that look in Mr. Pitt's eye, like nineteenth-century literature has nothing to do with going to business school or medical school. Right? Maybe. Mr. Hopkins, you may agree with him, thinking, 'Yes, we should simply study our Mr. Pritchard and learn our rhyme and metre and go quietly about the business of achieving other ambitions.'

Mr Keating then invites the boys to 'huddle up' around him as he confides in them: 'We don't read and write poetry because it's cute. We read and write poetry because we are members of the human race. And the human race is filled with passion. Medicine, law, business, engineering, these are all noble pursuits, and necessary to sustain life. But poetry, beauty, romance, love, these are what we stay alive for.'[70] In the same vein, C. S. Lewis argues that literature enlarges our being. In *An Experiment in Criticism* he writes that literature 'admits us to experiences other than our own.'[71] Good books – whether novels, essays, or poetry – give us windows into other worlds. In John Keating's words, we are members of the human race, and maturity in this regard is measured by our willingness and capacity to see beyond ourselves. As we explore the worlds in which others live out their lives, as we enter their feelings, their joys and sorrows, their hopes and fears, we ourselves are enriched as human beings. Indeed, it may well be that the primary goal of literature is to make us more human. Lewis goes on to say that through literature we become 'a thousand men' and yet remain ourselves. So our *humanity* is enhanced as we read: we become more fully human as we enter the worlds of others, more human in the sense that we do not allow ourselves to be stifled by a narrow parochialism that limits our awareness of the lives and circumstances of those who may be very different from us. Reading enables us to 'transcend our own competitive particularity'

Literature also exists for the joy of the reader, echoing the Horatian dictum that we should read not just for our instruction, but also for pleasure. In referring to the pleasurable aspect of stories, I am not necessarily referring to form, although the aesthetic structure, balance, and style of a story understandably give pleasure just as good poetry leaves one with a sense of satisfaction in the way words, images, and rhythm convey meaning. But there is pleasure, too, just as gazing at a majestic mountain peak fills one with wonder and joy. God has given all good things for our enjoyment, including good literature, which has intrinsic power to please. Whenever I read Keats or Wordsworth, Dickens or Shakespeare, it is a pleasurable experience. The utilitarian perspective is that aesthetic beauty may act as a catalyst for the meaning of the words to penetrate the mind, touch the heart, and move the will.

Many years ago I was one among several Christians asked by a pastor to name an author whose writing we were enjoying most at the time, along with a specific title. All those who responded before me referred to a Christian book that had overt religious or spiritual themes . . . until I mentioned a book by the Australian author Morris West. There was a pregnant pause, as if I had said something heretical! The irony is that West, who was a superb storyteller, wrote about the human condition from the perspective of a deep, though not always explicit, Catholic faith. There are some Christians whose library consists of nothing else but Christian books – testimonies (lots of these), devotional classics, Christian biographies, and the like – perhaps even some fiction written by Christian authors. I am not against Christian books per se, and there are many fine volumes that fall squarely within this category. But compared with the wealth of literature available today, embracing both the classics and contemporary writings, they do not sufficiently represent, as a single category, the contents of what may be described as a 'good bookshelf' . . . more about that later.

Redeeming language

In this chapter we can touch on only a few themes relating to the value of literature in human experience. It is self-evident that in Western society we live in an age of multimedia technology that threatens to hijack any attempts we might make, however well-intentioned, to expose ourselves not just to the richness of classical and contemporary literature, but to the power of language itself. Another enemy of reading is the pressure of time under which we live today. The layout of newspapers has been adjusted over the years to cater for the harried and the hurried, with abbreviated copy, emotive headlines, and more easily digestible vocabulary. The problem today is not that most people cannot read – they choose not to read: illiteracy in the modern world has been replaced with 'aliteracy.' To a very large extent this is because we live in a visual age – there is little incentive in contemporary society to switch off the all-pervasive television set or to cut down on video-watching habits, though the recent phenomenon of the *Harry Potter* books has encouraged more reading among younger people (and some older ones too!) than ever before. The movie version of the *Lord of the Rings* trilogy has also generated substantial book sales of the same title, which is a welcome outcome. But the ever-increasing march of technology, which imprisons many young people today in a self-absorbed world of iPods and earphones, threatens to undo even these meager successes. The transmission of truncated text-messages, in which emasculated language masquerades as authentic communication, further erodes the beauty and richness of human vocabulary. In a phrase, language needs to be redeemed.

In saying this, I do not want to minimize the importance of understanding the technology through which much of our communication occurs. If Christians are to have a realistic impact upon today's e-generations, then it is appropriate to discern how the church might respond sympathetically to the opportunities presented by the revolution in electronic communication. However, the benefits of the Internet age should not blind us to its obvious disadvantages: web users typically browse, or sample, cyberdata. They demand hard information, readily accessible, and requiring minimum evaluative effort. Language is sacrificed in the cause of efficiency. Words are no longer gifts to be savored, but tools to get results . . . and Christians are not exempt from this temptation to degrade language. If the community of faith is to have an influence for good in the world, then it must adopt a positive and welcoming attitude towards the contribution of the literary disciplines, placing itself in the vanguard in the redemption of language. Malcolm Guite expresses this exceptionally well: 'The concern of literature to use language well, to cleanse and purify it, to redeem its words from the captivity and abuse to which the powers of this world continuously subject them, is bound up with the redemptive purposes of God who chose that his Word should be born as one who had to learn to use words.'[72]

Earlier, I suggested that the church has the peculiar task of being not just relevant, learning to speak the language of the culture, but prophetic in its redemptive presence in the world.[73] This means that Christians are not to succumb to the diminishment of language that has so impoverished contemporary culture; rather, they have much to contribute by engaging with good literature in order to be enriched in their understanding of human life – their own and that of others. My contention is that we need to read good books if we are to grasp afresh the real meaning and power of language . . . and then to employ that language in a redemptive way.

In George Orwell's political novel *Nineteen Eighty-Four*, which portrays a world characterized by the mindless obedience of a people who are manipulated by totalitarian bureaucrats and politicians – the Inner Party – and watched over by 'Big Brother,' the author demonstrates in a frightening way the power of language to delude the population. The authorities introduce a new language, 'Newspeak,' as a psychological strategy to control thinking. Orwell himself writes that political language 'is designed to make lies sound truthful and murder respectable, and to give an appearance of solidity to pure wind.'[74] People are not coerced into using 'Newspeak': rather, they are immersed in the language as it is broadcast through the media, which are controlled by the all-pervasive Inner Party.

I do not want to suggest that language today has been contaminated as radically as represented in Orwellian society . . . though some may bewail the impoverished use of language by those in authority today, including our educators. Punctuation is not a strong point in today's English curriculum – Lynne Truss observes that a child sitting an English exam in the middle of the last century would be asked routinely to punctuate the sentence: 'Charles the First walked and talked half an hour after his head was cut off.'[75] That would test more than a few middle-school children today! Even more disturbing is the grammatical ignorance of many *teachers* in our schools today, such as the common fault of inserting an apostrophe in the possessive *its* when writing on the whiteboard. T. S. Eliot was probably very close to the mark when he suggested that words have lost their precision in the way in which we use them. In 'East Coker,' the second of his four related poems collected under the title *Four Quartets*, Eliot is concerned to restore meaning to language, but he is weighed down by the failure of language to express what he wants to convey. Words are 'shabby equipment always deteriorating' – but he has no other tools at his disposal, so he will do the best he can: 'For us, there is only the trying.'[76] Eliot's meditation on language is bleak, but we need to hear him if we are to effectively redeem language – both grammar and vocabulary – from its captivity to triviality and imprecision.

Of course, we should not sacrifice quality for quantity, but the sort of reading that I am advocating here has to do with what John Milton once described as the benefit of books 'promiscuously read.' C. S. Lewis read voraciously as a teenager at home, described in *Surprised by Joy*:

> I am the product of long corridors, empty sunlit rooms, upstair indoor silences, attics explored in solitude, distant noises of gurgling cisterns and pipes, and the noise of wind under the tiles. Also of endless books . . . There were books in the study, books in the drawing-room, books in the cloakroom, books (two deep) in the great bookcase on the landing, books in a bedroom, books piled as high as my shoulder in the cistern attic, books of all kinds reflecting every transient stage of my parents' interests, books readable and unreadable, books suitable for a child and books most emphatically not. Nothing was forbidden me. In the seemingly endless rainy afternoons I took volume after volume from the shelves.[77]

What is good literature?

The visual media employ words in a secondary sense – they are selected to reinforce the visual impact. But books – and here I mean *good* books – are dependent upon the way words are selected and put together, and our exposure to those words will influence the way we use words ourselves. Quite simply, the more good books we read, the better. This, of course, raises the question of what is a 'good' book. There is no obvious answer, and definitions are inevitably very subjective. Perhaps one measure of whether a book is good or not is to ask whether it treats someone as a 'reader' or a 'consumer.' Veith claims that 'modern bookstores are filled with shallow, salacious, badly written books that are travesties of true literary art.'[78] While there may be some truth in his assertion, many bookstores offer a wide variety of books, ranging from the trivial and tawdry to the brilliant and beautiful. In the same way that food may be described in the language of 'fast' and 'slow' (see Chapter 2), we might say the same of literature. A Slow Book movement may be the antidote to the literary junk that is so often available in our bookstores today. Perhaps a book may be described as good if it encourages us to appreciate its contents in a reflective and thought-provoking way, not only because of the value of its content but also because it has been well written. The immediate emotion may be one of pleasure, and literature that delights and entertains us is undoubtedly a legitimate outcome: we are robbed of the playful and recreational dimension of our humanness when we insist that reading always has to have some obvious utilitarian benefit. A well-written detective novel can be just the thing we need after a hard day's work or when we are on holiday.

We have suggested in the paragraph above two features that may be regarded as intrinsic to a 'good book' – content and what we might call 'quality of writing.' Before developing these two literary aspects, it is helpful to ask if there is such a thing as 'Christian literature,' and whether or not the elusive quality of 'goodness' has something to do with its explicit Christian nature. The twentieth-century English poet W. H. Auden once commented that there can no more be something described as Christian art than there can be a Christian diet. This is certainly true with respect to an author's 'quality of writing': how a poem or novel is written – its structure, characterization, and use of various literary devices – has nothing to do with it being Christian or not. If I have a raging toothache, I do not demand that I go to a 'Christian dentist'; more important is that I go to a *good* dentist, meaning one who has a reputation for good dentistry.

My colleague, Mark Worthing, has written a book on Christian ethics, and in an early chapter he asks the question, What is Christian ethics? He notes: 'Christian ethics is more than ethics taught within a Christian context or by a Christian person.'[79] He goes on to identify a number of key attributes of a specifically Christian ethics: its community context, its New Testament orientation, its Christocentrism, its obligation only for those who are followers of the Way, its focus on discipleship, and its distinction from theological and theistic ethics. With this in mind, we might argue that a piece of literature may be described as Christian insofar as it connects in some way with the Christian worldview as presented in the Bible, and specifically in the New Testament. It is perfectly possible for a Christian to write about such topics as pornography and profligacy, but it is how they are treated that defines how Christian the material is.

Ryken suggests that it is useful to speak of the ways in which a work of art *intersects* with Christianity.[80] In the same way that some theologians talk about the creation exhibiting signs of the Trinity (*vestigia trinitatis*) – in other words, we can discern the marks or imprints of God in the created order, because this universe in which we live is God's creation – it may be helpful for us to speak of a work being Christian to the extent that one is able to discern distinctly Christian themes such as forgiveness, grace, wholeness, community life, and redemption. In that sense, we may be close to coming to some understanding of 'goodness' in terms of a work's correspondence to the goodness inherent in the Christian worldview.

An example might help here. George Eliot's *Silas Marner* is the story of a weaver who, having been falsely accused of stealing some money in a northern industrial town, now lives a hermit-like existence in the fictional English village of Raveloe. Gradually he begins to accumulate his own hoard of gold, a mechanical process admirably described by Eliot: 'His life had reduced itself to the mere functions of weaving and hoarding, without any contemplation of an end towards which the functions tended.'[81] One evening, he returns to his cottage, and utters a 'wild wringing scream' when he finds that his cache of gold has been stolen. Shortly afterwards, an exhausted and unkempt little two-year-old girl, whose mother has just collapsed in the snow, is attracted by the gleam of light from Silas Marner's cottage, and she curls up on the hearth and falls asleep. When Silas discovers her, he interprets the 'tramp's child' as a gift from God, and raises her as his own, naming her

Eppie after his mother and sister, a blessing granted to replace his lost gold. The narrative is set within the framework of village life and the unscrupulous motives and actions of the more well-to-do inhabitants of the community. The novel comes to a satisfying end as Silas' gold is returned to him and Eppie returns Silas' love in the face of claims from the father who had abandoned her.

George Eliot was raised by her parents as a middle-of-the-road Anglican, but renounced Christian doctrine at an early age. However, *Silas Marner* is a story replete with religious themes, such as the loss and rediscovery of faith, the tenderness of family life, and the interconnectedness between community and faith. Eliot's treatment of human nature is reflected in her portrayal of Silas as a gentle, kind, and honest man, in contrast to the two disreputable sons of prosperous Squire Cass. He displays a capacity for love and goodness, and the novel highlights the themes of hope and redemption in the midst of great personal loss and isolation. We are made aware of Silas' faith in God in good times and in bad: when he is framed for robbery his faith, though 'benumbed,' is still intact; and when he discovers little Eppie, he says: 'It's come to me – I've a right to keep it.' Ultimately, however, Silas' faith seems to be grounded in a trust in human goodness as much as in God, mirroring Eliot's own journey.

In its subject matter and treatment of human life, *Silas Marner* is undoubtedly a 'good' book, and it resonates with all that is true in a Christian sense: while not explicitly a Christian book it clearly intersects powerfully with the Christian faith. The novel, described by the critic F. R. Leavis as 'pure perfection,' is also 'good' because it is written exceptionally well. A number of literary features stand out: symbols and metaphors that draw out the character of the main participants in the story, especially Silas; the structure of the tale, in which the social life of the village is played out against the backdrop of Silas' relationship with the community; and the moral and spiritual development of the central characters.

In his 1998 novel *Enduring Love*, Ian McEwan writes a riveting and unforgettable story that centres on a man with an obsessive disease known as de Clérambaut's syndrome. In its plot, characterization, and psychological tension, the narrative engrosses the reader, making it without doubt one of the finest novels in recent years. Its opening chapter is gripping and filled with suspense, heralding the unfolding of a powerful psychological thriller. It does not explicitly, or even implicitly, intersect with Christianity – but this does not disqualify it from being a 'good,' even great, book. It treats a specific human condition truthfully, and in this respect its handling of the impact of delusional homoerotic love signifies the book as 'good' because we cannot avoid dwelling on its contents in a reflective and thought-provoking way. The subject matter may not be agreeable, but that is not the point. As Christians, we cannot close our minds to topics that we find difficult or offensive to handle on the grounds that they are distasteful. If we are to engage with our contemporary culture, we need to make ourselves aware of the reality of life around us. However, this is a far cry from gratuitous exposure to shoddily conceived and even more shoddily written fictional, human-life dramas designed to appeal to the lowest common denominator.

The richness of poetry

What we have discussed about language in this chapter is true, of course, of other literary forms besides prose. C. S. Lewis, in a much-quoted chapter in his *Christian Reflections*, discusses the 'Poetic language' employed by John Keats in 'The Eve of St Agnes.'[82] Lewis contrasts the rich and evocative language of Keats with two other forms of language, which he calls 'Ordinary language' and 'Scientific language.' Here is the first stanza of the poem:

> St. Agnes' Eve – Ah, bitter chill it was!
> The owl, for all his feathers, was a-cold;
> The hare limp'd trembling through the frozen grass,
> And silent was the flock in woolly fold:
> Numb were the Beadsman's fingers, while he told
> His rosary, and while his frosted breath,
> Like pious incense from a censer old,

Seem'd taking flight for heaven, without a death,
Past the sweet Virgin's picture, while his prayer he saith.

Ordinary language would state bluntly that 'it was very cold.' Scientific language offers greater precision: 'there were thirteen degrees of frost.' But here we have an example of the power of poetic language combined with a rhythmic structure that powerfully conveys the reality of the 'bitter chill' that Keats is seeking to describe. The language is poetic in the sense that it employs images and symbols in such a way as to enable the reader to imagine what it must be like to feel the extreme cold of that night. Poetic language – whether employed in prose or poetic structures – is therefore vicarious in its capacity to touch the heart and mind of the reader. We should note here that language does not have to be complex and erudite to communicate. Rachel Buxton points out that Robert Frost's diction is essentially commonplace, 'earthed in the fundamental elements of life,'[83] and it is this quality of plainness that Frost skillfully exploits in his poetry. She quotes Frost: 'Words must be the ordinary words that we hear about us to which the imagination must give an iridescence. Then only are words really poetic.'[84]

The Nobel prize-winning Irish poet Seamus Heaney's early poem, 'Digging,'[85] which he once described as a 'course grained navvy of a poem,' is nonetheless a good example of the way simple words, together with metrical variety, can be employed to convey, in this case, the poet's early wrestling with his vocation. Having been raised in a farming family, Heaney compares his 'squat pen' unfavourably with his father's 'clean spade,' suggesting a sense of awkwardness about his literary profession. But he resolves his personal tension by the end:

> The cold smell of potato mold, the squelch and slap
> Of soggy peat, the curt cuts of an edge
> Through living roots awaken in my head.
> But I've no spade to follow men like them.
>
> Between my finger and my thumb
> The squat pen rests.
> I'll dig with it.

In its attention to metrical shape and the way words are chosen and structured, poetry even has the power to transform lives. In a recent interview, Heaney expresses his belief that if we approach poetry in a state of ready attentiveness, we may experience tiny, delicate inner changes that 'can become part of the memory system, part of the value system within an individual life. And if enough people attend like that within a society then there is a general strengthening of possibility and something that might be called healing, a growth of culture.'[86]

Poetry is often dismissed by those who regard it as being too 'highbrow,' perhaps too remote from the realities of everyday life. While some poetry – and prose – can be notoriously difficult to read and interpret (Langland's *Piers Plowman*, Coleridge's 'Kubla Khan' and James Joyce's *Ulysses* come readily to mind), for the most part the benefits of perseverance are well worth the effort. Christians 'should never forget that the poets who wrote the poetry of the Bible loved not only God and his truth *but also poetry*.'[87] There are many Christians who are diligent in their Bible reading but fail to comprehend the rich poetic nature of much of the Old Testament material. For example, a particular feature of Hebrew poetry is parallelism, which 'superimposes two slightly different views of the same object and from their convergence . . . produces a sense of depth.'[88] Whether through contrasting pairs of lines – as in Proverbs 11:19, where we read that 'the truly righteous man attains life, but he who pursues evil goes to his death' – or in synonymous parallelism, in which much the same thought is repeated, the reader's enjoyment of the text is enhanced through the symmetry and rhythm implicit in the poetic form. Occasionally new insights may be gleaned, but parallelism generally functions artistically rather than interpretively.

The book of Ruth

In order to more fully appreciate the literary artistry of the Bible, it is helpful to consider one of the better-known biblical narratives. In *Dancing in the Dark* I briefly examine the literary merits of the Old Testament book of Ruth.[89] If we probe beneath the superficial exterior and examine the book as a literary work of art containing significant theological insights, we discover that it is a narrative that has been carefully constructed in the best traditions of Hebrew literature. Throughout the book there is a dominant motif of emptiness–fullness. The thematic development in Ruth is complemented by its structural artistry, in which the typical Hebraic features of symmetry and parallelism predominate. This is particularly noticeable in Chapters 2 and 3. In both scenes, among the harvesters and on the threshing floor, a meeting takes place between Boaz and Ruth, with Boaz enquiring about the girl's identity and blessing her for her kindness (firstly to Naomi, then to himself). Ruth then returns to Naomi with barley from Boaz, and the next course of action is discussed.

Thematically, Ruth's reception of barley from Boaz and presentation of it to Naomi prefigure the birth of Obed, thus carrying the narrative forward to the sense of fulfilment that dominates the end of the story. The heightened sense of expectation afforded by these literary devices reinforces the emptiness–fullness motif that gives the story its underlying unity.

Other literary refinements add to the narrative's artistic shape. The book is in the form of a short story, or novella, and Campbell identifies a number of key attributes associated with this form-category: brevity, a plurality of episodes, a distinctive and well-wrought structure, an element of fiction, and a purpose for which the story was written.[90] In addition, word play is common throughout the narrative, and through a masterly use of sentences the author helps the reader to make the transition from one act of the story to the next as the narrative unfolds. This is particularly evident in the final verse of Chapter 1 as Naomi's despair contrasts with the hope offered by the harvest: the author 'by this exhibition of perfect poise convinces us beyond any doubt that all is well.'[91] There is also a careful managing of pace, which keeps the story moving without damaging the important scenes of encounter between the central figures. Childs has observed that the theological witness of Ruth is inseparable from its form: the literary and theological are dependent on one another.[92] The story does not explicitly declare God's providence in the face of the calamitous events recorded in Ruth, suggesting that more often than not God works in a hidden way in people's lives, working his purposes out 'behind the scenes.' We see in the superb literary artistry of the book a means by which *God's activity is revealed in its hiddenness.*

The presence of such literary merit within the biblical text should encourage those Christians who are cautious about reading literature to be more adventurous in their reading habits. Throughout this chapter I have emphasized the importance of reading *good* literature, and Christians will gain more by doing this than by confining themselves to reading just Christian literature (however that may be defined). Exposure to the way different writers express ideas in the form of poetic images, imaginative description, narrative structure, and character portrayal – features that are present throughout the Bible – cause us to identify with the reality to which good literature witnesses. The poem 'God's Grandeur' by Gerard Manley Hopkins is a magnificent testament to God's renewing grace in creation. When I read Tolkien's *Lord of the Rings* trilogy, I am made more aware of the nature of true friendship and of the way people are capable of misusing power. At times, novels and poems – and other artistic forms – can speak powerfully to us about such Christian themes as forgiveness and hope, or the compelling pressure of guilt so memorably portrayed in Fyodor Dostoevsky's classic novel *Crime and Punishment.* More disturbing themes, such as human vulnerability in the midst of social and political change in J. M. Coetzee's Booker Prize-winning novel *Disgrace*, or the hypocrisy of Soviet ideology in George Orwell's allegorical fable *Animal Farm*, resonate with the realities of life and offer us a window into the issues with which we need to grapple as responsible citizens in contemporary society.

Paying attention to the particular

In the preface to his novel *The Nigger of the Narcissus*, the Polish-born English writer Joseph Conrad observes that his task is 'by the power of the written word, to make you hear, to make you feel – it is, above all, to make you *see*. That – and no more, and it is everything.'[93] He goes on to anticipate that we might even discover 'that glimpse of truth for which [we] have forgotten to ask.' In the last chapter, I suggested that the experience of human life in all its fullness has to do with *paying attention* to this creation in such a way that we see it with new eyes. Good literature has the capacity to open our eyes to the essential particularity of human and physical life – this is especially so of poetry because of its powerful use of imagery. Stephen Spender claims that the poet's primary task is to 'think out the logic of images.'[94] The result is that we, the readers, are enriched in our awareness of what the medieval theologian Duns Scotus called the 'thisness,' or unique feature, of individual things. Poetry is particularly rich in its ability to accomplish this in the experience of the reader.

Many examples could be given of the power of literature to intersect with our humanity, enabling us to appreciate, engage with, and more fully immerse ourselves in the lives of others and in creation itself. Eugene Peterson insists that reading novels is one of the more serious activities in which a Christian pastor should be engaged. Novels, he claims, are fine ways to get across to busy pastors the importance of the particularities of story, person, and place.[95] Peterson's assertion applies not just to those who are engaged in pastoral ministry – it is relevant for all Christians. Our beings are enlarged, our horizons broadened. And there is an apologetic dividend to all this: as we read, we are encouraged, even inspired, to open our minds to the contributions of poets and writers who 'work away day after day, year after year . . . showing the story-shape of all existence, insisting on the irreducible identity of each person, and the glory of this piece of geography.'[96] If we are willing to take the time, we will come to realize that each place we enter through prose or poetry is a particular place, shaped by its own local features, and we will discover the value of treating each person we encounter – imaginary or real – as a distinct human being. We discover afresh the value of communicating the gospel in a way that pays attention to detail.

This emphasis on uniqueness and detail should not surprise us. Particularity fleshed out in the stories of ordinary people lies at the heart of the Christian gospel. Whenever we present the *grand récit* of the gospel we are confronted with the temptation to strip it of its narrative dimension in our desire to communicate the essentials of the Christian message. But the gospel is not a set of propositional dot points, but a *story* – the multifaceted story of God and his creation, and of a world made new through redeeming grace. And this story is played out in particular places among particular people. Whenever we read the Bible we are confronted with people with whom God deals in different ways – patiently, graciously, miraculously, sometimes in anger and judgment. We should not come to the biblical text ignoring such literary features as characterization and plot in a determined effort to keep our noses to the theological grindstone. Quite the reverse, in fact. It is only as we engage with the circumstances of life recounted in the Bible that we discover not only how God works in human life, but how different we are from each other. Leland Ryken maintains that a literary approach to reading the Bible 'helps us to recreate the experiences and sensations in passages. It takes concrete images seriously and does not regard them simply as a vehicle for something more important.'[97]

Imagination and fantasy literature

Whether we are reading the Bible or *Don Quixote*, a Ben Okri novel or Spencer's *The Faerie Queene*, we are encouraged to exercise our imagination, reading between the lines in order to 'enlarge our being.' Writing in a scientific context, Jeffrey Sobosan has this to say about imagination:

> My increased years have taught me that, like competence in all other things, competence in imaginative effort also takes deliberate and focussed attention. The listlessness of mental effort that often characterizes our behaviour, the refusal to attend to anything that is not immediately apparent or useful – the narcissistic temperament – can give way to intellectual passion only when the mind is diligently and carefully exercised over a wide variety of experiences.[98]

Further on, he reminds us that imaginative effort, while free-roaming, should not be undisciplined. Imagination is a gift from God and, along with other gifts, can be used in a way that is demeaning and dangerous as well as rewarding and productive. We all need to exercise constant discernment about what, and what not, to read.

Imagination, then, is a two-edged sword – it can be exercised negatively as well as positively. The primary emphasis in this chapter is on the salutary and beneficial aspects of imaginative effort. However, we should not blind ourselves to the more obvious danger areas, especially for Christians. Two areas that are frequently cited in this regard are sexuality and the supernatural, the darker side of which is manifested in pornography and occultism. In both cases, readers may find themselves exposed to stimuli that draw them into vicarious experiences, with potentially harmful consequences. We are each responsible for the extent to which we allow images and thoughts to enter our minds, and how much rein we give to our imagination. The apostle Paul reminds us that we are called to fill our minds with all that is true, noble, right, pure, lovely, and admirable (Phil. 4:8). Given the vast range of literature to which we are exposed today, great discernment is needed regarding our reading habits.

Before we focus on the genre of fantasy literature, a few brief words are in order regarding the vexing problem of what is acceptable from a Christian point of view with regard to sexual content in literature. While there is ample consensus among Christians, and others, regarding the degrading nature of pornography – Veith suggests that writers of pornography are 'prostituting themselves, selling their imaginations the way some women sell their bodies'[99] – there is considerable debate about how much and what sort of sexual content is acceptable in 'good' literature. Much hinges upon definitions, and Veith's discussion of such terms as obscenity, pornography, vulgarity, and profanity is a useful starting point.[100] The difficulty, of course, is that the violation of aesthetic decorum (his description of obscenity) cannot be measured objectively and, as Veith admits, the vulgarity in medieval classics like Chaucer's *Canterbury Tales* may be regarded as a valid expression of the lack of prudery in those times. We do not have the space in this book to enter into an adequate discussion of the description of sexual activity in literature, nor of the way the imagination can be stimulated through such portrayals. Besides, a hedonistic approach to sex, however salacious, is perhaps not the most objectionable offence in the literary domain – glamorizing violence and hate, encouraging prejudices and promoting oppression and injustice are moral evils that demand an equally forthright response. In this context, the issue of censorship is a problematic one, and past failures to have offensive material banned suggest that the Christian response should be marked less by banner-waving protests and more by constructive and intelligent criticism.

This is particularly true in the case of fantasy literature and its treatment of the supernatural realm, to which we now turn. Unfortunately, some Christian criticism of this genre in recent years has been, at times, rather shrill and ill-informed. Science fiction (SF), which overlaps with the fantasy genre, has been around for many years – for example, both *Frankenstein* and *The Strange Case of Dr. Jekyll and Mr. Hyde* are generally regarded as science fiction – but its boundaries are difficult to define with any precision. Essentially SF may be distinguished from fantasy because of its emphasis on the impact of science and technology in the development of the narrative, especially with regard to the physics of space and time. Fantasy literature takes us beyond the realities of our known world into imaginary realms, and may include such features as supernatural beings, magical powers, talking animals, and even time travel, as in Mark Twain's *A Connecticut Yankee in King Arthur's Court*. Its origins lie in the epic stories that can be traced back to the days of Mesopotamian and Egyptian mythology.

A brief comment on the development of fantasy literature may be helpful at this stage. The Epic of Gilgamesh, the earliest Sumerian versions of which go back to around 4000 BC, recounts the exploits of a great king who was two-thirds divine and one-third human. These story-telling elements in fantasy were continued in Greek and Roman mythology – not many schoolchildren today are required to read such classics as Homer's *Odyssey* or Virgil's *Aeneid* – and in the medieval period, the Norse and Icelandic sagas, which inspired Tolkien's

Lord of the Rings, are filled with powerful prose and poetic imagery. For example, the tenth-century Old English poem *Beowulf*, the oldest surviving epic in British literature, describes the adventures of a heroic Scandinavian warrior-king and his encounters with three great monsters. These and other classical and medieval fantasy epics laid the foundation for the mythological worlds and time periods explored in such works as *Don Quixote*, the satirical novel by the Spaniard Miguel de Cervantes in which the author mocks the idealistic chivalry of the Middle Ages, *Gulliver's Travels* – Jonathan Swift's satirical commentary on politics and human nature – and Lewis Carroll's *Alice's Adventures in Wonderland*.

One of the most important influences upon C. S. Lewis, whose fictional land of Narnia is one of the most celebrated examples of a fantasy world, was the nineteenth-century Scottish novelist, poet, and clergyman George MacDonald, whose novel *Phantastes* caused Lewis to observe, after a few hours' reading, that he had 'crossed a great frontier.' While much fantasy writing today is still in the form of science fiction, it is the realm of mythology that had the most profound effect upon Lewis and J. R. R. Tolkien, the authors of two of the most popular works of fantasy today – *The Chronicles of Narnia* and *The Lord of the Rings*. Recent movie versions have popularized the fictional adventures of the four Pevensie children and Frodo Baggins and his hobbit friends, along with the fantasy world created by J. K. Rowling in her *Harry Potter* series, although some are hesitant about bracketing Rowling with Lewis and Tolkien, regarding her as a literary lightweight in comparison. While most Christians find *The Lord of the Rings* and *The Chronicles of Narnia* imaginative and spiritually inspiring, far more questions have been raised not only about Rowling's literary merit but, more crucially, about her emphasis on witchcraft and wizardry, and the associated dangers of introducing young people to occult practices.

The relationship between Tolkien and Lewis at Oxford University was crucial in the latter's conversion to Christianity. As the two of them went for a walk one evening by the river in the grounds of Magdalen College with their mutual friend Hugo Dyson, they discussed the nature of myths. Lewis expressed to Tolkien his belief that myths were lies and therefore of no worth, even though 'breathed through silver.' Tolkien replied that myths were not lies – they were, in his opinion, the only way we can really communicate truths that would otherwise elude our understanding. 'We have come from God, Tolkien argued, and inevitably the myths woven by us, though they contain error, reflect a splintered fragment of the true light, the eternal truth that is with God.'[101] The realization that myths could be true revolutionized Lewis' thinking, and was instrumental in his acceptance of Christianity. In his literary output, the mythical features of imaginative literature became the principal way of conveying the truths of the Christian faith, enabling readers to 'unthink' false images and discover what Lewis describes as 'myth made fact'[102] So the fictional narrative format of fantasy, drawing on the literary conventions of parable and allegory, became, for Lewis, the primary means of portraying the 'Christian myth.' 'Lewis' whole enterprise in helping his readers grasp biblical truth was a process of demythologizing the false and remythologizing the true.'[103]

The concept of remythologizing lies at the very centre of *The Lord of the Rings* and *The Chronicles of Narnia*. It is precisely because both Tolkien and Lewis were thoroughly Christian that their masterpieces of fantasy – to which we should add Tolkien's *The Hobbit* and *The Silmarillion* (which describes the mythological background to *The Lord of the Rings*), and Lewis' famous cosmic trilogy *Out of the Silent Planet, Perelandra,* and *That Hideous Strength* – are shot through with Christian truth. There is a reality that we can connect with in these works that contrasts sharply with, for example, the imaginary world of Rowling's Harry Potter. Rowling frames her narrative around a worldview that employs wizardry and witchcraft as the means of pitting good against evil, but her value-system is not grounded in Christian truth. Does this make her less 'Christian'? Probably, but that should not lead us to dismiss her fictional writing out of hand. 'Potterworld' contains many important themes about life, such as friendship, loyalty, and courage – human virtues that are imaginatively woven into the fantasy world created around Hogwarts – with the result that the battle between good and evil is often seen to depend upon these qualities more than the display of magic. Even Harry's own magic is at times not as effective as that of his friend Hermione! And who would not want to play a game of Quidditch if they had the chance, or race up and down the moving staircases at Hogwarts? The fun and adventure that Harry and his friends experience appeal to the escapism in us all, though others would argue that, precisely for this reason, their magic is dangerous and deceptive, leading young minds astray and encouraging experimentation with the deceptive forces of occultism.

Besides this last claim, critics of Rowling argue that she fails to locate her fantasy world in the real-world duality that is so evident in the mythological works of Tolkien and Lewis. While the conflicts in Middle-Earth and Narnia present a clear-cut dualism between light and darkness, the magic that Harry and his friends learn at Hogwarts is more ambiguous, favoring white over black witchcraft. Furthermore, reality is manipulated for trivial as well as for more serious reasons. This, say Rowling's critics, opens the door to a slippery path that runs all the way down into occultism. It is difficult to refute this allegation, as the Potter novels have in some cases fueled a fascination with the occult among young readers. The answer, though, is not to ban the novels on the grounds that they are inherently evil, overly magical, or morally suspect, but to engage critically with them, seeking to identify points of contact and departure, both ethically and thematically, with the Christian gospel. This point, of course, applies to all fantasy literature, but it is easily forgotten in the midst of the spate of Christian criticism that has been directed at the *Harry Potter* novels in particular.

Many books and articles have been written showing how the fantasy worlds of Tolkien and Lewis and Rowling connect with the gospel. While most readers would agree that the first two write with much greater depth and imagination, drawing from a strong Christian faith and vision, all three deal in their own way with important gospel themes. Julian Jenkins, in a review of the first *Harry Potter* novel, suggests that all great fantasy literature examines in some way the use and abuse of power.[104] In *Lord of the Rings*, for example, Tolkien demonstrates convincingly the extent to which power can destroy unless it is used to serve others. This is especially evident in the self-sacrificing love of Aslan in *The Lion, the Witch and the Wardrobe*, which contrasts strikingly with the abuse of power by the White Witch, who keeps the land of Narnia in perpetual winter until her hold on power is destroyed. Many other gospel themes are discernible in these fantasy texts, including temptation, betrayal, death and resurrection, forgiveness, judgment, loyalty, individual worth, and ultimate hope in the midst of fear and darkness. While the Harry Potter novels engage with a number of these themes at various levels, and while many children – and adults – regard them as 'a cracking good read,' they lack a distinctly Christian worldview and at times display a moral relativism among the young heroes – for example, lies and trickery – that is at odds with Christian behavior.

As the father of three children, one of my enduring memories is the joy I experienced as I read *The Chronicles of Narnia* to each of them in turn. Having read them over and over again, I can say with conviction that they are stories that speak not only to the child but also to the adult. They contain truths that are timeless, and uniquely encapsulate the gospel message in a way that communicates powerfully to those who are drawn into the tales of dwarfs and talking animals, of adventures on high seas, of magic and deep mystery, of ordinary children caught up in a world not their own, of evil spells and strong enchantments, of a lion, a witch, and a wardrobe.

The fantasy works that we have briefly discussed here reflect 'splintered fragments of the true light,' and in their own way offer us access into the real world to which we belong. Each of us is invited into the story portrayed, and as we are drawn in we discover the power of imagination at work in our lives. Some accomplish this more successfully than others, and it remains the responsibility of the reader, guided by parents where appropriate, to distinguish between the good, the bad, and the ugly. This, ultimately, is what discernment is all about when it comes to literature. 'To read or not to read' – even in today's 'aliteral' age – is not nearly as important as the question, '*What* are you reading?' How we act in response to that question will have a significant impact on our lives as members of the human race.

4

Seeing God in the Creative Arts

*A plea to break out of our captivity to fear and to embrace
the arts as an affirmation of life*

Girl with a Pearl Earring is the
title of Tracy Chevalier's
imaginary account of the
circumstances leading to the
creation of the famous
masterpiece of the same
name by the seventeenth-
century Dutch painter
Johannes Vermeer. A young
Protestant servant girl
named Griet is allowed into
the artist's studio. She soon
displays an intuitive appreciation of Vermeer's craft,
and begins to offer him

advice and help as he paints. On one occasion Griet asks
Vermeer, who converted to Catholicism at the age of twenty-
one, why there are paintings in Catholic churches. Vermeer
responds:

> 'A painting in a church is like a candle in a dark room – we
> use it to see better. It is a bridge between ourselves and God. But
> it is not a Protestant candle or a Catholic candle. It is simply a
> candle.'
> 'We do not need such things to help us to see God,' I [Griet]
> countered. 'We have his Word and that is enough.'[105]

Vermeer then goes on to say that Protestants, like Catholics, see God everywhere, in everything: 'By painting everyday things – tables and chairs, bowls and pitchers, soldiers and maids – are they not celebrating God's creation as well?' This celebration of God's creation in human artistic endeavor – examined in the last chapter with specific reference to prose and poetry – needs further exploration, and affirmation. There is a powerful myth prevailing in many church circles that maintains that Christians are inevitably engaged in a form of 'cultural warfare' with mainstream popular arts, especially the visual, and audiovisual, arts. This reflects the dualistic paradigm discussed in Chapter 1, where we observed that tensions remain among Christians about how enlightened we should allow ourselves to be as far as the entertainment world goes. Steve Turner, an English poet and writer, records his early experiences of this tension, based on the reasoning that 'most art was created by unbelievers and could therefore damage our spiritual health.'[106] It was okay to get involved in the arts, so long as the end goal was 'outreach': 'Thus we had movies with tissue thin characters and threadbare plots that moved inexorably toward climactic conversions.'[107]

But engagement with art is surely to be applauded because, as we pointed out in the last chapter, our beings are enlarged: we become more fully human in the sense that we encounter, in some mysterious sense, what George Steiner calls the 'real presence' of God. For Steiner, experiencing the aesthetic, whether in poetry, painting, music or any other artistic endeavor, is what he calls 'a wager on transcendence,' because of his passionate belief that a transcendent reality grounds all genuine art. The Anabaptist theologian Duane Friesen echoes this conviction when he describes aesthetic experience as 'our sensual response to the way our cosmos and the world is ordered' – it is also, at the same time 'an integral part of our response to God, the Creator of the cosmos.'[108] The cry of 'art for art's sake' is too narrow a view, and rings hollow in the ears of those who recognize the essential continuity between the creative faculties and human experience.

Art also speaks to us in moral terms because of its (maybe hidden) impact upon the way we think and behave. Some art, of course, is so trivial and banal, so commercialized in its intent, that it rightly earns Steiner's label of 'the pornography of insignificance.' While Christians are called to be vigilant and discerning in the light of the contemporary consumerist culture, they would do well to acknowledge Madeleine L'Engle's observation that great artists 'keep us from frozenness, from smugness, from thinking that the truth is in us rather than in God, in Christ our Lord.'[109] L'Engle goes on to suggest that exposure to art helps us in our quest for truth: might we often be closer to God when we are beset by doubt than when we enclose ourselves in rigid certainties?

Art as communication

In this chapter our focus is on a wide range of creative artwork, embracing such media as film-making, music, painting, and sculpture.[110] As with all forms of communication, we are immediately confronted with the problem of interpretation. In 1953 M. H. Abrams wrote a book called *The Mirror and the Lamp*, in which he analyzed the literary criticism of the Romantic period.[111] He suggests that the literary critic – and here we might extend that to refer to all artistic criticism – needs to take into account the relation of art to four objects: the artist, external reality, the audience, and the internal characteristics of the work itself. These four coordinates translate into his classical model of the four major approaches to critical theory. In his exposition of the arts as 'gift,' Friesen identifies three of these coordinates: the gift that is given to the artist; the way that gift is expressed in a work of art, such as a novel or painting; and the gratitude with which that gift is appropriated and enjoyed by the public. In likening them to what Peter Berger calls 'signals of tran-scendence,' he implicitly incorporates art's relationship to external reality and places it within a broader theological framework.[112]

In *My Name is Asher Lev*, the first of Chaim Potok's two novels about the life of a Jewish painter named Asher Lev, the author traces the development of the gift of drawing in the young boy to manhood. In the sequel, Asher is in middle age, and the plot centres on the succession plans concerning the aged *rebbe* of the Ladover Hasidic community. In the first novel, Asher's father, a key figure in the Ladover cause, spends much of his time absent from their Brooklyn home, founding yeshivas in different parts of the world. The gulf between father and son creates deep tensions in the life of the family. Against this background, Asher is apprenticed to a famous artist, who encourages him to paint what he sees, and it is this insight – and inner impulse – that causes him to paint the two works *Brooklyn Crucifixion I* and *Brooklyn Crucifixion II* that lead to his excommunication from the local Ladover community. In the second novel, *The Gift of Asher Lev*, the artist, now married, discovers that his recently deceased uncle has willed to him a valuable collection of paintings. One day Asher climbs the stairs to his uncle's study, and gazes at the paintings mounted on the walls: 'The tiny color planes in the Cézanne, like the pieces of a riddle, exquisitely explored, investigated, probed, resolved, each daub of color another piece of his answer to the greatest riddle of all: how we see and think the world.' Throughout the two powerfully written novels, Potok enables us to grasp this essential reality: all true artists are impelled to communicate what they *see*.[113]

Contemporary hermeneutical theory attributes increasing importance to the role of the reader or viewer in the interpretive task. Confronted by a stone sculpture we might reasonably ask ourselves, What does this work of art do *for me*? But, in the light of Abrams' elegant model, that should not be the end of our questioning. The sculptor doubtless has a message to convey, encouraging us to discover what we can about the intention behind the work. Furthermore, we might want to enquire whether or not the artwork expresses some truth about the world in which we live. Finally, might there possibly be something intrinsic to the sculpture that is embedded in the work itself, such that the stone contains an inner reality that says something to us irrespective of the intention of the sculptor or the referential field of the viewer? The clever use of materials in a sculpture or the vivid application of colors in a painting may appeal to us aesthetically without our having to probe for a meaning that may not be there! In our aspirations to become artistic critics, we 'must be careful not to claim for artists or artistic works what they are not.'[114]

Questions like those in the paragraph above demonstrate the complex interpretive grid within which we are all involved when confronted with a specific work of art. Some people insist that a movie or painting is only 'true' if it expresses some aspect of truth that coheres explicitly with the real world. For example, a movie that demonstrates the beauty of friendship or the obscenity of rape may communicate those realities in a powerful way, and is therefore 'true' in its representation of human life. However, art does not merely describe *what is*: 'through the artist's imagination, it adjusts and manipulates a portion of the world, to allow its mystery to be unlocked.'[115] Artists are not obliged to mirror reality in a simplistic way. The abstract imagery of a Kandinsky painting has the power to communicate the elemental themes of life and death in a way that other more realistic compositions are frequently unable to accomplish.

We need to acknowledge that abstraction, novelty, and exaggeration, even distortion, are all grist to the artist's creative mill. Cartoonists may overstate a person's facial features, and theatrical farce may draw on improbable situations – in both cases exaggeration and distortion help us to appreciate the reality that is there. The Catholic fiction writer Flannery O'Connor writes: 'I am interested in making up a good case for distortion, as I am coming to believe it is the only way to make people see.'[116] In her essay, 'Writing Short Stories,' O'Connor refers to Franz Kafka's classic story 'The Metamorphosis,' in which the main character wakes up to find himself changed into a cockroach. She insists that Kafka confronts the reader not with unreality, but with the almost unbearable reality of the dual nature of human beings. This distinction between appearance and reality allows the artist the liberty 'to make certain rearrangements of nature if these will lead to greater depth of vision.'[117] For O'Connor, hidden truths are revealed through the use of the grotesque, enabling artists to transmit their own vision of reality in imaginative ways that might shock or startle.

A similar example can be found in *The Voyage of the Dawn Treader*, one of C. S. Lewis' Narnian stories, in which the obnoxious Eustace Clarence Scrubb finds himself transformed into a dragon after falling asleep on a hoard of gold, dreaming dragonish thoughts. Eustace's own metamorphosis leads to an admission of his own self-centredness, and his subsequent 'undragoning' by Aslan represents a symbolic baptism that reveals our inability to transform ourselves. Lewis may have had his own wrestling with pride in mind – he once confessed in a letter to his great friend Arthur Greeves to being 'a conceited ass.' This is the same phrase he attributes to Eustace in *The Voyage of the Dawn Treader*, whose metamorphosis into a dragon serves as a powerful reminder of the human struggle with greed and self-importance.

A disturbing example of artistic distortion can be found in Edvard Munch's well-known expressionist painting *The Scream*, in which the Norwegian artist appears to portray the agony of humanity assailed by isolation and despair. Theories abound as to the actual motive for the painting, with some critics suggesting that Munch's mental instability might have been a contributory factor. Whatever the reason, the painting, reproduced a number of times by the artist and translated into a lithograph so that it could have worldwide distribution, is a potent expression of the

reality of existential angst and a vivid depiction of the inner pain that is a part of the human condition today. Though a visual distortion of reality, it is nonetheless 'true' insofar as it imaginatively witnesses to the actuality of deep human emotion. The Spanish cubist painter Pablo Picasso once said that 'art is a lie that makes us realize the truth.'

Of course, there are many examples of character distortion

that serve a more light-hearted and humorous purpose, and which are no less real in their effect. The field of light entertainment abounds in caricature, a popular example of which may be found in the exaggerated portrayal of the Prime Minister, Jim Hacker, and the civil servant, Sir Humphrey Appleby, in the celebrated BBC comedy television series *Yes, (Prime) Minister*. The programs have been universally admired for representing the reality of British political life. Former British Prime Minister Margaret Thatcher once commented that its closely observed portrayal of what goes on in the corridors of power had given her hours of pure joy.

Truth and interpretation in art

Imagination and creativity – even the grotesque – therefore play an important part in the truthfulness of art. But this does not imply an anarchic freedom that seeks to break free from the givenness of the created order. Begbie argues that 'artistic freedom consists in being properly related through Christ to that world which was brought into being and is sustained 'through him.' '[118] He quotes the insights of the Russian composer, Igor Stravinsky, who acknowledges that the seven notes of the chromatic scale provide him with a compositional freedom that he would not have if confronted by an absence of limits. Theologically, Begbie interprets this limitation as a positive affirmation of the real possibilities implicit in God's original intention for all humanity, artists included. Creative freedom and objective order are therefore not incompatible.

Works of art communicate truth to us at the level of experience. Their primary appeal is to our feelings and emotions, rather than to our mind – this does not mean, of course, that we do not reflect deeply upon what we have experienced, but that the initial point of contact is at the emotional or intuitive rather than the rational or cognitive level. The arts also appeal to our imagination, as we discussed with reference to literature in the last chapter. But how does this correlate with the notion of truth? Ryken proposes four levels of truth in art: the truth about human values, especially our longings and fears; the truth that represents the way things are, specifically the contours of human experience or external reality; general truth about life as perceived and interpreted by the artist; and, finally, ultimate truths encapsulated in the notion of an all-embracing world-view.[119] Art is a form of language, and it accomplishes its communicative task in each of these areas with varying degrees of success. Much art undoubtedly achieves its purpose well, but sometimes a work of art may convey human values or the nature of reality in a shallow or vacuous manner . . . or it may convey intrinsically dishonest ideas in an artistically attractive way.

Pragmatically, the evaluation of artistic success depends very much on the purpose that a work of art is intended to convey, and how well that communication occurs. People, of course, respond differently to specific works of art: it is a matter of personal taste. As I walk through an art gallery, my friend who is with me may not share my preference for impressionist paintings or my appreciation of Picasso's cubism. So with my taste in music or the sort of movies I like to view. Consumers of art are as different as artists themselves, who compose and create according to their personal interests, preferences, and intentions. And that, of course, is at it should be – we have been created by God as unique human beings, shaped by our own background, environment, and genetic makeup, and the very diversity of our humanity is a rich expression not only of God's creative genius but also of the cultural fabric in which we live and move and have our being.

Our response to art is determined not only by our interpretation of its meaning, but also by our evaluation of its artistic and aesthetic merit. Wolterstorff's emphasis on the performative, or functional, role of art leads him to make an interesting distinction between *artistic* excellence and a*esthetic* excellence: citing Bartok's Fifth Quartet, for example, he argues that the musical work may be artistically excellent in the sense that it accurately conveys the meaning intended by the composer . . . but, in Wolterstorff's view, that does not necessarily render it beautiful.[120] Actually, artistic excellence and the communication of meaning may not be as closely correlated as Wolterstorff suggests: it is possible to appreciate a work of art without being aware of its immediate significance. I recently listened for the first time to the Benedictus from Karl Jenkins' *The Armed Man: A Mass for Peace,* and was profoundly moved by the sheer beauty of the music without being aware of its association with the consequences of war in human society. Furthermore, beauty may not necessarily be the most appropriate way of thinking about aesthetic excellence – linguistically, aesthetics has less to do with beauty than it has with enabling us to *feel* something (its antonym – anaesthetic – has to do with the senses being deadened!).

Consider these thoughts in terms of the technical ability of a painter. The artist's use of texture and brushstrokes, how layering is employed, the selection of colors used and the way perspective adds to the overall impact . . . these and many other aspects of the painter's craft determine the technical quality of the final result. So we might say that the painting achieves a certain degree of artistic excellence: it has a certain form and inner integrity that marks it out as an artwork of distinction. But of course it does not end there. Art communicates – it says something. And it does so through our feelings. And what it communicates is not value-free: because art is ultimately a commentary on life mediated through the personality of the artist, it has a moral dimension. Adopting Wolterstorff's categories, this has more to do with aesthetic excellence than artistic excellence, and in this regard Christians have just as important a voice in evaluating art as any other group of people.

Christians should bring to their engagement with the creative arts a distinctly Christian perspective. My comments in Chapter 3 about redeeming language and discerning the quality of 'goodness' in literature apply equally to other art forms. In that chapter, I cited the apostle Paul who writes in Philippians 4:8: 'Finally brothers, whatever is true, whatever is noble, whatever is right, whatever is pure, whatever is lovely, whatever is admirable – if anything is excellent or praiseworthy – think about such things.' While Christians may disagree over the relative beauty or truthfulness of a particular work of art, there is undoubtedly a distinctive ethical and doctrinal grid that should inform their evaluation. If, as we argued in Chapter 1, we are called to be salt and light, making a difference in the world, then we need to be on our guard lest we accommodate ourselves to less than godly standards in terms of what we see and hear in the name of cultural relevance. This comment applies not only to those who listen and watch – it applies just as much, if not more so, to those who seek to communicate through art. A fine example of a music band that has not sacrificed moral (and Christian) content in the interests of artistic excellence is the Irish rock band U2 which includes three Christians — Bono, The Edge and Larry Muller. The lyrics of the track 'Yahweh' on their album 'How to Dismantle an Atomic Bomb' make reference to life as a city that should be shining on a hill, reminiscent of Jesus' words in Matthew 5:14. Bono's passionate commitment to global justice is reflected not only in U2's music, but also in his public involvement in such campaigns as 'Make Poverty History' and his willingness to engage personally with leaders on the world political stage.

Apocalypse in pop culture

There is, of course, a fine balance to achieve as we engage with the creative arts. And because the world in which we live is broken and fragile, containing not only much that is good and beautiful but also the ugly and bizarre, Christians cannot afford to be too one-sided in their selection of what they are exposed to. It is too easy to be squeamish in the face of the many different expressions of art around us. For example, the film *The Shawshank Redemption* transports us into the sordid, drab, and vicious environment of a maximum security prison, and at times the scenes containing extreme language and brutal violence are overwhelming – but they are not at all gratuitous, and their inclusion is intrinsic to the film's message of hope and redemption. The movie needs the brutal to be beautiful.

Intimations of God's truth can penetrate us – even transform us – as we open ourselves to the creative endeavors of painters and poets, musicians and moviemakers. We begin to see new things that speak to us of the truth of a God who is freedom, love, and grace . . . and a God who knows and understands the

realities of the human condition. So pain, suffering, doubt, fear,
love, joy, and despair are played out in the images before us,
and we discover the truth about ourselves. All artists have this
great privilege of participating in God's creative energies,
whether they realize it or not. As our hearts and minds are
blessed or disturbed by the creative gifts of the artistic
community, we may, in the words of Seamus Heaney, hear 'a
music we would never have known to listen for.'

Jeremy Begbie relates the time when he addressed a mixed
audience at the London Institute of Contemporary Christianity,
and introduced the topic of improvisation in music. He cited the
compositions of Oscar Peterson, Dizzy Gillespie, and Beethoven,
commenting on their remarkable mixture of consistency and
unpredictability: 'I tried to show that something similar marked
God's ways with the world – reliable, but at the same time
constantly new and surprising. A few days later, I had an email
telling me about a man who through this talk recovered his
long-lost Christian faith, and with it his marriage.'[121]

Martyn Percy suggests that 'music is a gift, and as we learn to
read it, understand it and use it, we learn more about the God
who has given it. Gifts express the giver.'[122] He proposes a form
of theological modeling that likens the Trinity to jazz music:

> In thinking about the Trinity as music – jazz in this case – we are
> mindful of its combinations: its formal dimensions married to its
> innovative nature, and its capacity to cover a spectrum of needs
> from celebration to commiseration. And we are mindful of the
> different sounds that make up one sound, that is simultaneously
> scripted yet improvised, formal, yet free . . . The Trinity as jazz is
> not as strange as it first sounds. Jazz is a genre of music that is
> normally associated with freedom of expression and form. It is
> both transforming yet traditional; never predictable, and yet
> reliable. Order and freedom coexist, with passive listening turned
> into participation and communion; from an apparently tense
> synthesis of composition and improvisation, inspiration,
> liberation and dance can issue.

Percy argues that the analogy of jazz music delivers a
paradox that reflects mystery. Because jazz music draws us into
those open spaces in which we can find freedom, the music

reveals something of our need, as human beings, to participate in the life and communion of God as Trinity. This is similar to David Dark's suggestion that truth is revealed to us in the form of an epiphany, an experience that he describes in the language of 'apocalypse.' In his fine book articulating the major theme of this chapter, Dark makes an interesting reference to jazz music, suggesting that, at its best, it 'gives voice to the groaning universe anticipating a new day.'[123] This, he goes on to write, is the business of apocalyptic.

Dark rightly exposes the many misunderstandings that surround the word 'apocalypse,' the root meaning of which has to do with unveiling or revealing. The purpose of apocalyptic, he suggests, is to *show us what we are not seeing*, an insight that offers critical insight into the revelatory role of pop culture. Dark's use of the word 'apocalypse' is highly suggestive: its usual interpretation, particularly within the Christian context, confuses redemption with escape in its rejection of all that is of this world. It is a word that is rich with images of horror and destruction as the old gives way to the new, a scenario that resonates with dualistic notions of the irredeemable nature of the present physical creation. 'But genuinely apocalyptic expression is a radical declaration concerning the meaning of human experience. Its job is to reflect, in a deeply liberating fashion, the tensions and paradoxes that constitute our understanding of reality . . . apocalyptic offers a world that is and was and is to come, a world spinning inside (and outside) this one.'[124]

How does pop culture reveal these deep truths about ourselves and the world in which we live? In many ways, suggests Dark, but two in particular stand out. Firstly, in its concentrated attentiveness to the minute particulars of life, art has the capacity to penetrate all that is shallow, superficial, and contradictory in our lives. For example, *The Simpsons* portrays a dysfunctional family that is just like us – we laugh at their selfishness and ineptitude, and recognize in them an echo of ourselves. But when we watch inattentively we miss the point, rather like those who failed to 'get the point' of Jesus' parables: 'Unfortunately, the humility that is marked by a genuine readiness to know and acknowledge our own weaknesses and fears comes no more naturally to us than it does to the characters on *The Simpsons*. Yet without this humility of mind, no story, no art, and no apocalyptic can do its work on us. We walk through life unaffected, and forever consigned to an invincible ignorance.'[125]

A second way in which pop culture functions apocalyptically has to do with the slippery notion of 'goodness' which we discussed earlier. If art is good, argues Dark, 'it will have the ability to lift us out of one-dimensional thinking, means-end behaviour, and last ditch power drives that confine our lives.'[126] Significantly, Dark makes no distinction between good, beautiful, and truthful – what Colin Gunton calls the 'three great transcendentals of traditional philosophical enquiry.'[127] The three adjectives intermingle in his central thesis that they all have this remarkable capacity to *unveil*. And this unveiling – by the sheer goodness or beauty of a piece of art – directly challenges our hypocrisy and self-centredness if we are open to its power. This is art's Christian virtue: its apocalyptic power points us towards the actuality of the kingdom of God, which is not just a future hope but also a present reality.

The presence of the apocalyptic in art has to do with the gracious and sometimes shocking ministry of the Spirit in the world, who is ever at work to unveil all that is false, corrupt, and cruel as well as all that is true and whole and beautiful. It is the Spirit's privilege to unveil the kingdom of God, and he will accomplish this in ways that resonate with the culture of the day, immersing himself in whatever cultural 'texts' offer the best vehicles for communication. Of course, as we have already argued, no work of art is value-free, and the perspectives and prejudices of artists that contribute to the creation of a work of art need to be carefully discerned by the Christian interpretive community. Too often, however, discernment with regard to the popular arts has been characterized by a negative pursuit of all that is 'un-Christian' rather than a positive affirmation of God's life in creation. We noted in Chapter 2 that Christians need the wisdom to discern where the Spirit is at work, often in the unlikeliest places and in the most improbable ways. Grenz and Franke express this well with respect to the construction of human artefacts:

Because the life-giving Creator Spirit is present wherever life flourishes, the Spirit's voice can conceivably resound through many media, including the media of human culture. Because Spirit-induced human flourishing evokes cultural expression, we can anticipate in such expressions traces of the Creator Spirit's presence. Consequently, we should listen intently for the voice of the Spirit, who is present in all life and therefore who 'precedes' us into the world, bubbling to the surface through the artefacts and symbols humans construct . . . but always a voice that does not contradict the voice of Christian Scripture.[128]

This line of thinking endorses the view that a television series like *The Simpsons*, in spite of its cartoon irreverence and satirical content (perhaps, more to the point, because of it) is a vehicle for the Spirit. But we have to 'listen intently' for his voice, and we may easily miss him in the midst of the clamour of our culture. This is particularly apparent in the music scene, and many Christians find it hard to accept that contemporary music – especially, rock, punk, or heavy metal – may be a vehicle for the Spirit of God. Clearly, some of today's music does offend, especially when lyrics are merely a vehicle for gratuitously explicit obscenities. Earlier decades witnessed the rise of anarchic punk bands like the Sex Pistols, an anti-establishment group notorious as much for its vulgarity and unruly behavior as for its sneering vocals and a desire to shock and provoke. But behind the lyrics of many rock and punk songs there are genuine cries of pain and despair, as in the Smashing Pumpkins' 'Bullet with Butterfly Wings', a track on their enormously successful 1995 album *Mellon Collie and the Infinite Sadness*.

God, Mozart and 'heavy metal'

The incarnational character of Christianity proclaims the truth that God has chosen to make himself known as a human being in human culture and in the midst of the structures of society. The implication of this is something we have been fleshing out throughout this book. God is not distant from human culture but understands us and sympathizes with us as *cultural* beings.

This means that we should expect him to be revealed in the many diverse cultural expressions that make up a particular culture or society. In this section of the chapter we look at two very contrasting expressions of cultural life, both taken from the field of music: Mozart and 'heavy metal'. Some readers might gasp with horror that the two are embraced in the same paragraph! I confess to no great love of the heavy metal culture – rather the reverse, in fact – and the closest I have come to listening to any form of what I often describe as 'alternative contemporary music' is the music of the punk rock band with which my son-in-law was closely associated for many years. I am much happier in the company of Mozart. But personal taste is not the focus of this book.

Wolfgang Amadeus Mozart was, as we all know, a precocious genius. His death from a fever in his mid-thirties while working on his *Requiem* robbed the world of an astonishingly gifted composer, whose many works rank among the greatest classical masterpieces of all time. Haydn described him as the greatest composer known to him in person or by name – 'he has taste and, what is more, the greatest knowledge of composition.' Rossini claimed that he was the only musician who had 'as much knowledge as genius, and as much genius as knowledge.' Beethoven and Tchaikovsky were likewise in awe of his remarkable musical abilities, especially his capacity to create some of the most beautiful melodies known in the classical repertoire. Peter Shaffer's play, *Amadeus*, made into an Oscar-winning full-length movie – in which Mozart's relationship with Salieri, who is portrayed in the film as a jealous rival, is the central theme – presents Mozart as an immature and coarse young man, a portrayal regarded by many as unjustified.

In June 1956, Karl Barth, one of the Christian world's greatest theologians, paid homage to Mozart in a forty-minute lecture at the University of Geneva. He rejoiced that in Mozart's music 'the sun shines, but without burning or weighing upon the earth' and 'the earth also stays in its place, remains itself, without feeling that it must therefore rise in titanic revolt against the heavens.' He bowed before an art in which 'the laugh is never without tears, tears are never unrelieved by laughter.'[129] He also spoke about the reality and the peace that he experienced in an art that embraces nature, humankind, and God, which is as true to life as it is to death. Barth's testimony to Mozart's artistic genius is evidence of the power of music to reveal something good about human nature, specifically for Barth 'the sovereignty of the true servant.'

Of course, much else is communicated through Mozart's compositions, including the great human themes of love and death, especially in his operatic works. Great operas like *The Marriage of Figaro* (based on the stage play by the French playwright Pierre de Beaumarchais) and *Don Giovanni* (adapted from the tale of the legendary Spanish nobleman and philanderer Don Juan) are very Shakespearean in their treatment of love, intrigue, betrayal, and reconciliation. We recognize our own foibles and desires, as well as the realities of human nature, in the plots and subplots that are woven throughout the libretti of Mozart's collaborator, Lorenzo da Ponte. But it is the music that gives these two operas, and others, their lasting popularity. The composer also wrote some sublime sacred music, including his *Great Mass* – an unfinished composition like his *Requiem* – which is often interpreted as an expression of the composer's gratitude to God. No one, however, is really sure why he did not complete what many regard as one of his finest works.

If Mozart's music has universal accessibility and acceptance, the same cannot be said about 'heavy metal,' a musical genre that has had an enduring place within the many different youth subcultures over the last three or four decades.[130] Many Christians would be sympathetic with the view of the professor of religious studies who described it as 'a form of aesthetic terrorism'![131] However, such a judgment is hasty, and fails to recognize that music, at the most general level, is not just a means of entertainment but a way of seeing and interpreting reality. This is no less true of the heavy metal culture. A brief examination of what lies behind this particular music subculture and what Christians can learn from the genre is instructive.

Heavy metal began as an artistic reaction against the idealistic counterculture of the 1960s. Many metal bands and their fans acknowledge one band in particular, Black Sabbath, as the pioneering influence on the genre, although Led Zeppelin and

Deep Purple have played significant roles in the growth of the sound. The musical influences on the genre are varied, ranging from the grainy howl of primitive blues to the majestic sound of soaring baroque. But heavy metal is best known for the sheer volume and power of its sound, with its rhythms ranging from the highly syncopated and slow to mid-paced and blasting. Chordal structures range from minor dirges to atonal chromatic riffing. The complexity of the music is diverse too, ranging from simple rock structures to arrangements that are similar to intricate classical compositions. Vocals range from quasi-operatic melodic voices with clear enunciation of words to high screaming and distorted guttural-sounding growls.

But it is the raw power of the music that is its greatest attraction, offering a sense of 'power' to young people who feel alienated from modern life. In fact, the themes of conflict, violence, and death that pervade heavy metal lyrics reflect the genre's antipathy towards middle-class values. The emphasis on physicality in the music and in the lifestyle of its adherents can be traced to its working-class roots: Wenstein observes that bands and their fans come from working-class backgrounds or those disaffected with their middle-class backgrounds.[132] The music's physicality and lyrical content allow young people a 'safe place' in which to express a variety of emotions that society deems 'unsafe' or 'uncivilized,' or to deal with issues that are 'no-go' areas for discussion.

Nihilism is a pervasive feature of the music, though para-doxically there are strong undertones of the search for a utopian ideal...but an ideal of a world without the constraints of 'civilization' and organized religion, involving at times the desire to return to a pagan 'Golden Age.' Understandably, this appears threatening to the established social order, but a pagan utopian vision is, of course, a frequent theme in the classical music of Richard Wagner and in various strands of romantic literature. Many of the chaos images in heavy metal are mined from the Judeo-Christian tradition and the pagan sagas of northern Europe, and major sources of chaos rhetoric and imagery include the literature of Edgar Allen Poe, Tolkien and Milton's *Paradise Lost*.[133]

Satanism, neo-paganism and other forms of spirituality are common to heavy metal culture in its search for alternative answers to the fundamental questions of meaning and existence. Indifference right through to open hatred characterize attitudes towards Christianity and other forms of organized religion. For some musicians, such as Ihsahn, guitarist and singer in the black metal band Emperor, Judeo-Christian concepts like benevolence are despised as a sign of weakness, and Jesus is often regarded as a weak god in comparison with the deities of Norse mythology. The result is that many Christians have little or no time for those who are involved in the heavy metal scene, preferring to adopt the Niebuhrian 'Christ Against Culture' position – the only conceivable way of redeeming these musicians would be to extract them out of their music and their social networks.

Brad Bessell regards such an approach as counterproductive, giving rise to a form of 'social circumcision,' in which various cultural symbols – clothing, body piercing, hairstyles – would have to be left behind. Few, if any, would be willing to make such a jump. More relevant is the strategy adopted by the missionary organization Steiger International, a ministry of Youth With a Mission (YWAM), through the band No Longer Music (NLM). The band aims to penetrate heavy metal not by denying its culture, but by placing the gospel in the context of that culture with the aim of purging it of those elements that are destructive and evil.

Their lead singer comments,

> I never got into this for the music. A lot of bands want to be bands for God; with us it was the opposite. We were trying to reach people, and He told us to start a band. That's why we began, and it's been unbelievable because we made a decision from the beginning that we were going to be very clear about Who we believe and What we stood for.'[134]

NLM uses loud music and vivid drama to relate the narrative of the fall of humanity – spectacular video imagery, accompanying the music, overwhelms the audience, portraying humanity's need for Jesus. At one stage, a chain saw cuts through a wall and the band's bass player is hung upside down by his feet.

Heavy metal performers, as is true for all artists, are aware of the impact they can and do have on young people. To work

within their genre in order to bring transformation to the lives
of both the musicians and their listeners does not mean that we
automatically endorse or appreciate either the music or the
content of the lyrics. In his book on 'generation next' Barna
points out that 'we aren't called to love the culture, only to
recognize, understand and deal with it.' Rather than pompously
passing judgment on the rules by which young teens live their
lives, rules that might offend our sensibilities, we are called
instead to 'acknowledge the reality they are creating and to
address the reality that these rules exist and have influence in
their lives.'[135]

In the heavy metal culture there will be much that Christian
and non-Christian alike will want to reject. But the hostility
displayed by many of the bands should not mask the fact that
they are communicating, in the midst of their aggressive
protests against injustice and hypocrisy, a profound derision for
a form of Christianity that obscures the radical mutiny of Jesus
against the social order. If we are willing to engage with these
musicians we may come to realize how much they are doing us
a favor by confronting us – in a way that many will interpret as
both obnoxious and distasteful – with the idol that we have
created in the place of the radical Christ. Listening with open,
yet discerning, hearts to the culture of heavy metal brings the
promise of transformation not only to those who espouse that
culture but to those of us within the Christian community
whose first instinct may be to run as far as possible from that
culture – with hands clasped firmly over our ears!

The language of movies

In the early days of Hollywood, however, it was the eyes, not
the ears, which needed to be covered up! 'Picture houses' were
regarded as sinister assaults on the purity of the Christian faith,
with very little attention paid to the way movies might offer us
a window into the way things are. This does not mean, of
course, that movies are above reproach – far from it. Like
literature and other art forms discussed previously, there are
good movies and there are bad movies, judged according to

such criteria as technical or production quality and moral content. Movies, then, mirror life and also offer us a window into life – but, as Bryan Stone wisely reminds us, they are primarily a *lens*: 'We see only what the camera lets us see . . . Movies do not only portray a world; they propagate a worldview.'[136] So the same tests of discernment apply to movies as to art in general.

While the term 'industry' applied to films confirms the obvious fact that moviemaking is a commercial enterprise, its artistic credentials should not go unrecognized: '[t]here remains in human beings a deep hunger for images, sound, pictures, music and myth. Film offers us a creative language – an imaginative language of movement and sound – that can bridge the gap between the rational and the aesthetic, the sacred and the secular, the church and the world, and thereby throw open fresh new windows on a very old gospel.'[137]

Obviously, many films are produced which are primarily or totally concerned with entertainment – they may be escapist, like the *James Bond* or Wild West movies, or hopelessly romantic like the hugely successful *Sleepless in Seattle* and *Notting Hill*. Some science fiction movies also have that capacity and intention to simply entertain. The two archetypal film genres – the 'goodies versus the baddies' and the 'boy–girl romance' – may be regarded as typical of good escapist 'entertainment movies.' However, our concern here is with movies that engage with our culture in a way that evokes meaning and clarity about life and the human condition. For example, in Steven Spielberg's movie *Munich*, based upon the events surrounding and following the capture and murder of eleven Israeli athletes by the Palestinian Black September terrorist group at the 1972 Olympic Games, the Israeli Prime Minister Golda Meir is quoted as saying: 'Every civilization finds it necessary to negotiate compromises with its own values,' so justifying the secret war that she approves as revenge against the terrorist murderers. We inevitably find ourselves reflecting on the implications of such a statement.

Spielberg made the movie as 'a prayer for peace,' and clearly *Munich* resonates powerfully with the prevailing issues of political intransigence and violence that pervade the Middle

East today. But the film probes more deeply than this. In one entirely fictional scene the leader of the Israeli hit squad has the opportunity to sit down with a Palestinian who talks about his own longings for a homeland for his people. Screenwriter Tony Kushner, interviewed by *Time* magazine about the film, speaks about how his script deals with the Middle East question: 'It's not an essay; it's art. But I think I can safely say the conflict between national security and ethics raised deep questions in terms of working on the film. I was surprised to discover how much the story had to do with nationality vs. family, and questions about home and being in conflict with somebody else over a territory that seems home to both people.'[138]

Movies affect us in a number of important ways, summarized by Boorstin in terms of three Vs – voyeuristic, visceral, and vicarious.[139] As voyeurs, we can eavesdrop on events and situations that we have never previously gone through, experiences that range between the extremes of highly pleasurable to deeply disturbing. Earlier, I referred to *The Shawshank Redemption*, a film that transports us into the squalid and brutal world of a maximum security prison, where we are exposed to a dimension of life that would otherwise elude us. But the movie does more than highlight the obscenities of prison life: it also portrays the development of a true friendship between two men, a streetwise African-American criminal and a younger white bank official wrongly convicted for the murder of his wife. Watching the movie, we become voyeurs of something beautiful in the midst of brutality and despair. However, voyeurism may also be damaging to our spiritual health: the materialism, hedonism, and sexual permissiveness of contemporary Western culture are displayed regularly and approvingly in mainstream film and television, and Christians need to be constantly aware of their power to contaminate their lives.

Visceral, in the nonmedical context, has to do with the depth of our 'gut feelings,' reflecting the fact that many movies 'have the power to take us in their grip, to capture and hold our visual attention.'[140] In the film *Philadelphia*, Tom Hanks plays Andrew Beckett, a hot-shot young homosexual lawyer who is dying of AIDS; we feel for him because he comes over as a person with humanity and vibrancy, with a passion for life. Denzel Washington plays Miller, the black lawyer who represents Hanks when he is dismissed from the law firm because of alleged incompetence – though his AIDS and homosexuality are the real reasons. The film subtly presents the early contact between Beckett and Miller as two young lawyers, before the AIDS revelation . . . then the increasing distance . . . and finally increasingly closer contact as Miller begins to appreciate Beckett as a *person*, not just a caricature shaped by bigotry. Spielberg's *Saving Private Ryan* is another good example of a movie that takes hold of our emotions at many levels, especially during the opening twenty-five-minute sequence depicting the hideous carnage of war.

The word 'vicarious' has to do with feeling the experiences of others as if they were our own, and good movies accomplish this in the same way that good novels do – through the power of characterization and narrative flow. Vicarious experience is in one sense the opposite of escapist experience; we watch a *James Bond* movie to get away from real life. As we watch a movie like *Philadelphia*, or *A Time to Kill* (about a Negro in the racist southern states of America who kills two young white thugs for raping and nearly killing his little daughter) we begin to identify deeply with certain characters . . . even to the point of becoming one of the jury at the end of *A Time to Kill*.

Movies help us understand and critique our culture. *Dead Poets' Society*, for example, is a film that focuses on the importance of thinking for ourselves rather than simply conforming to what others expect of us. *The Matrix* and *The Truman Show* are both about enslavement and freedom. *The Matrix* is, as one reviewer wrote, 'the Technological Society come to its full fruition': a future society taken over by artificial intelligence machines. The matrix is a virtual reality computer program, the purpose of which is to turn humans into batteries (i.e. energy sources) for the machines to do their work. Tracing the etymology and current usage of the word 'matrix,' Mark Worthing observes that the word is apposite for 'the cyber reality that has enslaved the mass of humanity in the movie's storyline.'[141] *The Truman Show* conveys the same theme, but this time the enslavement is in the name of entertainment. The name of Jim Carrey's character, Truman, is significant, because, of all people, he is living a lie . . . and yet, paradoxically, he is typical of all of us, and so 'true man.' But Truman is not free, of course, and throughout the movie we are faced with the question of our own response to all that enslaves us in our own virtual worlds.

Robert Johnston offers six theological reasons why Christians should dialogue with movies, all related closely to each other.[142] Firstly, God's common grace is present throughout human culture, a theme that pervades this book, and needs no further comment. His second reason is that theology should be concerned with the Spirit's presence and work in the world. In the French film, *Ca Commence Aujourd'hui* (*It All Starts Today*), the film director Bertrand Tavernier pays tribute to the many people in society who are seeking to make a real difference to those who are caught in the endless cycle of despair and poverty. Set in a depressing industrial town in northern France, the hero is a schoolteacher, Daniel Lefebvre, who engages compassionately with families and children as they try and cope with crippling unemployment, an underfunded welfare system, and the resulting family dislocation and poverty. His life is portrayed as a daily struggle to bring life and joy into people's lives: Tavernier's passionate cry for justice actually contributed to needed changes in the French welfare system.

The film ends with an imaginative and creative trans-formation of the schoolyard and buildings into a colorful celebration of life, communicating hope in the midst of the squalid conditions in which many of the town's inhabitants live. Though fictional, the film was based on the real-life experiences of one of the screenplay writers, and throughout we are struck by the compassion and gentle strength of Lefebvre. While the film is not explicitly religious or Christian, it communicates the truth that God may be at work by his Spirit in suffering humanity in more ways than we care to think.

Johnston's next point is that we can hear God through non-Christians. God is active within the wider culture and speaks to us through all of life: here, we are reminded that God has his 'alien witnesses' throughout culture. He cites the example of *American Beauty*, 'a dark comedy and not for the easily offended,' with its portrayal of adultery and drug use, and frequent profanity and nudity. The film depicts Lester Burnham, a man who is shriveled inside – ignored by his wife, bored by his work, and unloved by his daughter. An infatuation with a young girl opens up his life to all that is possible, and he 'begins to smell the roses.' We learn that sadness does not have the last word. Vicariously, through Burnham, we too find ourselves embracing life.

Johnston's fourth point is that image as well as word can help us to encounter God: symbols and images are powerful catalysts for experiencing God. Again, this is a theme that we have been reinforcing throughout this chapter in the context of the communicative power of art. He then observes that theology's narrative shape makes it particularly open to interaction with other stories: Christianity is not a set of propositions, but a story, a story of God and his people. The narrative shape of film may speak to us powerfully because it offers opportunities to identify with central gospel themes, like forgiveness or community and the longing for love.

The movie *Antwone Fisher* is a compelling story about family brokenness and ultimate healing and forgiveness. The theme of family life is also given fine humorous treatment in the successful Australian comedy *The Castle*, which centres on the Kerrigans, a family that eats dinner together at the same time every night. The father Darryl (played by Michael Caton) unfailingly complements the mother on her cooking. They love each other, respect each other, and even though the eldest boy is in jail for armed robbery, they are all as proud of him as of each other. They live right next to an airport – in a *home*, not a house – which is about to be acquired for airport expansion. And so the battle begins. It is supremely a film that celebrates love, delightful innocence, and good old-fashioned family values in the midst of its satire, with an emphasis on simplicity, contentment, loyalty, and pride.

Finally, Johnston argues that the nature of constructive theology is a dialogue between God's story and our stories: 'our knowledge from Scripture is always a mediated knowledge. The interpreter, that is, has no access to the Bible except as he or she comes to it from one of theology's other resources,' which Johnston identifies as experience, tradition, culture, and the local church. So all cultural expressions – and these include movies – 'function as important resources for theological reflection. Movies need not be explicitly 'Christian' in their theme to be theologically significant.'[143] Of course, movies that *do* have an explicit Christian theme may challenge the very way we perceive or live out our Christian faith. One film that does just that is Lasse Halstrom's *Chocolat*, based on the book of the same name by Joanne Harris. *Chocolat* is a visually sumptuous film about the redemptive power of love, light, colour, and, of course, chocolate – a contrast to the grey, drab, lifeless French village controlled by the domineering Catholic mayor, the Comte de Reynard. In the book, it is the priest who is the villain – in the movie, he is the tool of the mayor. However, the victory of light over darkness, of joy over austerity, is given a twist. A woman called Vianne – together with her daughter and miscellaneous pagan 'white witchery' – is blown into the village by a 'sly wind from the north' and sets up her decadent chocolate shop (*chocolaterie*) right opposite the stone Catholic church, and opens it up during Lent.

The film presses all the right 'feel-good' buttons. However, one Christian reviewer of the book wrote that if it 'is a metaphor for the triumph of paganism over Christianity when the church fails to live out the gospel, then it may be of some value. If it is advocating freedom to follow the heart and not commit yourself to anything but the pursuit of personal happiness, then it is a seductively well-packaged box of chocolate-coated lies.'[144] While there is some validity in this warning, Michael Frost sees the film – and book – as something more than the showdown (or conflict) between legalistic Christianity and free-thinking paganism.[145] For him, the Comte and the church represent the formal institution, demanding allegiance and attendance. Vianne and the *chocolaterie*, on the other hand, represent the human face of friendship and community-building. Vianne gets involved with the people around her, who are gradually drawn into her web of love and caring . . . and in the process their lives are transformed, and color returns to the whole village.

Chocolat is similar in theme to *Babette's Feast*, a film in which a young French woman arrives among a strict religious community of puritans in Jutland, Denmark . . . Christians who do not know the meaning of grace. Babette's husband and son have been killed in the uprising in France in 1871, so she flees to a village in Denmark. For fourteen years she slaves away as cook and housekeeper, and when she unexpectedly receives a large sum of money from the French lottery she spends every penny of it on a feast for the grumpy, dour, old people. When they see the ingredients start to arrive – quails, a huge turtle, a calf's head, and many bottles of wine – two of the women, Martine and Filippa, are struck with terror that the meal is a virtual 'witches' Sabbath' and fearfully alert the rest of the disciples to the presence of evil in their midst. All agree that they will attend the dinner with their minds on higher things, as if they had no sense of taste – they will say nothing at all about the food or drink. Of course, everything changes once they start eating Babette's food!

For those who have ears to hear and eyes to see, both *Chocolat* and *Babette's Feast* highlight the contrast between religion and life, between a *graceless* Christianity and a *grace-full* Christianity … between a spirituality that denies our humanity and a spirituality that rejoices in our humanity. Movies like these are a testament to the power of film, as for all forms of art, to speak in an appealing and imaginative way to the truth that we live in a world in which there is no room for the legalistic 'split-vision worldview' that can rob us of the abundant life that Jesus came to give us.

5

Science: the Language of God?[146]

Seeking truth: in praise of a dialogue between bottom-up and top-down thinking

Carl Sagan, the American astronomer and planetary scientist, once quipped that to really make an apple pie from scratch, you must begin by inventing the universe. So when scientists go public with the claim that soon human beings will be able to create life in the laboratory, they fail to acknowledge – as they must – that the process inevitably begins with the availability of the basic raw materials that go into the creation of matter. Moreover, we live in a creation that exhibits many remarkable physical and chemical characteristics, a creation that is so fine-tuned that life as we know it today would not have been possible if conditions had been ever so slightly different. We might go further, and ask, Who actually designed the laws of physics in the first place?

The issues raised here focus on the interface between science and faith, an area that has received much publicity in recent years, not only because of the enormous strides made in genetic engineering with its inevitable ethical concerns, but also because of the attention given to such controversial issues as the 'intelligent design' (ID) movement, with its implications for the teaching of science in our schools. ID has given rise to vigorous – at times acerbic – debate, with many arguing that ID has no place in the science classroom. The eminent physicist and Nobel prize-winner Eric Cornell maintains that 'as exciting as intelligent design is for theology, it is a boring idea in science. Science isn't about knowing the mind of God; it's about understanding nature and the reasons for things.'[147]

The ID debate relates, in part, to the larger creation–evolution controversy that attracts fundamentalists on both sides, Christian and scientific, who typically see the issue in terms of creation *or* evolution, rather than acknowledge the possibility that God might actually work through evolutionary processes: the coexistence of creation *and* evolution has not been given the shelf room it deserves. In this chapter we will try to introduce some balance into the argument.[148] With regard to the disciplines of science and religion, there are many people who imagine that the two are incompatible. There are some who demand that they should be kept as far apart as possible – and their reasoning, as we shall see later, is not very convincing.

In Chapter 2 we argued that we need to reconnect with God's creation if we are to discover what it means to live fully human lives as participants in an inclusive and holistic 'creation community.' The privileged relationship that we are invited to experience not only with the God of creation but also with the creation of God draws us directly into the interface between science and faith. The grandeur of God lies not only in his sovereign glory as the Creator of all things, but also in the extraordinary diversity of his creation, unfolding over time in the human, animal, and natural realms. It is this rich and wonderfully complex creation that science is in the business of probing, investigating, describing, and seeking to understand. And many scientific discoveries about human life and the natural world are being communicated in an accessible and fashionable way to the general public through the media, especially television.

Media exposure

A few years ago Channel 4 in the UK presented a three-part series on the relationship between science and religion called *Testing God*. The series tackled many complex issues in a helpful and even-handed way, a far cry from the simplistic approaches adopted by those whose extreme views place them at opposite ends of the science–faith spectrum. The year 2005 saw a series of programs on television celebrating the centenary of the publication of three influential papers by the renowned physicist Albert Einstein, culminating in his famous e=mc2 equation. In his own time, Einstein became a media personality as his theories captured the public's imagination. In recent years Stephen Hawking, another scientist who has been hailed by some as 'the new Einstein,' has achieved cult status. Hawking has held the post of Lucasian Professor of Mathematics at Cambridge since 1979, and he became a household name not only because of his intellectual brilliance but because of his disability: he has suffered from the crippling motor neurone disease for nearly all his adult life. But this has not diminished either his private or public life. *The Times* proclaimed Hawking a superstar when he filled to capacity the Royal Albert Hall in London for a lecture on black holes. His most famous book, *A Brief History of Time*, has sold over ten million copies and been translated into more than thirty languages. In his own book on Hawking, David Wilkinson notes:

> He has played chess with Mr Data and Albert Einstein on *Star Trek: The Next Generation*, engaged in philosophical discussion with Homer Simpson, and done television commercials for telephone companies and opticians. He has even appeared on a Radiohead album track ... He is certainly the most famous scientist in the world and his every public pronouncement seems to be hailed with the kind of interest shown only to the 'A' list of rock and film stars.[149]

Another Oxbridge celebrity is Baroness Susan Greenfield, Professor of Pharmacology at Oxford University and Director of the Royal Institution of Great Britain, which has been in existence since 1799 for the purpose of 'diffusing science for the common purposes of life.' Greenfield has become a worldwide celebrity as a neuroscientist, and she was once heralded as one of the fifty most powerful women in Britain by the *Guardian* and ranked number fourteen in the list of the '50 Most Inspirational Women in the World' by *Harpers & Queen*. Her BBC television series *Brain Story* achieved much praise, though Christians might have noticed her claim (expressed a number of times in different ways) that all our beliefs and experiences are conditioned and controlled by the action of chemicals within our brains. Her reductionism is probably absorbed unquestioningly by millions of viewers, but it does not sit well with belief in God or the Christian understanding of the soul. It is another example of the way in which ideas are presented as fact, masquerading under the guise of so-called 'scientific' evidence. *Brain Story* is, in fact, an illustration of how subtly we find ourselves accommodating to the prevailing scientific worldview, in which claims are made about how the created order (in this case, the brain) works, some of which simply cannot be proved, given the current state of scientific knowledge.

The stem-cell and cloning controversies have generated a host of TV documentaries that keep these key issues alive for the general public, and rightly so. They are often highly informative, with important contributions presented in the areas of ethics, public policy, and legislation. The warning about human beings 'playing God' has become a clarion call against any form of genetic manipulation, and all of us – not just Christians – need wisdom and humility as we grapple with the complexities and capabilities of new genetic technologies.[150] Recently Channel 4 and PBS collaborated in an award-winning five-part series called *DNA*, which charts the comprehensive history of DNA science – from James Watson and Francis Crick's celebrated discovery of the double helix structure to the mapping of the human genome to the latest research – and examines its current, and sometimes controversial, applications and implications for the future. In the final program in the series, Watson argues for a new kind of eugenics – where parents are allowed to choose the DNA of their children – to make them healthier, more intelligent, even better-looking. While many people are drawn to such programs because they address controversial issues like eugenics and the sanctity of life, they are not the only things that matter in medical science. Palliative care, general surgery, disease control, alternative medicines, and many other concerns all find their place within the broader discipline of medical and health science.

The American nonprofit media enterprise PBS has produced many fascinating science documentary series, such as *The*

Elegant Universe, featuring Brian Greene, one of the world's foremost string theorists, and the controversial 2001 series *Evolution*, which examines evolutionary science and the profound effect it has had on society and culture. Of course, both series have had their critics – the former for being too speculative, and the latter for distorting the scientific evidence and incorporating a sharply biased view against religion. Besides programs like these that deal with contemporary issues in cosmology and biology, the continuing political debate over such issues as global warming, resource depletion, and the pollution of the environment has spawned a plethora of TV documentaries, conferences, and scientific papers, all of which have kept ecological issues very much in the public eye.

Concern for the environment has catapulted such luminaries as David Suzuki and Sir David Attenborough into the limelight. Suzuki's CBC TV science magazine show *The Nature of Things* has turned him into an international star. He is a third-generation Japanese-Canadian who has lately devoted himself full-time to environmental concerns, reflected in his TV series *The Sacred Balance*, as well as the establishment of the David Suzuki Foundation, which was founded in 1990 in order to develop 'a world vision of sustainable communities living within the planet's carrying capacity.' David Attenborough has had a distinguished career in broadcasting and has traveled widely, often to the most remote regions of the world, in his passion to communicate to as many people as possible the wonders of the natural world. An estimated 500 million people worldwide have watched Attenborough's thirteen-part series *Life on Earth*, with *The Living Planet* and *The Trials of Life* completing a remarkable trilogy.

Are science and religion opposites?

With so much popularizing of science, it is perhaps not too surprising that religion – the other half of the equation being examined in this chapter – has taken a back seat in their relationship. In their respective typologies of the science–religion relationship, two respected authorities, Ian Barbour and

John Haught, adopt the word 'conflict' to describe the assumed (and, in some cases, actual) position of irreconcilable difference between the two disciplines, even to the point of 'warfare.'[151] In a fascinating review of three books exploring the relationship between science and religion, Margaret Wertheim titles her discussion in *The Sciences*, a publication of the New York Academy of Sciences, 'The Odd Couple.' Her article is subtitled: 'Can science and religion live together without driving each other crazy?'![152] With Haught, I maintain that the two actually *need* each other because they 'ultimately flow out of the same 'radical' eros for truth that lies at the heart of our existence.'[153]

Karl Popper, perhaps the greatest twentieth-century philosopher of science, has argued that the scientific quest is not in fact a quest for absolute truth: rather, it is a quest for greater *verisimilitude* – a more accurate 'model' – in our understanding of reality.[154] The same is surely true with regard to the Christian faith. Who would claim to have the last word about the God who is greater than finite minds? One Christian writer put in the index at the back of his book a number of references to 'Truth, ultimate': the pages indicated are all completely blank![155] It is with this provisionality in mind that we might usefully approach the idea of dialogue in the relationship between science and religion. There needs to be a willingness for each to listen sympathetically to the other, along with an openness to adjust where it may seem appropriate, in order to avoid the charge of arrogance.

However, as noted earlier, the general impression gained by many people today is that science and religion are diametrically opposed: science deals with facts and religion deals with – to put it as charitably as possible – untestable dogma. Some would want to subvert the religious perspective as so much 'supernatural mumbo-jumbo,' hardly consistent with the scientific age in which we now live. Typical of this view would be the writings of the neo-Darwinist reductionist Richard Dawkins, the Charles Simonyi Professor in the Public Understanding of Science at Oxford University.[156] Dawkins, who was named 'Humanist of the Year' in 1996, occupies an intellectual position at the far end of the faith–science spectrum. He is fervently atheistic, and some fellow scholars complain that his mission in life seems to have shifted from popularizing science to waging an all-out attack on Christianity.

Alister McGrath, a noted adversary of Dawkins, has written a book that challenges Dawkins' central assumptions about the role of science in explaining the nature of reality. He cites a lecture given in 1992 at the Edinburgh International Science Festival, in which Dawkins described faith as 'the great cop-out, the great excuse to evade the need to think and evaluate evidence.'[157] In the second edition of *The Selfish Gene*, Dawkins goes so far as to equate faith with mental illness! For Dawkins, science really has fulfilled the need that religion did in the past of explaining such deep and mysterious questions as, Why are we here? What is the origin of life? Where did the world come from? and, What is life all about? McGrath's judgment is that Dawkins is 'a splendid representative of the no-nonsense 'one rationality fits all' approach of the Enlightenment.'[158]

In fact, if we adopt a historical perspective, we discover the existence of social and historical factors that have shaped the particular contexts within which the relationship between science and religion has been played out over time. The record shows that the two have not been pitched against each other over the centuries, as some would like us to believe. They have enjoyed a reasonably good, if unstable, relationship, punctuated by tensions that existed as the result of the dispute between Galileo and the Catholic Church at the beginning of the seventeenth century, the growing belief in the eighteenth century that perhaps the world was in fact a self-sustaining deterministic mechanism, in need neither of a divine author nor of a divine sustainer, and the Darwinian controversy in the middle of the nineteenth century.

Citing the example of Galileo in his relations with the Roman Catholic Church, Brooke reminds us that because both science and religion 'are rooted in *human* concerns and *human* endeavour, it would be a profound mistake to treat them as if they were entities in themselves – as if they could be completely abstracted from the social contexts in which those concerns and endeavours took their distinctive forms.'[159]

For example, Cardinal Bellarmine, who was the Vatican's key protagonist in dealing with Galileo and his support of

Copernicus' heliocentric model of the universe, had a far more open attitude to Copernican theories than is often supposed. Early on there were those within religious circles who were very much aware that the issues raised by the science–religion debate critically related to biblical interpretation, and it did no one any good – least of all within the Christian community – to insist upon one single, dogmatic interpretation of the biblical record. Furthermore, Galileo himself sought to relate his growing scientific understanding to his Christian faith. So, the Galileo affair is not a good representative of the 'pitched battle' scenario suggested by some.

On the basis of his observations regarding mass, space, and time, Isaac Newton was able to demonstrate that the world functioned according to certain mathematical principles. *The Mathematical Principles of Natural Philosophy*, or *Principia* as it came to be known, is perhaps the greatest scientific book ever written. Published in 1687, it contains a full treatment of Newtonian physics and their application to astronomy. These laws of motion and gravity gave rise to the mechanistic worldview, lending weight to Christian beliefs about a provident designer, and accelerating the subsequent rise of natural theology – from data and empirical observations 'down below' we can intuit the nature and character of the divine author, or Creator, 'up above.' Newtonian ideas were originally seen as consistent with Christian notions of divine creation – they helped us to understand how God was at work in his world – and Newton himself regarded God as the mediator of gravitational forces. But as the eighteenth century unfolded, other forces began to erode theistic interpretations of Newtonian mechanics: the Industrial Revolution and the major social and economic changes of the time were strong secularizing influences, along with increasing scientific endeavors.

In 1859 Charles Darwin published *The Origin of Species*, an evolutionary proposal that was not without its Christian apologists: there were those who supported what he had to say, and those who vigorously attacked him. At the famous Huxley–Wilberforce encounter in Oxford a year later, Frederick Temple, later to become Archbishop of Canterbury, responded favorably to Darwin's science, even to the point of advocating his ideas fully. Those who attacked Darwinism argued on the basis that belief in Darwinian evolution and belief in a Creator God were incompatible and therefore irreconcilable. So the debate was simplified down to creation *or* evolution.

In the twentieth century a philosophical movement called 'logical positivism,' with which the famous psychoanalyst Sigmund Freud was associated, was developed by a group of philosophers called the Vienna Circle. Freud believed that human beings were victims of unresolved inner conflicts, so challenging the possibility of a free and open relationship with God. So his views were entirely consistent with the logical positivists, who believed that only science had meaningful answers regarding knowledge, thus dismissing the metaphysical contributions of religion. Since science is 'provable' and religion is not, then religion can be discarded. However, what logical positivism failed to appreciate was that science's main focus is on questions of mechanism, whereas religion tends to focus less on mechanism than meaning. While this is still too simplistic a distinction, it does lead us to an alternative approach to the conflict hypothesis, that of *independence*.

Should we keep them apart?

In his book, *Rock of Ages*, the evolutionist Stephen Jay Gould presents science and faith as occupying different domains. His basic principle is known as NOMA, or 'non-overlapping magisteria': 'The magisterium of science covers the empirical realm: what is the universe made of (fact) and why does it work this way (theory). The magisterium of religion extends over questions of ultimate meaning and moral value.'[160] Perhaps the most famous expression of this independence of two valid approaches is what has come to be known as the 'Baconian compromise,' after Francis Bacon (1561–1626). One of Bacon's statements is called the 'two-books' statement – 'Let no man upon a weak conceit of sobriety or an ill-applied moderation think or maintain that a man can search too far, or be too well studied in the book of God's word, or in the book of God's works.'[161] In effect, Bacon sharply separated the two, and subsequent advocates of this approach have suggested that science and faith, though equally valid, are basically tackling different questions.

However, the independence approach fails to do justice to the common ground that science and faith occupy. We should avoid the two extremes of biblical literalism and fundamentalist scientism, both of which can prosper under both conflict and independence categories. There are many Christians and scientists who have spoken wisely about the need for dialogue, and to this group we might add church people too: Pope John Paul II once declared: 'Science can purify religion from error and superstition; religion can purify science from idolatry and false absolutes. Each can draw the other into a wider world, a world in which both can flourish.'[162] In an article in *Wired*, Gregg Easterbrook observes that 'the more scientists have learned, the more mysterious the Really Big Questions have become.'[163] Needless to say, Richard Dawkins and other reductionist scientists would argue that we just haven't given science enough time to find out the answers.

And they would have a point here. Take the intelligent design movement as an example. ID proponents argue that biology, at it most basic levels, displays an information-rich complexity that natural causes just do not seem to be able to explain. A better option is that an intelligent mind must be the cause. ID maintains that certain parts of living organisms are so complex, and composed of so many separate parts that cannot function properly on their own, that we cannot account for them in a reductionist fashion, as merely the products of blind selection. This is what is called in ID terminology *irreducible complexity*. ID is problematic, however, because it closes the door to further inquiry at the level of secondary causes, denying in principle our ability to learn how irreducibly complex structures were assembled. This places it dangerously close to a 'God-of-the-gaps' position, in which God is invoked only when natural explanations fail, disappearing from view when previously unexplained phenomena are given natural explanations.

The problem is that many scientists simply do not like to admit to any supernaturalism, and so any hint of an intelligence behind, for example, the design of the biochemical motors of bacteria flagella (a crucial ID example) is anathema to them. On the other hand, critics of ID argue that people like Michael Behe – a biochemistry professor at Lehigh University in the United States and a major figure in the intelligent design movement – suffer from a very unscientific failure of curiosity, creativity, and nerve. An intelligent response – if that is the language we are using! – would be to acknowledge that we simply cannot prove the case for or against supernaturalism, and so we are left to defend our position according to our personal belief system. And there is nothing wrong with that, so long as we are honest about it. But we need to be aware that if our case hinges upon not being able to explain irreducible complexity (a term originating within ID) scientifically, then we may find ourselves hoist on our own petard if science delivers a satisfactory explanation.

This example from the controversial ID debate highlights how important it is that all involved in the ID conversation adopt an attitude of humility: 'Rejection of evidence that cannot yet be measured with instruments in a laboratory is contrary to the scientific spirit of enquiry. It is time to move beyond dogmatic fundamentalism in both religion and science.'[164] Ultimately, science cannot give the final answer because science itself is changing, as twentieth-century developments in physics clearly show: 'Far from demystifying the world, as the reductionist agenda proposed to do, science is now opening up the horizon of an inexhaustibly indeterminate universe.'[165] The dialogue approach maintains that the sciences have much to learn from religious insights about the real world in which we live. Conversely, Christians need to listen to the voice (or, rather, the many voices) of the sciences, as they offer insights about how God's world works.

Learning from each other[166]

In an attempt to facilitate genuine dialogue with regard to God's relationship to the world, a number of scientists and theologians have recently begun to take seriously the idea of

God as the intelligent designer of an amazingly complex self-organizing system. To speak in these terms is not to resurrect the ID argument, which is usually presented as an alternative to Darwinian evolution – rather it is to take a much more holistic approach, acknowledging that God is involved in his creation in ways that not only approximate current evolutionary theories, but also reveal an astounding and surprising inventiveness.

Once we acknowledge the extraordinary physical properties and processes of our universe we may find ourselves asking metaphysical questions, Why is there anything at all? Who established the mathematical laws that enable the universe to function with such regularity day after day? One of the most important thinkers in the science–faith debate is Sir John Polkinghorne, a former Professor of Mathematical Physics at Cambridge University and a well-known theologian who has written widely in the area. He challenges us to consider what sort of thinkers we are. Do we start from the bottom up or the top down? In other words, is our instinct to start with a particular phenomenon or experience and seek to build our understanding of reality from that? Or do we prefer to start with broad, general principles, and then work downward from there?

For example, a 'bottom-up' thinker observes the changing weather patterns in a particular location, and then probes to see what they might say to us about the world in which we live. Another example would be the investigation of strands of DNA – the basic building blocks of life – in order to contribute to an understanding of what it means to be a human being. 'Top-down' thinking works in the opposite direction. Christians believe in a God of love who has made all things well. They might also want to assert that God acts in certain ways in the world (though there will be disagreement among Christians as to how exactly he acts). These fundamental beliefs then influence how events or experiences such as earthquakes, shooting stars, and human suffering are interpreted.

The important point to recognize here is that the two approaches *need not imply conflict*, because they are both, in different ways, tackling the same sort of questions. Both are attempting to get to grips with the nature of reality. The 'bottom-up' approach relates closely to the scientific way of looking at things. Bottom-up thinkers 'feel it is safest to start in the basement of particularity and then generalize a little.'[167] The 'top-down' approach presupposes some form of metaphysical framework – such as a Christian theistic framework – within which to interpret the nature of reality. In common with other Christian scientists, Polkinghorne argues that we cannot simply reduce the amazing complexity of creation to purposeless physical matter. There has to be more behind it all, he claims. How do you explain the amazing power we have to understand the physical world? The physicist Paul Davies acknowledges that there must be a Mind behind everything scientists see, although he chooses not interpret this in terms of the God of classical Christian theism. In one of his books he writes:

> Through my scientific work I have come to believe more and more strongly that the physical universe is put together with an ingenuity so astonishing that I cannot accept it merely as brute fact. There must, it seems to me, be a deeper level of explanation. Whether one wishes to call that deeper level 'God' is a matter of taste and definition. Furthermore, I have come to the point of view that mind – i.e. conscious awareness of the world – is not a meaningless and incidental quirk of nature, but an absolutely fundamental facet of reality. That is not to say that *we* are the purpose for which the universe exists. Far from it. I do, however, believe that we human beings are built into the scheme of things in a very basic way.[168]

And human beings somehow have a mind to grasp this amazing reality, reminiscent of Einstein's famous remark that 'the only incomprehensible thing about the universe is that it is comprehensible.'

Polkinghorne points out that scientists are now generally agreed that the universe is so finely tuned (the so-called 'anthropic principle') that if you were to change the laws of nature (gravity, or electromagnetic forces, say) even the tiniest bit, the universe would be sterile and boring, and nothing like the fruitful place that we know it to be (and that includes you and me!). Consider for a moment the presence of beauty in the world, the source of moral choice, and the reality of spiritual encounter, or worship: Polkinghorne speaks about the 'irreducible ethical element' present in our understanding of reality. All this suggests that behind the extraordinary physical reality, of which we are a part, there is a God who wills it all into existence. The universe has purpose.

Polkinghorne goes on to highlight the necessity for dialogue between science and faith by articulating a number of assertions that reflect their essential interdependence.[169] Both, for example, are concerned with the rational exploration of what is the case: scientists are interpreters in their search for an understanding of the nature and pattern of the physical world, and must therefore be open to correction. The same is true for Christians as they seek to interpret reality through the lens of faith. What is more, the Christian notion of the Word conveys something that is more than emotionally or spiritually satisfying – it conveys coherence and order, embracing reason or Mind: the Creator God is a *rational* God. Similarly, one of the most remarkable things about the world in which we live is that it can be understood *mathematically* – there is beauty and elegance in the equations that describe the universe.

In 1977, the IBM computer scientist Benoit Mandelbrot discovered a geometric form known as a 'fractal,' a word that he coined in 1975, derived from the Latin verb *frangere*, meaning 'to break.' Einstein had added to three-dimensional space a fourth dimension, time. Mandelbrot discovered that there existed space – fractional space – *between* the dimensions, leading to the idea of fractal dimensions. This opened up the way for the world of nature to be described in mathematical terms. An important principle underlying fractal geometry is that, again and again, the world displays a 'regular irregularity,' a reality previously unnoticed by scientists until Mandelbrot developed some mathematical tools for describing the remarkably consistent patterns inherent in such physical phenomena as coastlines, snowflakes, mountains, and clouds. In 1979, Mandelbrot was working on some mathematical iterations on the computer when he discovered a geometrical form which generated an extraordinarily complex structure, capable of an infinite number of magnifications. The resultant images are stunningly

elaborate and beautiful. The English mathematician Roger
Penrose declared that the Mandelbrot set 'is not an invention of
the human mind: it was a discovery. Like Mount Everest, the
Mandelbrot set is just there!'[170] An Italian theoretical chemist by
the name of Giuseppe Del Re comments that '[t]he universe
disclosed to us by science appears to be the most beautiful and
glorious thing imaginable, endowed with an internal mysterious order reminiscent of fractals, an eerie by-product of the
mathematics of complexity.'[171] As Christians who believe that
God is the author of all creation, we may want to declare that
Mandelbrot was discovering *what is already there*.

Serendipity is a word that scientists sometimes use to describe
the rewards of scientific research. After all the hard work of
investigation and experimentation, of theories dashed and ideas
discarded, there comes that moment when it is all worthwhile –
like Mandelbrot's set or Crick and Watson's discovery of DNA.
Scientists are excited today about the possibility of drawing all
their theories together in the form of a Grand Unified Theory
(GUT). Christian believers are similarly imbued with a sense of
expectation and wonder as they contemplate the grandeur of
God. This is so not only as we meditate on the glorious truths of
the gospel, the God who has come to us, and the hope of
resurrection life. Surely there is excitement too as we open
ourselves to the divine mystery that somehow integrates all the
many diverse aspects of human experience.

Earlier, we made reference to a concept known as the
'anthropic principle,' which has often been illustrated by the
following story. Suppose you are about to be executed by firing
squad. Ten men aim and shoot, but you discover to your
amazement that you are still alive. That requires an explanation!
Is it rational to shrug and say, 'Well, that's just the way it is!'?
You surely want to know *why* it happened. The same question
applies to the fine-tuning of the universe. How can it be that the
world is such a fruitful and habitable place, to the point that the
slightest change in the laws of nature would topple its
incredible life-supporting stability and coherence? Is it enough
to say, 'Well, that's just the way it is!'? Now, there are only two
rational explanations regarding the firing-squad illustration.
One is that there were trillions of executions taking place that

day, and you happened to be the lucky one in which all the sharpshooters missed. Or else, they were all on your side. If we translate that to the 'anthropic principle,' either there are trillions of universes, and ours happens to be the one where everything comes together which makes you and me possible. The other explanation? Someone's on our side! There is divine purpose behind the fruitful fine-tuning of our universe.

Scientists have shown that only a universe as large as ours could have lasted the fifteen billion years that are needed to bring into being the nuclear furnaces of stars which produce the carbon and oxygen necessary for human life. So the universe needs a very long history in order to *become* what God has always intended it to be. Christians could interpret the process of evolution as the *history that is necessary* for the Big Bang to become God's fruitful universe that we know today. Through a divine mix of regular and reliable (but not rigid) laws of nature, and irregular and unpredictable happenings, God in self-limiting love allows his creation to evolve with the freedom with which he endows it.

Polkinghorne also points out that science and faith have common ground in that they are both problematic. The problem with the latest developments in science is that they are decidedly nonrational! Traditionally science has dealt with the 'how?' questions relating to reality, with the 'why?' questions left to faith. But now scientists acknowledge that they cannot explain how quantum theory works – except to agree that it does work. Christian theology has its intractable questions too. There are some obvious ones – like the problem of God and suffering. The response that human beings are given free will, and that creation has a freedom given to it by its Creator, go some way to answering the problem . . . but not fully. We will return to some of these ideas a little later on in this chapter.

In his historical survey of science, the astrophysicist John Gribbin quotes the words of the great science fiction writer Isaac Asimov:

No one can really feel at home in the modern world and judge the nature of its problems – and the possible solutions to those problems – unless one has some intelligent notion of what science is up to. Furthermore, initiation into the magnificent world of science brings great aesthetic satisfaction, inspiration to youth, fulfilment of the desire to know, and a deeper appreciation of the wonderful potentialities and achievements of the human mind.[172]

No one should underestimate the problems faced by both science and faith in today's complex and troubled world, in which technology has opened up the possibility of enormous changes in the way in which we view life and how to live it. But neither should we underestimate the opportunities presented by a sympathetic dialogue between the two.

Does God play dice?

The twentieth century has witnessed some remarkable developments, perhaps none more astonishing than the revolution in the way in which we understand the science of matter and energy. Physics is not as predictable, as rigidly Newtonian or mechanistic as once thought. Many scientists who also happen to be Christians – and there are more around than is commonly supposed! – are beginning to allow for the possibility that the physical world is endowed with an open future that allows for God's providential action. In 1961 Edward Lorenz, Professor of Meteorology at Massachusetts Institute of Technology, accidentally discovered the so-called 'butterfly effect' in his computer simulations of weather patterns.[173] The 'butterfly effect' was coined to reflect the phenomenon of a butterfly's wings stirring the air over China that several weeks later gives rise to storms over Canada! However accurate our weather forecasts may be, they still cannot account for the unpredictable. Here we enter the realm of quantum physics, which describes the unpredictable operation of electrons at the subatomic level. Quantum theory, which is based on prob-abilities, offers a logic that is at odds with the either/or logic that characterized earlier (Newtonian) physics: it is the logic not of 'either A or B', but of 'both A and B.'[174] Einstein struggled with the underlying idea that chance was a player in the cosmic drama: while his theories of relativity were pivotal in the collapse of the Newtonian worldview, they did not shake his deterministic outlook. Faced with the uncertainties implicit in quantum mechanics, he famously observed that 'God does not play dice with the world.' But this is precisely what quantum theory seems to imply, with its inherent probabilistic structure.

The quantum view of the world departs from classical assumptions in a number of important ways. Firstly, as noted above, the deterministic paradigm has given way to an emphasis on probabilities, such that uncertainty and probability are inherent features of quantum reality. We should remember here that we are dealing with subatomic reality, so that we cannot immediately translate quantum insights, which are significant at the submicroscopic level, into the macroscopic world. The desk at which I am sitting as I type these words is still a desk, a concrete reality in the macroworld of my experience. Nonetheless, in the quantum context, it is also a ferment of interacting subatomic particles. Secondly, the reductionist perspective has given way to a more holistic understanding and approach to physical reality: the emphasis is on the interconnectedness of parts such that *wholeness* is the primary reality rather than the reductionist's passion for microscopic units. A third distinguishing characteristic of the quantum world is the concept of nonlocality, which, very simply, refers to the interaction between particles of matter across vast distances of space. This reflects a radical interconnectedness that points towards an underlying order in the universe.

The implications of the new physics of the quantum world challenge those views of God that regard him as a divine clockmaker, a deistic God who set the whole universe in motion, and then withdrew to allow it to function according to some predetermined and unchanging principles of operation. Rather, God's involvement is hidden and at times (but not always) unpredictable – his activity is discernible through faith and not experiment. Both science and faith offer us here a God who acts not only according to predictable natural laws – such as the rhythms of the seasons that reflect his faithful character – but also in an open, indeterminate way. The nonlocality principle embedded in quantum mechanics is highly suggestive of a universe that is a holistically interconnected reality, in which – at the quantum level – particles interact interdependently according to some guiding principle.

How do we interpret this 'guiding principle'? Perhaps the complexities of quantum mechanics have opened up to us one possible way in which to understand how the Spirit of God may be at work in creation. In *The Trinity, Creation and Pastoral Ministry*, I suggest that the creative and recreative Spirit is the vitalizing Spirit, active from the moment of the big bang, releasing life and possibility as creation unfolds and reaches towards its intended goal. In fact, to speak in this way is to posit a continuity between the Spirit who enlivens and sanctifies us in our relation to God and the Spirit who enlivens us in our relation to the created world. To deny this continuity is to polarize spirituality and vitality, isolate the soul from the body, and embrace a dualism that conflicts with the biblical understanding of what it means to be made in the image of God. We will close this chapter with reference to this important doctrine of humanity, but before we do, we need to revisit a theme that we introduced in Chapter 2, a theme that lies at the heart of the science–faith debate, What is the relationship between God and creation?

Creation's freedom

In Chapter 2, we explored in Trinitarian terms the nature of the God who has made space for the world within himself, and who loves this world with a passion that ultimately led to the incarnation and the cross. The language of incarnation speaks of a God who stoops down from on high to take his place among sinful human beings. W. H. Vanstone, an English parish priest, argues that Christ's self-emptying (*kenosis*) in his incarnation, far from impairing the fullness of his revelation of God, contains the very heart and substance of that revelation, which is of a kenotic God who is ever self-giving in authentic love.[175] Vanstone has touched upon something that is at the heart of incarnational theology, namely the way of love as the motive for *kenosis*. God is not separated from his creation, indifferent and uninvolved. It is a mark of his great love, and of his freedom too, that he has chosen a relationship with human beings that is given its fullest expression in the incarnation (and ultimate suffering) of his Son. We might also understand God as one who freely limits himself out of love so that his *physical* creation might experience freedom in all its fullness. So the doctrine of *kenosis* speaks to us of a God who has freely chosen and accepted self-limitation for the sake of the freedom of *all* that he has created, human and nonhuman. The American philosopher Diogenes Allen writes:

> When God creates, it means that he allows something to exist which is not himself. This requires an act of profound renunciation. He chooses out of love to permit something else to exist, something created *to be itself* and to exist by virtue of its own interest and value. God renounces his status as the only existent – he pulls himself back, so to speak, in order to give his creation room to *exist for its own sake.*[176]

It is clear that this idea radically conflicts with the totally determined mechanistic universe of Isaac Newton. God is viewed here as one who acknowledges *free natural processes* as well as human *free will*. He respects the unfolding of his universe with its own inbuilt laws, initial conditions, and potentialities, as well as respecting human beings as free agents created in his image. God freely allows his creation to become what he has purposed it to be, neither distancing himself deistically from his creation nor overruling those free, natural processes that determine the unfolding of the universe through a creative interplay between chance and law.

This is a perspective that not only challenges the classical determinism of some conservative Christians but also the reductionism of those scientists like Richard Dawkins and Stephen Jay Gould who insist that the universe is a meaningless and purposeless zigzag path of evolutionary development, without any intelligence or reason behind it. According to these scientists there is no need to posit an author behind nature, because ultimately all things are reducible to scientific explanation: there is no ultimate or purposeful goal in creation, let alone a divine plan.

The notion of 'free natural processes,' however, is consistent with a God who is 'involved creatively in an open-ended process that involves both randomness and lawfulness.'[177] The freedom that God grants to his creation means that there will inevitably be what we might call gains and losses within an evolutionary framework. Pain and suffering are intrinsic to natural growth. In this context, it is helpful to distinguish between the suffering that derives directly from human sin and contaminates human life and the environment (for which we are responsible), and death and disease, which are the natural prerequisites for the evolution of life (for which we are not responsible). This inevitably leads to the question, Why did God create a world that requires life to evolve through death? Why create a world in which pain and suffering and disease so readily take root?

Consider Tennyson's poem *In Memoriam*, which includes the following well-known lines:

> Who trusted God was love indeed
> And love Creation's final law –
> Tho' Nature, red in tooth and claw
> With ravine, shriek'd against his creed.

There are no easy answers to why God has brought into being – by whatever means – a creation that is 'red in tooth and claw.' Does this not challenge Christian notions of a benevolent God, who has made all things well? What sort of God would allow one animal to rip apart another for food? What response do we have when natural disasters afflict the planet, such as the recent horrifying tsunami on Boxing Day 2004, caused by a thirty-kilometre rupture in the seabed in the Indian Ocean? Perhaps the most helpful response to the problem of natural evil in the physical creation is one that takes into account the findings of modern physics, which present us with a picture of the universe that is characterized by the most remarkable mathematical elegance and relational interconnectedness. In such a universe, the quantum features of randomness, risk, and unpredictability are necessary attributes of the emergent self-organizing processes that are inherent in the very fabric of creation.

Perhaps we need to acknowledge that we live in a universe that exists, in the words of Keith Ward, 'by opposition.' The continent of Australia, which is now my home, regularly experiences devastating bushfires, during which vast tracts of forest are consumed by fire. Bushfires, though they can lead to the tragic loss of life and property, are all part of the natural processes. While human neglect and sinfulness repeatedly contribute to increased fire risk, bushfires are essential to clear areas and allow new growth, and this process is critical to ecological health. Ward writes:

> It is of the nature of the energy of which [the material universe] is constituted to destroy as well as to create, to renew itself precisely by destruction, and so generate the new by its own continual perishing . . . Its vast energies continually interact and annihilate one another, yet generate new properties in the process. In such a world-system of many delicately balanced energies, held in an elegant mathematical web of rational principle, capable of generating emergent properties, including all the mental properties involved in the existence of a community of free rational wills, the creative originating Will can act to form and realize the structures of the physical order and bring its diversity into final unity with itself.[178]

The idea of suffering and regeneration belonging together should not be strange to us, especially when we think of a woman in labor as she delivers her child! The same idea of life coming from death can be found in John 12:24, recording the words of Jesus: 'unless a grain of wheat falls to the ground and dies, it remains only a single seed. But if it dies, it produces many seeds.' One writer argues that 'struggle is the principle of creation. Struggle is always going on, and it is this struggle in which life is regenerated. Nature is always giving birth, regenerating, always in travail.'[179] So parasites and predation, earthquakes and erosion are all part of the deal: they are an essential part of the 'free natural processes' at work in God's good creation.

These are problematic issues for Christians, and there are no easy answers – there are many Christians, for example, who argue that the world in which we live today is the way that it is because of the 'fall.' Of course it would be wrong to dismiss the very real impact that human sin has had upon the environment. We do not have a good track record as far as looking after our planet is concerned. To live responsibly as human beings within the created order embodies a wide range of concerns, such as the treatment of animals, the environmental management of forests and waterways, and the allocation of resources for effective global stewardship, to name only a few. But the reality of human sinfulness is very different from arguing that *creation itself* has fallen – it may be more accurate to say that creation has been contaminated by *human* fallenness, and bears the marks of that alongside the gains and losses of evolutionary history.

Emergence and coherence

Central to the idea of creation's freedom is the concept of *emergence*, which is a term that describes what happens when an interconnected system of relatively simple elements self-organizes to form more intelligent, more adaptive, and complex higher-level behavior.[180] At the most basic level of understanding, emergence may be described as a 'bottom-up' process that represents 'a movement from low-level rules to higher-level sophistication.'[181] Fuller offers three simple examples in which emergent properties arise: water, a cell, and a human brain. Water molecules are not in themselves wet, yet combined with many others they produce 'wetness'; proteins, nucleic acids, and other chemicals are themselves not alive, but combined into a cell they become a living organism; finally, a neuron is not conscious, but acting together with other neurons it produces consciousness.[182]

Another example from nature comes from the world of ants. Here is a quote from the book of Proverbs (6:6–9):

> Go to the ant, you sluggard;
> consider its ways and be wise!
> It has no commander,
> no overseer or ruler,

yet it stores its provisions in summer
and gathers its food at harvest.
How long will you lie there, you sluggard?
When will you get up from your sleep?

All the commentaries I have come across indicate that here we have a reprimand against sloth – there may well be need of that for some Christians! But as a recipe for a more effective Christian life, this may not be the best passage to turn to: it may unintentionally encourage some in their striving and self-effort! But the discerning reader will recognize something else in these verses: 'It has no commander, no overseer or ruler.' And so it is with ants and colonies: there is no command structure telling the ant what to do. In a quite remarkable way ants participate in the life of the colony in a coordinated fashion not because they are carrying out orders from a leader, but because they respond at the immediate, local level to what's going on around them. They don't have a 'big picture' available in order to determine their behavior. This is a classic example of what scientists call 'bottom-up' emergence.

Increasingly scientists are becoming fascinated by this phenomenon of emergence. For example, how is it that seventy-five trillion cells can emerge into the complexity that is the human body? In a remarkable way, individual cells, with no bird's-eye view of the final outcome, self-organize on the basis not only of the DNA encoded within them, but also as they relate to the other cells around them. Can we expand our vision and begin to think of the universe in similar terms? When Galileo and Newton were developing their ideas about the cosmos, the dominating metaphor was a *mechanistic* one – we live in a clockwork universe that obeys the designer's instructions in a fixed, deterministic way. The poet John Donne, troubled by such an interpretation of the cosmos, wrote these famous lines at the beginning of the seventeenth century:

And new philosophy calls all in doubt,
The element of fire is quite put out,
The sun is lost, and th'earth, and no man's wit
Can well direct him where to look for it. . .
'Tis all in pieces, all coherence gone.[183]

Donne was bemoaning the fact that scientists had lost an understanding of the universe that emphasized the interconnectedness of all things. They were more concerned with deterministic causes than anything else. But recent advances in the fields of thermodynamics, relativity, and quantum mechanics remind us that the universe is a remarkable system in which every single event is related to everything else. This is what Donne meant by coherence.

In a recent book Giuseppe Del Re develops the thesis that we must now work with another cosmological metaphor in the light of current scientific insights about chance, complexity, and coherence. That metaphor is summed up in the title of his book, *The Cosmic Dance*. In his foreword to the book, Thomas Torrance writes these words: 'Del Re uses the 'Great Dance Image' to give meaningful expression to the dynamical order of the universe as a coherent, evolving pattern in which all things participate as if in a dance or a ballet, combining general harmony and coherence with evolution, randomness and irreversibility.'[184]

We live in a remarkable universe that is characterized by patterns and relationships that reflect a cosmic order that is both beautiful and wonderfully harmonious. Go out at night and spend half-an-hour gazing at the night sky and you may begin to be captivated by this way of thinking. But we must not be restricted to a reductionist viewpoint, imagining that the only way to explain such a wonderful universe is by working from the bottom up. Science and faith have much to say to each other here. Christians would want to argue that our sovereign Creator God has set in motion from the beginning of time a creation of the most wonderful and beautiful complexity, such that what some scientists interpret in reductionist language as 'bottom-up' emergence is in reality the unfolding of God's creation – so it all has causality from the 'top down'! All things, therefore – and that includes you and me as the apex of God's creative genius – participate in the unfolding of God's ultimate purpose, which is to reconcile all things to himself, whether in heaven or on earth (Eph. 1:10).

Science, faith and *imago Dei*

When the American physicist and mathematician Freeman Dyson received the 2000 Templeton Prize for Progress in Religion, he declared: 'Science and religion are two windows that people look through, trying to understand the big universe outside, trying to understand why we are here. The two windows give different views, but both look out at the same universe. Both views are one-sided, neither is complete. Both leave out essential features of the real world. And both are worthy of respect.'

In this chapter we have explored some of the critical interface areas between science and religion, and discovered how true Dyson's words are: they both look out at the same universe. The final chapter of this book is an attempt to draw together some of the threads woven throughout the various chapters, providing a robust theological framework within which to dispel all attempts to resurrect the sacred–secular divide syndrome. The substance of that final chapter has to do with the doctrine of the Trinity. In order to bring some closure to our discussion of the science-faith issue, we need to make some reference here to Trinitarian thinking.

In an earlier chapter, I suggested that we can discern the marks or imprints of the triune God of grace in the created order. Our thoughts in this chapter have led us to the realization that the universe brought into being by God is a remarkably interconnected and dynamic reality, and science is increasingly having to come to terms with this truth. But science is not alone in this understanding. Of all the religions in the world, Christianity is the most compelling in speaking of a God who has created a dynamically coherent universe that reflects his relational being. The reason for this lies in the nature of the Christian God as Father, Son, and Holy Spirit.

God, Christians argue, is actually God by virtue of the loving relationships that exist within the divine life. Father, Son, and Spirit are united in such union that it is impossible to imagine any one person existing without the others. *Perichoresis* is a Greek word that refers to this intense mutual indwelling of each other. It is an inclusive concept that directs us into the essential nature of God's inner being of community and dynamic relationality, whose energies are not contained within his inner-Trinitarian being, but spill out in other-centered love to all creation.[185]

The Trinitarian concept of *perichoresis* is helpful at a number of levels of reality, as well as between those levels. As a theological doctrine, it is helpful as a way into understanding the communion of being and action that is at the heart of the life of the Trinity. Pastorally, it is significant in expressing not only the relationship between God and human beings, who are invited to participate in the divine life, but also the nature of our life together as the people of God (so the church may be viewed as an image of the Trinity). Scientifically, the concept correlates with an understanding of the interconnectedness of all creation in a coherent, open-ended, and complex system.

It follows, therefore, that both science and faith have this in common: both speak of a dynamic and relationally rich universe, characterized by both human and nonhuman realities. Scientists probe these realities in order to better understand them, and we have much to learn from their efforts. What is more, though we are the unique creation of God, our physical origins lie in the ashes of dead stars, and when we die to dust we will return: the particles that comprise you and me will be reconstituted in other forms throughout the universe. Of course, as Christians we declare that there is more to life after death than that! We look forward to an eternity in God that goes beyond, but nonetheless *includes,* physical existence – but a physicality that is peculiar to the conditions of the new creation that we anticipate with eager expectation.

The point I want to emphasize here is that, more than we often realize, we, as human beings, belong in the 'creation-community' and we are privileged to experience – at a deeply personal level – our own interconnectedness with all of creation. As those who are made in God's image (*imago Dei*) we reflect God's relational life; and as we discussed in Chapter 2, that involves being caught up in what Moltmann has called the 'creation-community,' a community of both creatures and environments contributing to a 'web of life on earth.' We cannot – we dare not – distance ourselves from God's creation. To do so is to fall into the very dualism that has infected the church for much of its history. It would also deny the Trinitarian nature of the God who has made space for the world within himself, and who embraces all of his creation with a love that only seeks the best for all that he has made.

Not only does *imago Dei* encapsulate in all its richness human participation both in God's inner-Trinitarian life and in his magnificent creation; it also explains why people throughout the ages have sought to understand through the sciences the physical universe in which they are privileged to participate. To be made in God's image expresses both the desire and the capacity to *investigate* God's world, as well as the act of *living* human life within the created order. To prise science and faith apart is to rob ourselves of the joy of discovery that is one of God's most precious gifts to us.

6

Actions Speak Louder than Words

Politics as 'the art of the possible and not the reign of saints' –
the reality of power, compromise, and influence

In a memorial lecture in Adelaide in 2003, the Australian
Foreign Minister Alexander Downer attacked the public
comments of some church leaders, accusing them of becoming
'amateur commentators on all manner of secular issues on
which they inevitably lack expertise.' In his address, he quoted
the former Bishop of London, Graham Leonard, who once
commented: 'Bishops and theologians in their public utterance
are remarkably vague and uncertain about matters which their
faith should teach them with certitude but remarkably certain
and dogmatic on matters of considerable complexity and
ambiguity about which they have no particular expertise.'[186]
    The bishop's comments relate particularly to his concern
about liberal ideas penetrating the church, but they are apposite
in the context of concerns expressed by Downer and others
about the relationship between politics and the church. In
common with statements by many other politicians, Downer
claims that he is not against church involvement in political
debate; what irks him is ill-informed criticism of politicians and
political decisions, too often motivated by the pursuit of what
he describes as popular political causes or cheap headlines.
Others, however, argue that what is perceived by some as
Christian leaders entering the 'popularity stakes' represents
genuine – if at times hasty and misguided – attempts to
contribute to political debate.

Not too many people today would openly argue that politics and faith have nothing to do with each other. They converge precisely because both have to do with making a difference in this world. Both are concerned with creating conditions that enable people to realize what Aristotle once called *summum bonum*, the 'good life.' In Chapter 2 we argued that it is artificial to divorce spirituality from issues of social justice and compassion and care for the needy, and emphasized that worship has to do with getting involved in God's world precisely because that is where he is involved. The important questions today have less to do with whether or not faith and politics mix, but what sort of mix we should advocate. How does the faith–politics relationship work out in the nitty-gritty of public life?

Individual or collective influence?

In an attempt to make sense of the interface between Christian faith and public life, Chris Sunderland writes: 'The essential task of any good politic is both to creatively uphold the social order and accept appropriate challenge.'[187] He cites two important figures in eighteenth-century English society: Edmund Burke, who had a love for social order, and Tom Paine, whose sympathies lay with those who were squeezed out of the social system, leading to exclusion and unjust treatment. For Sunderland, maintaining the status quo while at the same time allowing for challenge and change is what good politics is all about.

But there is an inherent difficulty in such a thesis. In his landmark study in ethics and politics, *Moral Man and Immoral Society*, the great American liberal theologian Reinhold Niebuhr (not to be confused with his brother H. Richard Niebuhr, whom we met in Chapter 2) argues that all social cooperation on a larger scale than the most intimate social group requires a measure of coercion. In his judgment, the coercive factor, while unable to preserve the unity of social life in and by itself, is nonetheless always present. The consequence is that politics will forever be 'an area where conscience and power meet, where the ethical and coercive powers of human life will interpenetrate and work out their tentative and uneasy compromises.'[188]

Niebuhr's scepticism about the resistance of conscience to coercion may be well founded, but capitulation is not inevitable. When British MP Stephen Timms, who at the time of writing is also the Minister for Pensions, joined the Labour Party in 1979 he struggled with his conscience: 'I had this view that I was going to find myself facing some ghastly moral dilemma where the Party would tell me to do one thing and my conscience would tell me to do something different.'[189] His testimony is that, although he has had to face some difficult decisions that required him to reflect deeply on the issues involved, thinking through the faith perspectives involved, he has not had to compromise with regard to his conscience. Timms is one of a number of Christian MPs who meet regularly across party lines to pray for each other. They are also dependent on the support and prayer of their local church communities.

Niebuhr's central point is that power and politics are inevitably intertwined. But he was a man who was caught between two theological worlds – while he abhorred the fundamentalist tendencies of conservative theology, with its authoritarian dogmatism and potent kingdom 'messianism,' he struggled with the failure of liberal theology to tackle the real evils of society. Liberal Christianity was not only too moralistic, it was ultimately hopelessly optimistic, 'too naïve about human nature to be called Christianity.'[190] Niebuhr's realism led to charges that he failed to offer any genuine prophetic vision of what a good society should look like. Ultimately, it is perhaps his failure to espouse a radical kingdom theology that weakens his political analysis, at least from a Christian perspective. Dorrien's summary is particularly apt: for Niebuhr, Christian realism had to do with 'human striving, conflict, and sin over which God ruled as sovereign . . . The presence of the kingdom inaugurated by Christ and vivified by the Spirit was not a reality that shaped his ethical thought.'[191]

This brief assessment of Reinhold Niebuhr's thinking in the 1930s, fueled by the miseries of the Great Depression, is helpful because it points us to a major tension in the relationship between politics and Christian faith. Niebuhr was impatient with liberal Christianity's moral idealism because it failed to recognize the inherent inability of social groups to subordinate their collective egotism to what he calls 'a pure morality of disinterestedness.' The implication is that Christian political influence – at least in terms of moral persuasion – may be most effective when channeled through motivated individuals rather than through collective groups initiated and organized to achieve what they deem to be socially desirable goals. The veteran British MP Tony Benn announced on his retirement that he was leaving the House of Commons in order to concentrate on politics! He was convinced that he could make more of a difference by playing an active part in the political process outside Westminster. Benn's personal decision should not, of course, be regarded as a recommendation against joining political parties, or canvassing for a seat in Parliament, in order to accelerate needed social changes. As the old saying goes, there is more than one way to skin a cat, and political influence can be exercised any number of ways, as we shall note throughout this chapter.

I suggest that Christians are politically most powerful when they live and act in society in ways that reflect the ethics of the kingdom of God. Politics and Christian faith converge precisely because Christians are members of the human race, along with everybody else, whatever their creed or colour. However, such a view should not be taken as a denial of the potential impact of political pressure groups, lobbying for changes in such areas as education policy, human welfare, and social injustice. A case in point is the Jubilee Debt Campaign, which seeks to relieve the debts that have mounted over the years as a result of the loans made to the poorest countries of the world. It has been estimated that 80 percent of the massive human chains that formed in protest against the injustice of these debts consisted of Christians. Much of the initial planning and direction of the campaign came from the churches, and Gordon Brown, the Chancellor of the Exchequer at the time the campaign was launched under the title of Jubilee 2000, was in no doubt that the campaign had been the major force in influencing public opinion. The Jubilee 2000 director credited Tear Fund, the evangelical relief agency, with providing financial support that averted collapse at a critical stage.[192]

Stephen Timms, who is heavily involved in the resurgent Christian Socialist Movement in Britain, suggests that there is a new social activism at work in contemporary British politics, giving rise to the comment of a newspaper columnist that 'it is no longer Morris, Keynes and Beveridge who inspire and change the world – it's Leviticus.'[193] On his personal website, Timms outlines his understanding of what is involved in 'Christian socialism':

> It is clear from the Bible that Jesus was not only a man who empathised with people's problems, but was a man who took action to change them. It is my hope for this generation that people who are committed to following the lifestyle of Jesus will seek to engage in politics and with the political authorities, as Jesus himself regularly did. I hope that people will feel that they can work with the social justice priorities which this Government has established. Equally, it is important the Government can learn lessons from the churches and other faith communities, because many of the most imaginative ideas for tackling Britain's social problems are emerging from faith-based projects which are tackling them.[194]

Not only in Britain, but also in many other countries throughout the world, there is evidence of initiatives undertaken by faith communities at both local and national levels that seek to alleviate poverty, encourage community, provide basic essentials, and foster healing. These initiatives complement the social welfare support available through government funding. Niebuhr's fear of a loss of real moral power in human groups through a diminished capacity for self-transcendence leading to unrestrained egotism is altogether too negative a judgment. Certainly the dangers are present – but they should not be allowed to outweigh the value of organized action and negotiation in order to achieve desired outcomes.

The seduction of power

The nineteenth-century historian Lord Acton is best known for his insight that 'power tends to corrupt, and absolute power corrupts absolutely.' In an address delivered to members of the Bridgnorth Institute in England on 28 May 1877, on 'The History of Freedom in Christianity,'[195] Acton cites the Renaissance Italian diplomat Niccolo Machiavelli, who believed that 'the vigorous use of statecraft necessary for the success of difficult schemes would never be made if governments allowed themselves to be hampered by the precepts of the copy-book.' Machiavellianism, of course, has now become a byword for the denial of moral principles in political affairs, and the advocacy of a pragmatism in which the end justifies the means. In his address, Acton presents a strong historical case for his thesis about the corruption of power, highlighting in particular the extent to which the clergy, who had once served the cause of freedom so assiduously in the strife against feudalism, were, in the pre-Reformation era, enslaved to royalty, with the church allied to the state throughout Europe.

When Luther launched his attack against the Catholic Church at Wittenberg in the sixteenth century he was savage in his indictment of the church's practice of selling indulgences in order to perpetuate its power. But he also inadvertently unleashed a new wave of people-power as the German peasants embraced their newfound freedom. Luther was caught in the struggle to which I referred earlier, the tension between upholding the status quo and encouraging change. As Sunderland rightly observes, his support of the state's repression of the peasants, enshrined in his 'two kingdoms' theology, has been instrumental in convincing a number of Protestant Christians to adopt a hands-off approach as far as politics is concerned; rather than get involved in the power game, Christians are better advised to retreat into a private pietism . . . which, of course, is to buy into the dualistic agenda. As we have seen already, such an approach has little to do with Christian discipleship – it represents a form of 'religious cop-out' that bypasses the struggle and discernment needed in political involvement for the sake of the kingdom.

In the midst of this necessary involvement, the power issue will not go away. Power *is* seductive and it *does* corrupt. Examples of those who stand firm are sadly outnumbered – at least, it *seems* that way, to judge by media accounts – by the many who succumb to the temptation of power. Corruption in high places is not confined to the secular world where business and political interests hold sway. Richard Foster has written persuasively about the dangers of money, sex, and power in Christian life,[196] and this seductive triad has corrupted the ministries of a number of high-profile Christians in recent decades. Christians are tempted as much as anyone else to do the wrong thing for what may seem at the time to be all the right reasons. And political temptation is no exception. An American law professor once wrote: 'Who wants to be a voice crying in the wilderness when we can be witnesses testifying before Congress? Who wants to be a prophet without honour in his own land when White House breakfasts are available? Who wants to store up treasures in heaven when there are elections to be won here on earth?'[197]

The attraction to Christian leaders of the immediate, the concrete, and the publicly recognized can be heady stuff! Something is happening at the visible centre of power, and this appeals to the human ego. But the power of the gospel is not of this kind at all: true power resides in the intrinsic nature of the gospel, which has nothing to do with personal ego and everything to do with Christ.

Alan Lewis powerfully exposes the church's 'self-destroying imitation of the world's success and plenitude'[198] in a number of key areas under the umbrella idolatry of a theology that bypasses the centrality of the cross. In similar vein to Hall's critique of North American Christianity,[199] Lewis argues that only in self-emptiness can the church, like Christ, discover its fullness: only in an other-centered commitment can the church reflect the ministry of Christ. Theology itself is criticized for its failure to divest itself of a lust for power and glory. Lewis' critique is directed at clerical leadership, but his analysis needs to be heard by all Christians who are seeking to make a difference in the world: *beware the seductive pull of power!* Lewis' antidote to power is an acceptance of weakness, for God calls us in spite of our failings, not because of our manifest strengths and abilities. A renewed understanding of power, grounded in servanthood, resides not in privilege and position but in the Spirit of Christ crucified: 'My grace is sufficient for you,' the Lord reminded Paul, 'for my power is made perfect in weakness' (2 Cor. 12:9).

Subversive infiltration

It is important to understand that power is not a bad thing in itself. The Greek word *dunamis*, from which we get 'dynamite', is used frequently throughout the New Testament to describe God's power at work in creation and through individual lives. It is used especially to describe the reality of the Holy Spirit at work in the lives of believers. In Acts 1:8, Jesus tells his disciples that 'you will receive power when the Holy Spirit comes on you; and you will be my witnesses in Jerusalem, and in all Judea and Samaria, and to the ends of the earth.' When Peter spoke in the name of Jesus Christ to the crippled beggar in Acts 3:12, the apostle said to the astonished crowd: 'Why do you stare at us as if by our own power or godliness we had made this man walk?' Power to witness and power to heal – *dunamis*, the dynamite of God at work in his world!

Political engagement, therefore, has nothing to do with the divestment of power for fear of its contaminating influence, but everything to do with how Christians might exercise power in such a way as to avoid the corrupting temptations so eloquently identified by Lord Acton. The language of power here is, of course, derived from and predicated on the reality that Christians are privileged to participate in the powerful work of the Holy Spirit who is ever at work in the world, seeking to bring about healing and reconciliation from the vantage point of the gospel. I would like to examine this understanding of power in the context of political action from the perspective of the church as a faith community, as well as in individual Christian lives.

With regard to the actions of the church in the world, the German theologian Helmut Thielicke writes about 'the law of infiltration and subversion.' In developing his argument, he discusses the church's task of 'political preaching.' The church is not just the sum of individual Christians – each Christian is called to exercise his or her freedom, such as the freedom to vote for this or that political party, but the church must always live, speak, and act without prejudicing the decision of its individual members. How, then, he asks, is the church to speak 'without on the one hand falling victim to timeless abstractions wholly divorced from the situation, whereby it does nothing but issue very general and for the most part very trivial appeals to conscience, and without on the other hand actually meddling in the situation, falsely construing it as one that directly involves a man's stance before God?'[200]

Taking a historical perspective, Thielicke acknowledges the church's works of mercy and many acts of private charity: we have recorded some of these already within the contemporary social setting. However, he roundly condemns the church's political apathy in the face of social injustice, an apathy that 'drives the forlorn victims . . . to resort to revolution.' He rejects simplistic revolutionary solutions that fail to recognize the radical difference between the kingdom of God and the world, while at the same time recognizing that the church is called to make a stand on the issues of the day, impelled by the Holy Spirit and not by the spirit of the age.

At this point Thielicke is clear in his dismissal of political and social programs advanced by the church: the church is not the product of human initiative. So, for example, to combat social oppression in such areas as Latin America with violence on the basis that the end justifies the means is to fall into a pragmatism that misunderstands the nature of power. Thielicke offers a response that is less overt but more theologically robust. Arguing from the basis that Hellenism infiltrated the embryonic Christian world through gnostic ideas, he asks whether a similar process might not apply with regard to the Christian church's influence upon the world. He presents his law of subversive infiltration not as a pragmatic attempt to master the world – as apparent, for example, in some conversionist agendas in America – but as 'a law of action which is grounded in the nature of the Christian message itself.'[201] The example he gives comes from Paul's letter to Philemon, in which he offers a response to the vexed question concerning the New Testament's silence about a social order that tolerates slavery. By sending Onesimus, a slave, back to his master as a Christian brother, which is precisely what Paul does in writing to Philemon, he does something that is radically new. Paul's action presents 'a way that is diametrically opposed to that of slavery morality . . . at this point at least the order of slavery will have been shattered from within . . . this particular structure of society will have been undermined. *The changing of persons will necessarily mean the changing of the order.*'[202]

The transformation of the social order is, for Thielicke, only an incidental by-product of the changing of lives. Political action by the church is therefore indirect: 'it does not debate *things*; it aims at the conversion of *persons*.'[203]

It is important to understand that Thielicke is not recommending abstention from political action. Nor is he advocating personal conversion as the *only* route for political action. His focus on the church resonates with the view of John Howard Yoder, who argues, on the basis of an exegesis of Paul's affirmation of the role of the church in the world in Ephesians 3:8–11, that 'the primary social structure through which the gospel works to change other structures is that of the Christian community.'[204] Ultimately, Thielicke's proposal for subversive infiltration is offered because of his fear that the church might capitulate – as it too often has in recent years – to the powerful lobbies that seek, in their own subversive way, to overturn the values and commands of the gospel. In other words, we are not to play them at their own game: the power of the gospel is altogether different, and ultimately more effective, than that which characterizes the vast majority of political action today.

The position advocated here echoes two of H. Richard Niebuhr's 'church of the center' categories, as described in Chapter 2. These are 'Christ Above Culture,' involving a willing and intelligent cooperation of Christians with non-believers in carrying on the work of the world, while yet maintaining the distinctiveness of Christian faith and life, and 'Christ and Church in Paradox,' in which Christians live in the world as redemptive presence, but without the clarity of binary opposition more evident in the former. How might Christian political engagement look under the label of 'subversive infiltration'?

A good example is in the area of school education, which has become for many Christians a major cultural battleground. Christian conservatives in such first-world nations as United States, Britain and Australia are beginning to challenge the growing emphasis on politically correct values that, in the words of Kevin Donnelly, a prominent Australian educationalist, 'champion a left-wing view of the world enmeshed in the culture wars against conservative values.'[205] The 'left-wing' agenda seeks to combat what education unionists describe as a curriculum base that favors privilege and meritocracy. In place of fundamental educational standards that reinforce the 'three Rs,' classroom discipline, and high-quality teaching, the curriculum pushes the pendulum towards such politically charged areas as gender, ethnicity, and class.

As a result, critics of the new 'trendy' curriculum, for example, denounce the obsession with Marxism as an appropriate template for the analysis of literature, especially texts like Shakespeare that predate the particular 'ism' being promoted! Controversy also surrounds the status of literature in the English curriculum where literature has been subsumed under the general category of 'text.' The idea is that students should be taught to analyze texts in terms of contemporary power relationships. This is known as 'critical literacy,' which has been defined as the analysis and critique of the relationships among texts, language, power, social groups, and social practices. Central to critical literacy is the deconstruction of texts in order to resist bias and manipulation. Political correctness is the name of the game. So *Snow White and the Seven Dwarfs* comes under scrutiny because living happily ever after is defined as 'marrying the prince,' and *Thomas the Tank Engine* reinforces a capitalist hierarchy, as mainline passenger trains are considered superior to goods trains! Children are denied the joy of reading for pleasure and are encouraged to become 'active meaning makers.'

Many other examples of the conflict between right-wing and left-wing values may be cited. And this, of course, is precisely where the battle lines are being drawn. The battle for the minds of our children lies at the heart of the current clash in education content and standards, and Christians have a very real part to play in the unfolding social scenario. Rather than rise up in protest, taking action on the streets, and lobbying for more Christian values in schools, concerned parents might be better advised to get involved in their local PTAs (parent–teacher associations), or seek a place on the board of governors. Faithfully engaging in the real world, seeking to persuade others in a redemptive way, lies at the heart of Christian political action, and ultimately may achieve more lasting results.

Many Christians recommend sending their children to Christian schools, although there are others who are not so sure about their effectiveness, believing that the real battle for the minds of children is in the home and not the school. Moreover, critics of Christian schooling suggest that they do not adequately prepare young people for the real world after school. This is a debate that we do not have space to explore further in this book, but it represents a good example of the sort of issues that Christians are called to face as they live out their lives in the world. The appropriate response may be either collective (in terms of action flowing out of the convictions of a like-minded group, which may or may not be Christian in its primary orientation) or individual, and the degree of infiltration involved will differ from one situation to another. The important point is that Christians do not stand idly by, wringing their hands in despair as if they had no political clout. They do, more than they realize. And one group that has sought more clout than any other in the history of Christian political involvement is the 'Religious Right' in the United States. And it is anything but subversive in its approach!

The rise of 'Christian politics'

In an intriguing assessment of the Christian Right in America,[206] Grant Wacker, who is Professor of the History of Religion in America at the Duke University Divinity School, asks, How could the Christian Right flourish in the sunlit progressivism of the Age of Aquarius? He defines the Christian Right as a coalition of evangelicals who care enough about the political goals of the Christian Right to leave their pews and get out to vote and non-evangelicals who care enough about the political goals of the Christian Right to work with evangelicals. The movement had its early origins in the twentieth century in the debates over biblical interpretation and the creation–evolution controversy (the 1925 Scopes trial was a landmark event), with the perceived threat of communism accelerating its rise in the latter half of the century. But its real growth was stimulated by a number of important social and cultural developments in the 1960s, such as the civil rights movement, the hippie youth culture, feminism and the sexual revolution, and the sanctity of life debates.

In the face of these challenges to traditional conservative values, Christian leaders like Jerry Falwell and Pat Robertson presented an alternative evangelical platform, emphasizing the supreme authority of the Bible, particularly in family life and human relationships. The four cornerstones of their worldview have been summarized by Wacker as follows: firstly – and this represents its most visible cornerstone – moral absolutism, including the fixity of sexual identities and gender roles, the preferability of capitalism, the importance of hard work, and the sanctity of unborn life; secondly, the assumption that metaphysics, morals, politics, and mundane customs stand on a continuum – so, ideas about big things like the nature of the universe inevitably affect little things, such as how individuals choose to act in the details of daily life; thirdly, government's proper role is to cultivate virtue, not to interfere with the natural operations of the marketplace or the workplace; and, fourthly, the assumption that all successful societies need to operate within a framework of common assumptions.

Beyond these four cornerstones, the Christian Right sees itself in an all-out war against the secular world, especially with regard to the secular media, the public schools, and the enemies of the traditional family. Its overt siege mentality places it very much within a dualistic frame of reference. Its members ally themselves naturally with the Republican Party, particularly in its affirmation of traditional moral standards. Similar connections are evident in Britain, with the Conservative Christian Fellowship – grounded in a strong moral agenda – operating as a forum for believers in the British Conservative Party. Interestingly, the Christian Socialist Movement in Britain, which is less overtly evangelistic, emphasizes issues of justice and in this respect its association with the Labour Party parallels the justice concerns of the American Democratic Party. It is too early to evaluate the impact of the Family First Party in Australia in terms of party political affiliation and influence, but its moral agenda, especially with regard to family values, makes it a more natural ally with Australian Liberals rather than the Labour Party. As a political party in its own right, Family First, which evaluates every piece of legislation according to its impact on family life and values, may be in danger of narrowing its focus and failing to achieve a broad enough policy platform to attract a large number of votes. In addition, its own strong link with the Assemblies of God denomination may be as much a disadvantage as an advantage. However, its influence in government through the allocation of preference votes in the 2004 Australian federal election, though disproportionate to its size, has kept the major parties on their toes. This may be its most important role within the parliamentary process.

It is apparent that a political alignment in Christianity is occurring that parallels the traditional party political divide, particularly in Britain and the United States. From time to time there are reports that the two sides are seeking common ground, but fear of exclusivism or compromise is always a problem. Of course, Christians should not necessarily seek to resolve their different social and political emphases: disagreement and debate are essential to a healthy democracy. How individual Christians respond will depend very much on how far their Christian convictions guide them, especially with regard to the morality–justice spectrum.

One worrying concern voiced by Christians on both sides is the 'slippery slope' syndrome. On the one hand, the high moral ground epitomized in the Christian Right may lead to the sort of fundamentalism that fails to acknowledge the strong tension between the authority of Christ and the claims of culture, characteristic of Neibuhrian 'paradoxical dualism.' Further-more, the danger of being sucked into political power games is always present whenever fundamentalist programs are pitched against the prevailing political climate. On the other hand, the economic justice and social libertarian portfolio inherent in such groups as the Christian Socialist Movement tends to favor private ethical choice in such areas as abortion and euthanasia, with the consequent danger not only of a drift away from the exercise of moral responsibility, but also of a hypocritical split between private practice and public utterances (or even behavior).

As a final observation, we may note that the Christianity–politics relationship is not one-way. Whenever there is a rise in Christian involvement in the political process, the benefits cut both ways, and for the political parties the reality of the relationship is ultimately tested at the ballot box. And this, of course, the various Christian groups know very well. Not only do we see Christian leaders seeking to exert their influence through lobbying, attending prestigious breakfasts, and jumping on to the political merry-go-round, but savvy political leaders are careful not to offend key Christian groups, especially those who might hold the electoral balance in their hands. Again, the temptation among Christian leaders to succumb to the overtures of high-profile political figures is an ever-present reality, a temptation that may compromise their gospel stand. The reality is that 'Christian politics' in the form that we have discussed above is almost certainly here to stay, at least in the foreseeable future, and all Christians need to reflect and pray about where they will place their cross when it comes to election day. Wisdom dictates that, more often than not, the choice is between the lesser of two evils. As Michael Cromartie rightly points out, 'politics frequently requires prudent and principled compromise . . . it is the art of the possible and not the reign of the saints.'[207] Or, in Reinhold Neibuhr's words, politics is 'the method of finding proximate solutions to insoluble problems.'[208]

Actions speak louder than words

In Colossians 3:12 the apostle Paul writes: 'Therefore, as God's chosen people, holy and dearly loved, clothe yourselves with compassion, kindness, humility, gentleness and patience.' Christians are called to live by the Spirit, manifesting fruit that includes such attributes as patience, kindness, and gentleness. However, when confronted with views different from their own, Christians may display one of three different responses. Some will shake their heads in despair, bewailing the state of the world, and retreat into their private, comfortable faith-spaces, lacking the courage of their convictions. At the other end of the spectrum, there may be those who, in the words of the Christian philosopher and ethicist Richard Mouw, contribute more to the problem than the solution: 'Well-known clergy tell their followers that the time has come for a 'battle' against the forces of unbelief. The TV cameras show Christians on the picket lines, angrily shaking their fists at their opponents.'[209]

Mouw is concerned about the lack of what he calls civility, a simple 'public politeness' or courtesy towards others. However, this does not mean that we sacrifice convictions: there are times, he insists, when it is appropriate to manifest some very uncivil feelings. Quoting some lines from Yeats' poem 'The Second Coming,' Mouw pleads for more 'passionate intensity' about our convictions. 'The real challenge,' he argues, 'is to come up with a *convicted civility*,'[210] an ungainly phrase, but one that helpfully expresses the balance that Mouw is trying to convey. It is this course of action that represents the third way for all Christians, who are called to live as salt and light in the community. A good example of one who follows this path is the American author and Christian political activist Jim Wallis. He founded the magazine *Sojourners* in the 1970s while studying at seminary in Illinois, and in 1976 wrote his first book, *Agenda for Biblical People*. He continues to serve as the editor of *Sojourners*, encouraging Christians to rediscover their call to live in the world as pilgrims, loving and serving the world without conforming to it.

But Wallis is interested in more than words. Raised in a Midwest evangelical family, he soon found himself appalled by the racial segregation in his church and community: 'The contradictions between the simple and self-justifying world view of my childhood in the church and a growing awareness of the world and its atrocities caused havoc through my teenage years, The cracks became cleavages as the harsh facts of racism painfully penetrated my consciousness in my youth in Detroit. I felt shocked, betrayed, angry, and painfully implicated in the brutal realities of white racism.'[211]

He began to live and work among the black churches and neighborhoods of inner-city Detroit, and became involved in the civil rights movement and antiwar protests. His convictions led him along a path of radical discipleship, convinced that morality and justice are two sides of the same coin. In his recent book, *God's Politics*, he challenges the political left to widen the language of moral values by including within its scope such issues as poverty, the environment, criminal justice, and war. His purpose is to expose more critically the narrow program of the political right and encourage the Democrats to put forward an action agenda that synthesizes justice and morality consistent with godly principles. He once claimed that the Right was attacking him for 'trying to help the Democrats get religious language so they can win an election!' His crusading zeal has won him many supporters and he is a frequent and popular speaker at meetings and rallies across the country.

But at heart Wallis is an activist, not just a clear and penetrating thinker. In 1995 he convened Call to Renewal, a national network of churches, faith-based organizations, and individuals working to overcome poverty in America. Evolving from a gathering of nearly 100 religious leaders, the movement is based upon four core values: overcoming poverty, dismantling racism, affirming life, and rebuilding family and community. Those who participate in Call to Renewal pledge themselves to work to influence local and national public policies and priorities, while growing and developing a movement of Christians committed to overcoming poverty.[212] While Wallis' commitments take him far and deep into the national political landscape, he recognizes that political action can be effective at many other levels. Accordingly, both concerned individuals and local faith communities are encouraged to seek ways in which they might act in order to combat the disparity between rich and poor people.

Wallis' original vision of 'the church's biblical identity as a new community which is a sign of the kingdom in history, an alien society of God's people whose life and action is intended to play a prophetic and decisive role in the world'[213] remains at the core of his 'convicted civility.' It is a vision shared by many others, and corresponds to the biblical affirmation that the people of God are summoned to be a hospitable people. Hospitality also resonates well with the notion of civility. Christine Pohl reminds us that hospitality 'reflects God's greater hospitality that welcomes the undeserving, provides the lonely with a home, and sets a banquet table for the hungry.'[214] Richard Gollings, who was involved for many years in church planting in Mexico City and Tijuana, tells the story of two yearly migrants to the urban construction industry who were welcomed by a local pastor to share his dinner, and given a free room in the *templo* where his family lived. The notion of hospitality is evident here in the missionary heart of the local pastor: likewise, the local church is called into being as a 'covenantal community,' including and enabling 'community obligations to strangers and outsiders.'[215] There is two-way dynamic involved here: strangers are welcomed into the Christian community, which at the same time moves out from its comfortable centre of familiarity and intimacy into costly engagement with others. Ultimately, actions speak louder than words.

Nowhere is this more evident than in the reforms that followed John Wesley's open-air preaching in Britain and America. In the nineteenth century the social fabric of both countries was transformed, as a number of Christian leaders, inspired by a social conscience that emerged out of the Evangelical Revival, began to make their presence felt in the political landscape. One of the most famous was William Wilberforce, who was the inspiration behind the Clapham Sect, a 'brotherhood of Christian politicians' in Britain through whose efforts the slave trade in the colonies was abolished. Their influence was felt far and wide throughout the nation, extending to education, workplace reform, gambling, parliamentary reform, and many other areas where injustices existed.

Another key figure during this time was Lord Shaftesbury, a politician whose efforts to alleviate the plight of women and children working in the slums, and especially in mines and factories, under the most appalling conditions, caused his biographer to write of him: 'No man has in fact ever done more to lessen the extent of human misery, or to add to the sum total of human happiness.'[216] Similar reforms were evident on the other side of the Atlantic, associated particularly with the ministry of Charles Finney, who mobilized an army of volunteers engaged in social reform. These great advances in justice and righteousness – themes that resonate both with Old Testament prophecy and Jesus' radical call to discipleship in the New Testament – have not, however, been as evident throughout the twentieth century as evangelicals concentrated less on social reform and more on preserving their identity in the face of liberal onslaughts. What is indisputable, though, is the fact that Christians – whether they are operating inside or outside the established political structures – have the power to make a very real difference to society, reflecting the historical ministry of Jesus, whose life and teaching was, in the fullest sense of the word, political.

Writing about Jesus' ministry, John Stott, whose worldwide ministry has focused especially on the twin themes of evangelism and social action, offers a narrow and broad definition of the word 'politics.' According to its narrow definition it is 'the science of government.' However, if politics is concerned with the whole of our life in human society, then it is, more broadly, 'the art of living together in community.' It is in this broad sense that he argues that Jesus' whole ministry was political:

> In the ... narrower sense, he clearly was not [involved in politics]. He never formed a political party, adopted a political programme or organized a political protest. He took no steps to influence the policies of Caesar, Pilate or Herod ... In the other and broader sense of the word, however, his whole ministry was political. For he had himself come into the world in order to share in the life of the human community, and he sent his followers into

the world to do the same. Moreover, the Kingdom of God he proclaimed and inaugurated was a radically new and different social organization, whose values and standards challenged those of the old and fallen community. In this way his teaching had 'political' implications.[217]

There is a Franciscan blessing that reflects this 'political calling' to all who claim to be disciples of Christ, a blessing that has to do with the way we live our lives in the midst of suffering and oppression:

> May God bless us with discomfort at easy answers,
> half-truths and superficial relationships,
> so that we will live deeply in our hearts.
> May God bless us with anger at injustice, oppression
> and exploitation of people and the earth,
> so that we will work for justice, equity, and peace.
>
> May God bless us with tears to shed for those who suffer,
> so that we will reach out our hands
> to comfort them and change their pain to joy.
> And may God bless us with the foolishness to think that
> we can make a difference in our world,
> so that we will do the things which others say cannot be done.

In his own ministry Jesus had a profound concern for the material well-being of the poor and disadvantaged – he made a difference by his actions, challenging those who were self-righteous and indifferent. Likewise, as followers of Jesus, Christians are called to live redemptively as 'the salt of the earth' and 'the light of the world' (Matt. 5:13–14) in the communities and neighborhoods in which they live.

The politics of sex – an example of civility

In this chapter we have focused on a number of public issues that lie at the heart of the political debate, such as education and social justice. But there are many other issues about which

Christians are right to be concerned, such as the role of the media, the fragmentation of family life, the problems of global warming and environmental degradation (briefly discussed in the last chapter), industrial relations, the terrorist threat, the technological revolution, emerging trends in sexuality, the challenges of an increasingly elderly population . . . the list goes on. All of these areas are grist to the political mill. Their importance will wax and wane over time, but none of them will go away. They all demand wise and discerning response from the Christian community. It is not the purpose of this chapter to offer solutions to issues over which there may be deep divisions. Certainly the Bible may offer clear guidance in some areas, but this is not always forthcoming in others. What is critical at all times – however patent the biblical position may seem to be to its adherents – is the appropriate Christian *attitude,* and Mouw's concept of civility, discussed earlier, is particularly helpful.

Let's see how this might work out in the area of sexual behavior, a moral issue that is fundamental in the political agenda of the Religious Right. The wide range of topics embraced under the umbrella of sexuality include, for example, sexual promiscuity, early-age sexual activity, adultery, same-sex relationships, the AIDS epidemic, pornography, sexual fantasy, sex education, sex in the media, and the related topics of contraception and abortion. There is no one Christian slogan that does justice to the complexities inherent in the debates over these numerous aspects of human sexuality and their manifestation in contemporary Western culture. But Christians should be united by civility, adopting an attitude of gentleness and courtesy without losing the cutting-edge convictions that drive them. And that is important: if sexual values are important to the health of a society, then Christians should be in the vanguard when it comes to preserving those values. Our own interpretation of truth should never be the casualty in political debate and engagement.

Mouw devotes a chapter in his book *Uncommon Decency* to how to be civil about sex.[218] He readily acknowledges that there is a preoccupation with matters of sex in some Christian quarters, and not just among evangelical Protestants. But the primary role of sex in human life, both socially and privately, suggests that the issue cannot be sidelined as yet another irrelevant football thrown into the political playing-field by those who should be concerned about weightier matters. That said, the starting point for Christians is to be honest about their own sexuality. Mouw cites the words of a godly minister, who, when he became aware of a younger colleague who had been caught in an adulterous relationship, said: 'I have no business feeling self-righteous. If my own sexual history were made public, there would be no major scandals. Nothing to get me defrocked. But I would still be ashamed – *so* ashamed!'

The truth, as Mouw so helpfully points out, is that we are all casualties of our fallen nature. Ray Anderson, one of Mouw's colleagues at Fuller Seminary in California, argues that running through the center of human sexuality is the element of the tragic:

> When the beauty and promise of human love and intimacy are linked with the capacity for sexual desire and fulfillment, no experience will prove adequate and completely fulfilling . . . Redemption from the tragic does not guarantee perfect fulfillment of every capacity or desire. It does offer grace to bear with what must be borne, and to sublimate self-gratification in one area to self-fulfillment in another. Every human being is a sexual being and will experience some degree of the tragic in this area.[219]

Honest self-awareness will go a long way to guaranteeing civility in political discourse in this, as in many other areas of life. This is the first of what Mouw calls 'guidelines for sexual civility.' His second is to avoid oversimplifications, including taunting the opposition with catchy slogans that only serve to widen rather than close the gap. He then advises us to remember our own collective sexual sins, coupled with the need to curtail irrational fears. For example, in the area of homosexuality, the church has been inexcusably harsh over the years, and the accusation of homophobia, though often inappropriately applied to Christians by the homosexual lobby, leaves a sour taste in the church's mouth. The church's treatment of divorced people and its negative attitude towards sex also contribute to the long history of sexual oppression that has characterized the church community. All Christians should humbly examine themselves in order to identify any irrational fears that may frustrate constructive political engagement. Mouw's final guideline is to cultivate what he calls 'sexual empathy': to acknowledge that all human beings have been lovingly fashioned in God's image is to begin to identify with others in their situations in life, however much we may disagree with them.

Finally, Mouw addresses the issue of public policy and the role of Christians with regard to sexual issues. His central point is that, though we are called to maintain clear standards of sexual behavior *within* the community of faith, we are not entitled to *demand* those same standards within society. We may regret the reality of alternative sexual behaviors in society, but the Christian calling is, in the first instance, to shine as lights in the darkness, not to insist that everyone do as we do – which, given the recent track record of the church in the matter of child sex abuse, is a matter of deep regret in itself.

There are, of course, many different ways in which individuals and church communities may witness to their beliefs with regard to sexuality. For example, one simple strategy with regard to obscene content on television is to telephone the TV channel in question to register a complaint. It is a legal requirement in many countries for these complaints to be logged and measured against a broadcasting code of conduct, and a flood of complaints – particularly if they carry the implied threat of boycotting the channel – may have the desired effect. In America, the Parents Television Council has become a major national force in the crusade against indecency, with nearly half a million complaints lodged against the Federal Communications Commission in 2005 compared with only 111 in 2000.

More generally, seeking to influence legislation is, of course, the right of any citizen, and this can be accomplished in any number of ways – getting informed about important issues, sharing in public debate, lobbying MPs, voting in elections and taking part in demonstrations. But always done with civility as well as conviction. Faith and politics are inextricably entwined, and individual Christians and local faith communities are privileged to influence contemporary society through their political activities. Politics has to do with making a difference in this world: it is a 'doing' word. The tragedy is that when all is said and done, there is often more said than done.

7

Is Capitalism a Dirty Word?

Redeeming work from its captivity to the economy and reclaiming business for the kingdom of God

In 1999, with the forces of communism shattered, delegates of the World Trade Organization gathered in Seattle to discuss trade and tariffs in the global economy. They were not alone: thousands of protesters had also arrived in the city to disrupt proceedings. What ensued next has come to be known as 'the Battle of Seattle.' Protestors marched, waving banners, and locked arms to block the entry of delegates. Some began to vandalize nearby property. Police used tear gas and rubber bullets to disperse the crowds. The scenes became uglier on day two of the summit as riot police moved in with a violent crackdown; demonstrators, most of whom had come to protest peacefully against the human rights abuses and environmental pollution caused by international trade, panicked, and many bystanders were caught up in the mayhem.

Subsequent protests in Prague, Quebec, and Genoa over the following two years against such organizations as the International Monetary Fund, the World Bank, and the G8 summit of rich nations attracted large crowds of demonstrators, and were marked by similar violent scenes. In recent years, however, demonstrations have not been as vigorous or well-attended, with the exception of the 2006 G20 summit in Melbourne, where hundreds of anti-globalization supporters, some masked, attempted to dismantle security barriers surrounding the hotel where finance ministers and bankers were meeting. Many of the protesters were involved in pitched battles with police armed with batons. Up to this time, violent demonstrations had been supplanted by a new form of resistance, epitomized by the emergence of the World Social Forum (WSF), a direct rival to the World Economic Forum. The WSF was set up in 2001 to coordinate strategies against capitalism and globalization, and over the last few years many satellite groups have been established on a regional basis.

The competing Forums represent two sides in the debate over the ethics of capitalism, and it is a debate that Christians cannot disregard. For many people, whether or not they belong to the Christian faith, 'capitalism' is a dirty word. It immediately conjures up images of exploitation, injustice, corporate greed, and the perennial offence to humanity, and to God, of the rich–poor divide. Taking a global perspective, the many examples of people living in abject poverty, of women and children forced to work eighteen hours a day in sweatshop conditions, and of poor people being denied the benefits of pharmaceutical research in order to alleviate diseases like malaria, challenge the argument that capitalism might actually have some good points.

However, this is a challenge that we need to take up. I wrote in Chapter 1 that for some Christians an unreal dualism can shape the way life in the commercial world is perceived: businesspeople live according to secular principles, and God's people live according to spiritual, or sacred, principles. My own background in business, working in the oil industry and subsequently as a university lecturer in marketing management, set the scene for much personal struggling as I attempted to reconcile the commercial realities of marketing with my growing Christian faith. Initially, I was tempted to reject the business world as unhealthy and contrary to godly life, but further reflection convinced me that the gap between what I had taught in a university business school and what I was doing in Christian ministry was not so yawning after all!

In this chapter we will address the relationship between the two by firstly looking at the contribution Christianity can make to business. In other words, Christians should regard the management of the world's resources as part of the mandate given to human beings to care for the earth and provide for one another so that we might live fully human lives. How we go about that is a legitimate Christian concern. However, that is only one side of the coin with regard to the relationship between Christianity and commerce. The other side of the coin asks the question, Does business have something to contribute to Christianity? We might call this 'the management of ministry,' a corresponding rubric that relates to the application of business principles within the church and other Christian organizations.

Closing the gap – a theology of work[220]

In order to tease out more fully the first side of the coin, a useful starting point is to consider our theology of work. Contrary to some perceptions, work is not to be regarded as a necessary evil; in fact, quite the reverse. Work is a gift from God to humanity, as Dorothy Soelle points out in her book *To Work and to Love*. She recounts an occasion when she became impatient with her daughter's progress at school, and went to see her teacher to ask when the children would start to work. The teacher's response – 'Can't you see what's going on here? Don't you see that these strong workers, these children, are building a town with their blocks?' – affected her profoundly, betraying her 'spiritually-impoverished' view of work: 'His response changed my mind, moving me from a myopic, production-oriented perspective on work to a more humane understanding of work. I discovered the meaning of work in its three essential dimensions: self-expression, social relatedness, and reconciliation with nature by way of this experience.'[221]

Soelle considers, firstly, what work does *for the worker*, which shifts us from an outcomes-based approach to work to one that recognizes human beings' innate need to create. In her summary of Dorothy Sayers' 'Gospel of Work,' the American theologian Laura Simmons writes: 'all work must allow people to fulfil their vocation by being creative; if it fails to do so, it is cheating them of their essential humanity.'[222] Soelle invites us to reflect on Walter Habdank's remarkable expressionist wood-cut *Treadmill* (or *Tretmühle* in German), 'a poignant image of work as a curse.'[223] The woodcut highlights a number of aspects of what work means for many people today – monotonous grind, alienated labor, powerlessness, solitariness, and despair. This picture is a wretched distortion of the way work is meant to be for all people.

Both Soelle and Sayers are passionate in their quest to redeem work from its captivity to economic forces, and to restore it both ethically and spiritually as an expression of human dignity. In 1960 Douglas McGregor made an important distinction between what he calls 'Theory X' and 'Theory Y.'[224] Theory X describes an approach to human motivation based on direction and control – the 'carrot-and-stick' model. Implicit in this interpretation of human behavior is the premise that most people dislike work and will avoid it if they can; therefore, coercion and a system of reward and punishment are necessary in order to achieve organizational objectives. This approach is advocated as an appropriate strategy in the light of the perceived majority preference for security rather than personal enterprise.

However, argues McGregor, the principle of direction and control is unable to provide human beings with the deeper satisfactions which are necessary if organizations are to be maximally effective. He proposes an alternative approach, which he labels Theory Y: 'The central principle which derives from Theory Y is that of integration: the creation of conditions such that the members of the organisation can achieve their own goals *best* by directing their efforts toward the success of the enterprise.[225] The Theory Y approach to the management of human resources is based on a number of key assumptions: people do not inherently dislike work – work, in fact, is as natural as play or rest; the capacities of individual self-control, commitment, and responsibility are strong motivational traits in human behavior; and creativity and ingenuity are widely distributed among people and not confined to a select few. The symbiotic nature of Theory Y is such that both the organization and each individual member gain by working cooperatively in the pursuit of mutually beneficial objectives.

An example from the business world powerfully illustrates the principles of Theory Y. At the age of eighteen, a Brazilian entrepreneur named Ricardo Semler joined his family's ailing engineering business, Semco, when it was on the verge of bankruptcy. He challenged the traditional corporate notion that when workers bring their bodies to the factory they leave their minds at the door. He decided that the company's major strength was its people, and his innovative management style turned the company into one of the fastest-growing organizations in the country. Semler's management philosophy is based on the principle of trust. In his book *Maverick!*, which outlines his radical proposals for corporate efficiency,[226] he argues that nothing is as revolutionary as common sense! Adults should be treated as adults, not adolescents, and offered the opportunity to exercise control within their work environment.

Early on in his management career Semler noticed that workers at the company were not being consulted, and he realized that there must be a better way to motivate them. Gradually his business philosophy took shape under the guiding thesis that the goal of any organization is ultimately to do something worthwhile: profits should be regarded as a survival mechanism that serves this ultimate goal. Through a process of experimentation, key operating principles were introduced which transformed Semco. These included such radical steps as recycling the leadership team on a rotating basis; freeing the staff to set their own salaries and to hire and fire their own bosses; encouraging all employees to audit the company's books; developing a generous employee profit-sharing scheme; passing control back to the workforce; and promoting the concept of teamwork among the employees. Initially, the system was abused by a few, but the overwhelming majority respected the freedom given to them and responded by working with greater commitment and loyalty.

Semler's primary focus is on people and what is important to them: human beings are not numbers in a big corporate machine. This view also challenges the traditional emphasis on the benefits of economies of scale: small units may actually be more productive than large-scale operations because of the increase in morale and the value of people working together in smaller units. Commenting on the renowned Hawthorne experiments conducted by the industrial sociologist Elton Mayo from 1927 to 1932, which studied the relationship between teamwork, morale, and productivity, Sayles and Strauss conclude that employees 'want more than just to have friends, they want to *belong*. One can sense that he is part of a larger organization only by indirection, but the shared experiences of one's immediate colleagues are among the most meaningful and potent sources of job satisfaction.'[227]

In *The Seven-Day Weekend* – a seductive book title, if ever there was one! – Semler describes his company in the following way: 'We're just a living experiment in eliminating boredom, routine, and exasperating regulations – an exploration of motivation and passion to free workers from corporate oppression.'[228] Semco is an excellent example of a business that takes seriously what has come to be known as the 'work/life balance,' a concept that has spawned a growing number of agencies specializing in consulting with businesses about their work practices. Many companies throughout the world are beginning to adopt strategies such as flexible working hours, family friendly measures, employee assistance programs, and flexible leave arrangements. These go a long way towards alleviating many of the enormous pressures many people experience in the workplace.

Soelle's second essential element of good work has to do with its societal dimension, expressed in terms of its impact upon the community. She highlights the ever-present threat of unemployment, which cuts workers off from their channels of communication with society, leading to a sense of alienation and low self-worth. One possibility is to encourage the unemployed to engage in socially valuable projects, fostering what Peter Maurin has called 'a society based on creed instead of greed.'[229] At the other end of the spectrum, the Protestant work ethic has given rise to workaholism – in the United States, many workers have sacrificed their annual holiday entitlements (already low in comparison to those in Europe) at the altar of work. And even when they do go on vacation, many cannot tear themselves away from their cell-phone or email! We have been conditioned to a way of work that destroys what it means to be and to relate.

Sometimes, of course, it is not a choice that we make – it is imposed upon us. Chris Sunderland, a biochemist and ordained Anglican who is involved in the interface between the Christian faith and public life, writes of one young man who works for a major retail chain, who recently got married and also become a Christian:

> Yet he is allowed only one weekend in twelve off work. His wife works as an estate agent. How are they supposed to maintain friendships or keep up with relations, let alone one another? How can he nurture his new faith adequately? His plan is to get out of retail. That means lots of study in the evenings and is yet more pressure on their young marriage.[230]

For Soelle, this pressure on human life in the workplace is paralleled by pressure on creation itself. This is her third dimension – work as reconciliation with nature. In today's global economy, resources are extracted from the environment with scant regard for sustainability, with many companies and governments paying only lip service to the growing crisis in global warming and resource depletion. It is time to be more responsible, and time is running out. Christians especially have an important voice here in proclaiming that this is *God*'s creation.

Work, then, *humanizes* us by connecting us to our inner being, to one another and to the wider society of which we are a part, and to creation itself. Work is holistic in its capacity to enhance our lives mentally, emotionally, physically, and spiritually.

Ultimately, then, work is worship, because through the gifts that we are given by God we express our lives in all their fullness and so glorify God in our humanity. It is for this reason that we cannot, and must not, separate the Christian faith from the world of work. Work is not a necessary evil but a necessary good, and to reduce work to its monetary reward is to rob it of its power to enhance human life. If work is something that needs to be redeemed, can we claim the same for the system, capitalism, which places labor in the service of capital? Or is capitalism incompatible with Christianity, in need of replacement rather than redemption?

Capitalism – blessing or curse?

Lesslie Newbigin is forthright in his condemnation of the 'exuberant capitalism' of the past 250 years, which he predicts 'will be diagnosed in the future as a desperately dangerous case of cancer in the body of human society.'[231] But is that assessment too negative? Can anything good come out of Athens? Are there any viable alternatives? From a Christian perspective, the biblical witness points to a number of criteria for determining the shape of the best economic system, some of which include: the supply of products and services for the enhancement of life; provision for the basic needs of marginal and disadvantaged people; fair and equitable means for resolving conflicts; meaningful work for all people; opportunities for people to contribute to the welfare of society as a whole; efficient and careful use of resources; respect for all nations of the world; an equitable spread of power and access to power; an equitable distribution of the benefits and costs of economic activity; protection of human rights; and finally, but not least, a recognition of the value and dignity of every person.[232]

No system meets all these criteria, and each economic system is ultimately only as efficient and fair as those who participate in it. Some critics of capitalism have exalted the merits of communism, but the historical record of the past 150 years indicates that those with a vested political interest in remaining in power have compromised the ideals of communism. Essential human freedoms have been curtailed – the system has not delivered on its promises, essentially because its Marxist ideal of human equality (a very Christian thing indeed) was deemed achievable by the elimination of the capitalist structures that had given birth to many of the social injustices of Marx's day. Communism's flaw was its conviction that the problem lay with the capitalist *system*.

However, capitalism's Achilles' heel lies not in its goal of wealth creation through human endeavor and entrepreneurialism, which offer the possibility of the enhancement of life for all humanity, but in the manifest failure of those who are an essential part of that system to equitably distribute that wealth around. Richard Foster has rightly identified wealth as one of the three seductive sirens of our age,[233] arguing that money, sex, and power are all fundamental to life, but capable of being channeled into destructive pathways in our lives. Paul reminds Timothy that it is not money itself, but the love of money that is a root of all kinds of evil (1 Tim. 6:10), and elsewhere Christians are exhorted to keep their lives free from the love of money (Heb. 13:5).

So the moral difficulty with capitalism 'arises not from it being a market system. We need ways of exchanging goods and services in order to survive.'[234] It is worth emphasizing that 'capitalism would still be the most effective system for creating wealth even if we chose not to consume what we have produced but to give it away.'[235] Moreover, there is considerable evidence to suggest that capitalism has improved the lot of many who might otherwise be far worse off. For example, when the USA decided to cease its imports of garments made by children under fifteen, many families in Bangladesh were hit economically as fifty thousand child workers were sent back home.[236] This is not to endorse child labor, of course, but to highlight the fact that we live in a very imperfect world, and the complexities of different economic systems need to be analyzed and measured with extreme care.

No one economic system has all the answers, and ultimately, alternative models of economic management, such as those espoused in socialist or Marxist nations, end up compromising somewhere along the line. As even Newbigin rightly notes, 'in their quest for equality [Marxist states] sacrifice individual freedom, as capitalist states in the name of freedom sacrifice equality. Yet neither system can survive except by modifying the rigor of its ideology.'[237] What is at issue for the Christian community is not whether or not we should demolish capitalism, but how we might 'think seriously about ways in which aspects of the current [capitalist] system might be humanised, improved, renewed and reformed.'[238]

This is a task that none of us can evade because, whether we like it or not, we are all implicated in the system that provides us with the quality and standard of life to which we have become accustomed. It is no good wringing our hands and bewailing the injustices of a system from which we derive comfort and convenience. As I write these words, I am aware that in the not too distant future I will be receiving a pension from the Church of England made possible by past and present investments in companies that may have behaved unethically in their trading practices. Do I refuse a proportion of that pension based on an estimate of how ethically the Pensions Board has managed its funds?

Richard Higginson is the Director of the Ridley Hall Foundation's 'Faith in Business' Project in the UK. In his book *Questions of Business Life*,[239] he uses the language of *mutual marginalization* to describe the relationship between Christianity and business – in practice, he argues, each has little time for the other, a position that he believes is contrary to God's purposes. Higginson's book is the fruit of seminars at Ridley Hall in Cambridge, and focuses primarily on how to obtain good business practice (corporately, globally and at the level of individual involvement) without seeking to demolish the capitalist ethos that infuses the global business environment.

It is arguable, therefore, that the real problem lies not in the system of exchange per se, but in the way those who have control in the system exercise their power. It is not the system as such that needs redemption; it is the people who are part of the system and who have a stake in its operation. And this, of course, is the message of Christianity: Jesus teaches us that the things that make us 'unclean,' including greed, come from *within* us (Mark 7:21). What Christianity proclaims is the need for a revolution in our hearts, not a revolutionary new system. And some businesspeople, though they may not subscribe to the Christian faith, seem to demonstrate clear Christian principles within the overarching framework of capitalism. Ricardo Semler's desire to enhance the lives of Semco's employees is an outstanding case in point. Another is Anita Roddick's 'profits with principles' approach to her Body Shop empire (more about that later in this chapter). For such people, the enrichment of human life and responsibility for the environment are more important creeds than the enlargement of their own bank balance – creed before greed, if you like![240]

There is also an increasing number of companies who are concerned for those who are less fortunate in society, echoing Soelle's plea that 'we need to ground our work in cooperation and mutual aid instead of in competition and the relentless economic war we wage against poor nations.'[241] For example, the American pharmaceutical giant Merck once chose to freely give away a drug that combated river blindness in West Africa because of the governments' inability to pay.[242] Many others, however, are either less altruistic or more wary, or both, and perpetuate practices in the workplace that not only stifle the enjoyment of life but lead to the destruction of life. Environmentalists and animal-rights activists, for example, regularly protest against production and marketing practices within the 'fast food' industry. Oil spillages caused by aging pipelines have poisoned water sources in parts of Africa, and destroyed the agricultural viability of the regions affected. Whether we take a domestic or global perspective, the central issue remains, How can Christians make a difference in the midst of what Newbigin calls the 'unremitting stimulation of covetousness' that he considers to be the driving power of capitalism?

Of course, it needs to be said too that ethical behavior is not the prerogative of the pious – far from it! Many Christian organizations paint a sad picture when it comes to the care of those who work for them, and there are tragic stories of those in senior positions of leadership and management whose behavior has been distinctly less than Christian. Ed Dayton expresses this well when he writes:

Now, there no doubt are men in management positions (both secular and Christian) who are operating in very unchristian ways. They are using their position to manipulate for personal gain; they are conducting their business in ways that violate accepted ethics or perhaps even the laws of the land. They may be dealing with other human beings in very unloving ways. But as I read most current management theory, it seems very Christian indeed! There is an increasing awareness that helping an individual grow as a person within the context of the organization's goal is good for the organization and good for the individual. Like good bus driving, the *rules* of a well-played game are reasonably obvious. The failure is not in the philosophy, or lack thereof, but in the practice. Again, we are reminded that it is not things that are sinful, but men![243]

Perhaps this is where Thielicke's 'law of infiltration and subversion' (introduced in the last chapter) comes into play again. In what ways might individual Christians and the Christian community at large engage in and with business in ways that are 'grounded in the nature of the Christian message'?

A redemptive approach to business

In his *Institutes* Calvin specifically legitimizes the ministry of the 'ungodly,' arguing that 'if the Lord has been pleased to assist us by the work and ministry of the ungodly in physics, dialectics, mathematics, and other similar sciences, let us avail ourselves of it, lest, by neglecting the gifts of God, spontaneously offered to us, we be justly punished for our sloth.'[244] To his list we might add the gifts of those who work in the world of business. Calvin's words are challenging and incisive, and invite Christians to reflect on their willingness to discern opportunities to participate in God's giftings in the business world. This, of course, reflects the underlying premise of this book.

A first step in the redemption of business practice, therefore, is to acknowledge the enormous breadth and range of the mission of the Creator Spirit, who seeks to draw us into a compassionate and humanizing participation in his reconciling mission in the world. The former Bishop of Winchester, John Taylor, is thoroughly inclusive in his understanding of mission, which

> embraces the plant-geneticist breeding a new strain of wheat, the World Health Organization team combating bilharzia, the reconstruction company throwing a bridge across a river barrier, the political pressure group campaigning for the downfall of a corrupt city council, the amateur dramatics group in the new cultural centre, the team on the new oil-rig, the parents' committee fighting for de-segregated schools in the inner city. The missionaries of the Holy Spirit include the probation officer and the literacy worker, the research chemist and the worn-out school teacher in a remote village, the psychiatrist and the designer, the famine-relief worker and the computer operator, the pastor and the astronaut. Our theology of mission will be all wrong unless we start with a song of praise about this surging diversity of creative and redemptive initiative.[245]

Taylor then offers three thumbnail sketches that reflect characteristic marks of the Holy Spirit at work in different situations. One of them involves an organization and methods (OM) study for a chain of city snack-bars. The OM adviser recommended rebuilding all the lunch counters on a curve in order to encourage conversation, and overcome the loneliness experienced by those sitting at straight counters.[246] In many similar contexts, Christians working in the commercial world have opportunities to influence the way we do business. In whatever area of work we are involved – corporate decision-making, human resource management, relationships with consumers, or deskwork in an office – we have an opportunity to live out our Christian values.

At times, our job may be on the line, especially if we are asked to do something that is ethically suspect, like lying to customers about the performance of a product, sacrificing production line safety in order to cut costs, or misrepresenting figures in a financial audit. The reality is that many Christians find it hard to combat the climate of half-truths and dishonest practices that prevail in their company setting, and may succumb to the temptation to compromise their faith, particularly if job security is on the line. A tricky area for many Christians centers on the issue of Sunday trading, which has now become the norm for many retailers; ultimately, in this as in many other areas, each person must decide on the basis of conscience, since we all have different priorities and perspectives on this matter. Scripture unfortunately is not always as clear about the specifics of ethical response as many of us would like!

Living faithfully as a Christian employer or employee represents probably the most effective way of influencing business practice. But it does not stop there. For the manager responsible for leading a group of employees in a company department, the ethic of love makes important demands. This is spelled out by Jeffrey Yergler with reference to the nature of servant leadership, which he interprets in the language of grace and forgiveness. One of Yergler's central theses is that 'grace applied thoughtfully, legitimately and ethically on the part of the manager, enhances the value of the person which then impacts the quality of the work produced. Conversely, when management exercises oversight and accountability without *any* expression of grace, it creates an environment of chronic low morale and, therefore, low (inadequate or insufficient) performance.'[247]

The notion of grace, suggests Yergler, is difficult to implement because of its initial association with 'soft' management. However, as discussed earlier, employees respond better to the motivational Theory-Y philosophy of management than to the 'carrot-and-stick' Theory-X model. In the Hawthorne experiments, researchers discovered, not surprisingly, a high degree of correlation between morale among the employees and productivity. This is precisely the same point made by Yergler, except that he explicitly introduces the concept of grace exercised by management as the influencing variable in the equation. The stimuli in the Hawthorne experiments primarily related to the perceived sense of working without coercion from management along with improved working conditions and a sense of teamwork experienced by the employees among themselves.

Yergler develops his thesis of grace by tying the term more specifically to the exercise of forgiveness in the workplace.

Citing the work of Robert Greenleaf,[248] whose writings focus on the concept of servant leadership, he observes that 'most leadership practices today are seldom about discerning what is needed by *others* but rather about buttressing what is needed to preserve *oneself* and one's agenda'.[249] With respect to the grace of forgiveness, Yergler claims that 'leaders and managers who eschew any hint of forgiveness and remain firmly ensconced in their 'right positions' *fail* to provide a fundamental intra-organizational example of servant leadership. Both consequences, though often hidden, are *tremendously* costly to the human spirit and organizational esprit de corp.'[250]

Enough has been written here to indicate how important it is for employers and employees alike to seek to act *Christianly* in the workplace, thereby not only enhancing the lives of those who belong to the organization, but also contributing to the likelihood of greater productivity. Commenting on the false values inherent in capitalist ideology, Newbigin argues that falsehood 'can be overcome only by the truth, and the truth has been manifested once for all in Jesus Christ. It is the business of the church to bear witness in the public realm to that truth.'[251]

Accordingly, the subversive infiltration recommended by Thielicke can be usefully accompanied by more direct action by Christians, adopting more politically overt responses to capitalist injustices, such as the global efforts involved in the Jubilee Debt Campaign, discussed in Chapter 6. In Australia, the federal government's recent controversial WorkChoices legislation has stimulated wide debate throughout the country. In a media release from the Australian Catholic Bishops Conference in November 2005, the bishops expressed concern that the legislation fails to promote employment growth, fair remuneration, and security of employment, and they question whether it promotes truly cooperative workplace relations and ensures the protection of the poor and the vulnerable. Two particular bones of contention have been the removal of unfair dismissal laws with respect to businesses with fewer than 100 employees, and the lack of provision of minimum wage guarantees.

A final strategy that we might keep in mind as consumers is one that has to do with the ethics of purchasing and investment.

If we believe that the capitalist system is here to stay, then we should consider how we might individually refrain from buying products that rely upon practices that spoil the environment or demean humanity, or investing in companies that have a poor ethical track record. A well-publicized example of a company that seeks to 'integrate principles with profits' is Anita Roddick's Body Shop. In her book *Business as Unusual*[252] Roddick recognizes the powerful role of business in the world, and working from *within* the market system she demonstrates her passionate belief that it is possible to create a profitable business while protecting and valuing humanity and the environment. Roddick is doing with Body Shop with respect to social responsibility what Ricardo Semler is doing with Semco with regard to human well-being. Both emphasize profits *plus* principles, and it is companies like these that should attract both our expenditure and our investment. We can make our difference.

The management of ministry[253]

All that we have discussed so far may be encapsulated under the rubric of 'the ministry of management' – seeing business as part of God's work in the world. We now turn to 'the management of ministry' with specific reference to the contributions that business insights and practices can make to the way Christians manage their affairs. Applying Christian principles to business is one thing – applying business principles to Christianity is another! In the New Testament, Jesus relates a parable, in which a dishonest manager, accused by his master of irresponsibly wasting what he had been given to look after, acted in a shrewd, though fraudulent, manner to preserve his own interests (see Luke 16:1–13). In his comment on the parable, Jesus commends the steward not for his fraud nor for his self-centered goals, but specifically for his wisdom and perspicacity: 'For the people of this world are more shrewd in dealing with their own kind than are the people of the light' (Luke 16:8).

The point of the parable is that those who have been given responsibility in the kingdom of God should be alert to all the

resources that may be available to them in the fulfilment of
what they are given to do. While Jesus goes on to connect the
parable to friendships and the stewardship of money, it is
helpful to consider his teaching in the context of opportunities
to draw from the wisdom of the world in the affairs of the
kingdom of God. May not those who work in business have
much to teach the 'children of light' with regard to the astute
management of resources? The chasm between Athens and
Jerusalem that characterized my early Christian life began to
close in my mind as I reflected on the contribution that
management could make to effective – and efficient! – local
church ministry.

Church leaders are often under great pressure within their
denominations to develop strategies for growth. In the second
half of the twentieth century, the Church Growth movement,
with which Donald McGavran and Peter Wagner are particularly associated,[254] unwittingly contributed to this pressure,
though, paradoxically, it also offered hope to those who were
struggling to get their local church out of ruts and into renewal.
The literature, tapes, seminars, and conferences spawned by
this movement seemed to promise new life: take the pulse, read
the signs, develop five-year plans, distribute questionnaires,
design new organizational patterns, set targets . . . the techniques and methodologies proposed were endless.

In its early days as a pioneer of church growth, the Institute
of Church Growth (ICG) under the leadership of Donald
McGavran promoted a missiology that emphasized kerygmatic
proclamation above incarnational presence. McGavran's
'theology of harvest' – in preference to a mere 'search theology,'
which he criticized for its failure to focus on results – was
unequivocally growth-oriented, and his emphasis on the
quantitative dimensions of growth led to charges of
triumphalism, which he cheerfully accepted. 'McGavran's
concern for the priority of evangelism in mission arose from his
own experience and involvement in the Christian mass
movements in India.'[255] Accordingly, his theology arose out of a
unique context, and may be fairly criticized for failing
sufficiently to allow for the incarnational dimension as a *primary*
mission focus. Furthermore, his pragmatic recommendations –

including growth methodologies, training programs and gift-discovery techniques – have at times obscured his overriding conviction that mission has to do with participation in the will of God. It is with regard to the implementation of that mission that the debate has been most heated.

Many of those churches that were enamored of ICG teaching in the early years discovered that for all their efforts nothing really changed. Pragmatism offered so much, yet delivered so little. The bookshelves of pastors were full of 'how to' texts, designed to get the local church out of maintenance mode into growth and mission; 'spiritually-loaded' numbers, especially seven and twelve, appeared in the titles (*7 Steps to . . .* or *12 Keys to . . .*) as if to guarantee divine authenticity or inspiration. Authors encouraged pastors to be success-oriented and growth-conscious, and a pragmatic 'what-works' business-oriented mentality began its subtle invasion of the pastoral ministry of the church.

The distinction to be made here is between *relying* on what the world has to offer and *'plundering'* from the world's inventory. An episode from the Old Testament may help us here. When God called Moses to lead the Hebrews out of slavery in Egypt, he added that he would 'make the Egyptians favorably disposed towards this people, so that when you leave you will not go empty-handed' (Exod. 3:21). So the Hebrews were enabled by God's grace to plunder, or spoil, the Egyptians of silver and gold and clothing, articles that they would find useful for their journey to the promised land. Likewise, the Christian community may find valuable resources available to them from the world of business to facilitate their ministry in the world, resources which are not exclusive to those who do not participate explicitly in the life of the church. Plundering is radically different from being seduced by the promises of success offered by the proponents of pragmatism. The ultimate idolatry in this regard for those who are charged with pastoral leadership is the espousal of a managerial approach to pastoral ministry that supplants the call to participate in the ministry of Christ in the power of the Spirit.

The church is called into being as God's chosen instrument to bring about his purpose and promise in the world. Any planning undertaken by the church must therefore be within a theological rather than a secular perspective. Ray Anderson points out that, theologically, the future 'is both a purpose and a promise that has come to the present, rather than being extrapolated out of the present.'[256] This important distinction has a great deal to do with the debate about the absorption of management techniques in order to accomplish the mission of the church.

Analyzing past data, projecting trends based on statistical analyses and surveys, setting appropriate targets, and organizing resources in an efficient and careful way in order to meet the objective of x percent growth in y years' time – such is the stuff of business management, and convincing and heady stuff it is at times. Nor is it all wrong. Its appeal is that you can get to grips with it; it smacks of efficiency and good stewardship, and it has the distinct advantage of being based on working models that offer hope. The theology of 'what works' can offer the stagnant church the possibility of digging itself out of the mud and continuing its journey along new and exciting paths.

But is that what God's church is called to do? Is the Christian community summoned to grasp hold of all the good things that the world has to offer by way of management efficiency, utilizing the tools and techniques of the business world as it tries to find its feet in the twenty-first century? Anderson is rightly concerned to emphasize that planning models are not wrong or inappropriate per se in the practice of Christian ministry; they have their place in mobilizing the community of faith in its witness in and to the world. What concerns him most is the very real danger of losing sight of God's vision when confronted by the attractions of what business has to offer the church.

Lessons from Semco

All this suggests that the minister as 'manager' needs to shift out of a linear, even bureaucratic, type of thinking in order to enter into the new things that God is always doing in the church and in the world. Some Christians disapprove of the notion of 'seeking a vision' for ministry on the grounds of its pragmatic connotations, but this is far too limited a perspective. Vision in itself is not wrong – it is only wrong if it is rooted in secular methodology isolated from the initiatives of the Spirit. Vision for ministry may be defined as 'a clear mental image of a preferable future imparted by God to His chosen servants.'[257] All that we have discussed so far is encapsulated in this definition, and the key phrase is 'imparted by God.' To have a vision for ministry is to be envisioned by God for *his ministry*. This, of course, has to do with the practice of discernment: those who are gifted by God for leadership within the church have the responsibility of seeking God's will and vision for their particular area of ministry within God's kingdom.

In order to bridge the gap between principle and practice, Myron Rush offers a number of helpful suggestions for those interested in applying a biblical philosophy of management in their own ministry situation: create a trust relationship between you and your group; give decision-making power to all individuals within the group; turn failures and mistakes into positive learning experiences for the group; constantly give proper recognition to the group and its individuals for accomplishment.[258]

McGregor's advocacy of Theory Y corresponds very much to these four principles, and we have already seen how this people-centered approach to management has been implemented with great success at Semco.

It is an interesting exercise to translate Ricardo Semler's management philosophy into the context of the Christian faith community. At the most general level, the relational emphasis implicit in his style of management is one that has been recognized in many studies of church growth and mission effectiveness. For example, the church planning consultant Kennon Callahan identifies twelve factors characteristic of healthy churches, concluding that the most effective churches are those that have concentrated more on his six relational factors than on the other functional or physical factors.[259] Anderson and Jones argue, on the basis that the church is not a task-oriented organization, that church planning 'requires a process based on its relational character.'[260] This relational emphasis needs to permeate all aspects of planning, as evident in a stimulating new approach to congregational change called Appreciative Inquiry, discussed in the next section.

The notion of leadership rotation in pastoral ministry is intriguing, and would certainly keep the leadership on its toes; however, it is debatable whether the Spirit's anointing for leadership would necessarily correspond to a strict rotational cycle! What works within a secular context may not be appropriate for spiritual ministry. Perhaps the areas that offer greatest reward for study and implementation in local church life are the principles of trust, teamwork, and organizational size. Trust is an indispensable quality in people management, and is a hallmark of good leadership; we might also agree with Bonhoeffer that it is safer to speak about 'leadership' as a particular gifting than to focus on the concept of the 'leader,' thus emphasizing the quality rather than the role: 'the focus of leadership is the person being led, the line of vision goes from above downwards, while the focus of the Leader is the Leader himself and the line of vision goes from below upwards.'[261]

Bonhoeffer was deeply troubled by Hitler's assumption of dictatorial control, and his uneasiness is one that Christians should rightly share when faced with similar claims to authoritarian leadership within the community of faith. Fear rather than trust characterizes the group over which such control is exercised. Some Christian leaders are unable genuinely to trust others because of their own deep insecurities, and so they become suspicious of those who seek ministry opportunities within the church. Some would prefer to remain with the status quo, obstructing forward movement and needed change, rather than take risks with people, even to the point of encouraging them to make mistakes!

Teamwork lies at the very heart of Christian ministry. Paul's teaching about the nature of the body of Christ highlights the essential unity of the community of faith: 'The body is a unit, though it is made up of many parts; and though all its parts are many, they form one body' (1 Cor. 12:12). We should not confuse the concept of teamwork with the notion of 'every-member-ministry.' Without fail we should affirm that every Christian has something to contribute to the life and ministry of the church; teamwork, however, relates to the way in which the diverse gifts of the body are offered and received. It speaks to us of attitude rather than action. In his letter to the Philippian Christians, Paul compares relationship within the church with the Trinitarian life of God, encouraging Christians to be 'like-minded, having the same love, being one in spirit and purpose. Do nothing out of selfish ambition or vain conceit, but in humility consider others better than yourselves' (Phil. 2:2–3).

The issue of size has a lot to do with the feasibility of teamwork at a practical level. The 'small is beautiful' philosophy with regard to congregational size corresponds to Semler's invitation to think small in the context of economic productivity. At times church growth literature has encouraged those in pastoral ministry to 'think big,' as if size were the authentic measure of spiritual success. While we must be careful that we do not despise those who promote this interpretation of church growth, we should offer equal encouragement to those who seek to minister within the 'small is beautiful' framework. Both trust and teamwork are more easily maintained within a smaller local assembly, though sadly neither is exempt from the abuse of leadership.

The lessons to be learned from Semco may be unrepresentative of the business community at large, but they do suggest the possibility of points of contact between the business world and Christians who want to become more efficient in the way they organize themselves. Therefore we appreciate the insights of management theorists and practitioners, but check always that they have been refined through the crucible of the cross. Critically, we ask, Do the insights we receive from the business world serve the purposes of God in bringing into being the new creation he has already promised?

Whenever we import approaches from business into the community of faith, we need to ask two questions. Firstly, does the methodology serve the ultimate, eschatological, new creation purposes of God? More specifically, does it serve God's revelation of his will for us, in this place where we now live and have our being? Secondly, if so, and because the end does not justify the means, is the methodology in itself a legitimate expression of the goodness and righteousness of God? Thus we are to constantly evaluate methodology in the light of theology and God's ministry in the world. Pragmatic methodology drawn from business management is valid if, and only if, it passes through these two filters, rightly giving preeminence to 'who' and 'what' over questions of 'how.'

Preparing for God's future

The idea of planning is not foreign to God. God has a plan for his creation, a plan that is unfolding through history until that time comes when all things in heaven and on earth will be brought together under one head, who is Christ (Eph. 1:10). He had a plan for the exiles in Babylon: ' "For I know the plans I have for you," declares the Lord, "plans to prosper you and not to harm you, plans to give you a hope and a future" ' (Jer. 29:11). More specifically, God may reveal his plans to his servants in the face of opposition and difficulty, as Jehoshaphat discovered when he prayed to the Lord: 'We do not know what to do, but our eyes are upon you' (2 Chr. 20:12) . . . and God's plan gave victory to the Israelites.

It is the privilege and responsibility of those in pastoral ministry to discern what is in God's heart as they seek to lead the church as his delegated 'managers.' People may propose, but ultimately it is God who disposes: 'Many are the plans in a man's heart, but it is the LORD's purpose that prevails' (Prov. 19:21). Christian management starts with the recognition that God has plans that need to be prayerfully discerned. It is in the execution of these plans that those in pastoral ministry can most usefully draw from the experience and wisdom of the business world.

Good management theory recommends the adoption of clearly defined objectives. Clear-cut goals present, for all involved in pastoral ministry, great opportunities for focused prayer, enabling a congregation to be specific in its understanding of and commitment to God's purposes. Good planning also requires that a faith community recognize its own strengths and weaknesses in the light of God's vision for its future. As a result, the resources and changes needed to realize the fulfilment of that vision will be more readily discerned – this is the auditing step in the planning process. Knowing what exactly is going on *within* the community of faith as well as *externally* within the ministry environment demands both honesty and perseverance. Business executives ruthlessly assess their internal resources of finance, human personnel, and technology, and their external environment in the form of competitive threats and market opportunities. Likewise, there is value in wisely and carefully discerning the inner strengths and weaknesses of a congregation, as well as appreciating the specific context within which pastoral ministry takes place.

A constructive model to help a congregation discover how to prepare for its future by appreciating its strengths is a process called, appropriately, Appreciative Inquiry (AI). AI is an approach that focuses on 'the generative and creative images that can be held up, valued, and used as a basis for moving towards the future.'[262] In his application of AI to the First Presbyterian Church (historically an ethnically Japanese church), located in Altadena, California, Mark Lau Branson treats the church as an organic, interpretive community, discovering how to draw on its own inner strengths, defined as significant 'life forces' that are available in stories and imaginations.[263] As the congregation explores these life forces, new habits and ways of living arise out of the conversations that take place, offering positive scenarios for the future.

Branson argues that Appreciative Inquiry is 'more than just a planning method – it is a way of seeing and creating.'[264] It describes a process of congregational reshaping that is grounded in the ongoing life of its members. However, it is not a random exercise. Though it relies critically upon people's self-understanding and memories, it follows a sequence of four steps – Initiate, Inquire, Imagine and Innovate – within the framework of a clear commitment to positive narratives and images. Branson's study is an excellent example of how a specific approach that has its origins in the discipline of organizational development,[265] can be tailored to a local church, or indeed to any Christian organization.

Following the auditing process, the next step is to explore both prayerfully and pragmatically – for God is not against pragmatism, but ever seeks to protect or redeem it from

ungodly influences – the various options available to fulfil
God's vision in the light of what has been discovered. Business
executives are accustomed to distinguishing between strategy
and tactics, a differentiation picked up in the church growth
literature. Strategic planning is broad, whereas tactical planning
addresses the details. For example, if a local congregation is
convinced of a God-given vision to engage more authentically
with the elderly in the community, then it may explore a
number of alternative strategies: the provision of a drop-in
center on the church premises; a visiting program involving
members of the congregation; special services geared to older
folk; a special 'Alpha' initiative among the elderly; prayer-
partnership programs; ministry opportunities in homes for the
elderly; the list is endless. These are the strategies that need to
be brought before God in prayer as well as before the
congregation with regard to practicality.

Of course, the possibility that the Spirit may lead the congregation into new, unexpected opportunities for ministry must
never be discounted. In his discussion of Appreciative Inquiry,
Branson cites the relevance of insights from chaos theory, which
is a term in the natural sciences that refers not to total disorder,
but to unaccountable natural processes in which extraordinarily
complex patterns arise unpredictably out of turbulence. He
notes:

> In churches, we often attempt to set up some order and purpose
> only to be repeatedly surprised. A sermon has unintended
> consequences, one program unexpectedly undercuts another
> program, or new energy arises when we sense only dissipation.
> As churches begin to use long-range planning, based on some
> kind of predictability, we often spend more time adjusting the
> plan than we did creating it originally . . . AI theorists hold that
> by embracing the chaos – gaining new perceptions, imagining
> new futures – we have a better chance at nurturing the life-giving
> forces that are available to us.[266]

For Branson, applying an Appreciative Inquiry approach
to church leadership involves 'order at the edge of chaos.'
He challenges the conventional 'business' model for church

management, with its reliance upon linear, hierarchical, cause-and-effect systems of behavior. Conventional management systems are *not* the stuff of church life, he argues:

> . . . this leads to management by separate functions, applying certain forces, measuring resources and output, maintaining power structures, and making changes by altering a power or a force . . . In this interpretive approach, the goal of church ministry is to find the staff and develop the programs that can fill the required pews. Business language fits this framework: products and services, marketing and sales, managers and marketers.[267]

What Branson is eschewing here is not management approaches per se, but those models that derive from a traditional, *mechanistic* model of business. His application of AI involves processes and sequences that resonate with sound and efficient ways of operating, seeking to obtain the most hopeful scenarios for the future. At the same, time, however, the AI process is thoroughly relational in its orientation, consistent with much contemporary rethinking about management practices.

Once the specific strategy or strategies have been discerned, the particular details can be worked out in relation to con-gregational strengths and weaknesses. This is the 'nuts-and-bolts' part of planning, in which every faith community finds itself involved at different times. At all stages everyone should be offered the opportunity to participate in God's vision for the church in its witness in and to the world. Congregational ownership of the vision, in all its myriad expressions, inevitably encourages the sort of commitment and unity that is sadly lacking in many churches today. The specific example of Appreciative Inquiry discussed above is one approach drawn from the field of management that seeks to promote the best and highest future for the faith community.

There is much for Christians to contribute to and receive from the world of business. To divorce the one from the other is to put our heads in the sand, and deny the theological reality that business is not separate from the kingdom of God, but can be a powerful reflection of God's activity in his creation. Men and women in the business community are privileged to live and serve redemptively in their calling either as employers or employees, making a real difference to the way in which we do business. But, as for all of the areas that we have been looking at in this book, the traffic is not just one-way. Management principles that have passed through the filters discussed in this chapter can assist us in the way we conduct ourselves as Christians, offering us the benefits not only of greater efficiency in the use of resources, but also of better ways of relating to one another and focusing on the future that God has prepared for us.

8

Nine Theological Theses

*Grounding the celebration of life in fertile theological soil –
nine theses that say 'yes' to God's world*

The ideas raised throughout this book offer the possibility of a
way of life that challenges the narrow parochialism and
superspirituality that are only too evident wherever church life
has been contaminated by the sacred–secular divide syndrome.
The title – *Celebrating Life* – says it all. I wrote in Chapter 1 that
God has created a good world in which he is intimately and
necessarily involved, and his presence is to be celebrated in
every area where men and women are active in social, political,
cultural, and educational discourse and behavior.

When those who previously have had no time for either the
Christian faith or the church see Christians engaging intelli-
gently and creatively in social and cultural life, contributing as
fellow members of human society alongside everyone else and
willing to learn from those who may not share their faith
convictions, then perhaps we may witness a new openness to
the things of God in people's hearts. They may sit up and take
notice – Christians are not people 'from another planet,' but
people 'just like us'! It could be the beginning of revival. This is
the promise of being willing to advance beyond the sacred–
secular divide syndrome.

In his fine collection of essays, *God in the Dock*, C. S. Lewis
writes perceptively:

It is not the books written in direct defence of Materialism that make the modern man a materialist; it is the materialistic assumptions in all the other books. In the same way it is not the books on Christianity that will really trouble him. But he would be troubled if, whenever he wanted a cheap popular introduction to some science, the best work on the market was always by a Christian . . . The first step to the re-conversion of this country is a series, produced by Christians, which can beat the *Penguin* and the *Thinkers Library* on their own ground. Its Christianity would have to be latent, not explicit.[268]

Of course, Lewis was a bookish man and his own forte was in the literary arena, so it is understandable that he should focus on that particular aspect of culture. But his point applies across the whole range of contemporary cultural life and behavior. Francis Collins, for example, is a highly regarded scientist, head of the Human Genome Project . . . and a convinced Christian, who has both the standing and the desire to promote scientific insights without compromising his faith. The political world has witnessed some outstanding Christians – in Chapter 6, I referred to the Clapham Sect, a 'brotherhood of Christian politicians' in Britain through whose efforts the slave trade in the colonies was abolished, as well as more up-to-date examples of Christian political activists like Jim Wallis. Kevin Rudd, an Australian federal Labour politician whose Christian convictions are well known, consistently urges us to embrace Bonhoeffer's vision of 'a just world delivered by social action, driven by personal faith.'[269] The former director of the National Economic Development Council in the UK, Sir Fred Catherwood, a former President of the Evangelical Alliance and Vice-President of the European Parliament, has actively demonstrated his Christian faith throughout his international political and business life. In the world of the creative arts, Bono of the rock band U2 is a stellar example of a Christian living out his faith in the glare of international publicity.

Many other well-known figures could be cited – Christians who are high-profile figures in their field of endeavor. The reality, of course, is that there are many others who are faithfully living out their Christian beliefs in unheralded ways in the local community, latently not explicitly. The apostle Paul writes to the Christian church at Thessalonica: 'Make it your ambition to lead a quiet life, to mind your own business and to work with your hands, just as we told you, so that your daily life may win the respect of outsiders and so that you will not be dependent on anybody' (1 Thess. 4:11). Elsewhere, Paul enjoins his readers to work at *whatever* they are doing with all their heart, as working for the Lord (Col. 3:23). Christians are privileged to *fully participate* in society, seeking always to make a difference whatever their vocation may be.

In his stimulating book entitled *The Spirit of Life*, Jürgen Moltmann argues that the essential obstacle to our experiencing the full life that is ours in Christ is to be found in our passive sins, not our active ones: 'for the hindrance is not our despairing attempt to be ourselves, but *our despairing attempt not to be ourselves*, so that out of fear of life and fear of death we fall short of what our own lives could be.'[270] We often fear treading out into the unknown, preferring the safety of familiar things – that is not something to despise, of course, for it reflects the inbuilt tendency many of us have for security and safety. But the gospel encourages us to move beyond the security of our own comfort zones into a life of adventurous trust in God, a life in which we discover our full humanity as we celebrate 'the 'yes' and 'amen' to creation.'[271]

In a thought-provoking discussion of the impulse towards adventure which is God's gift to human beings, Paul Tournier reminds us that the word 'enthusiasm' literally means 'feeling God within oneself.' Specifically, it is to be an adventurous person, willing to embark on risky and perhaps dangerous pursuits. Tournier suggests that all of us are endowed with this spirit of adventure. This instinct 'may be cloaked, smothered, and repressed, but it never disappears from the human personality. The timidest pen-pushing clerk will disclose under psychoanalysis, and particularly in the analysis of his dreams, a secret nostalgia for the adventure which he has sacrificed to security.'[272]

To be made in God's image is to be enthused by the same spirit of adventure that animates him. God's music is the music of life, the music of adventure, the music of going on a journey full of anticipation and a sense of discovery. To be willing to take risks, to step out into the adventure of living, which is God's gift to us all, is to see life through new eyes. We discover that there is a whole new way of life available to us in God which has everything to do with enjoying our humanity and God's good gifts to us in his creation.

Shaping the theology

With this in mind, I would like to offer in this final chapter a number of theses that ground the ideas in this book in fertile theological soil. Good theology always precedes good practice, and so, mindful of Martin Luther's famous publication of his ninety-five theses in 1517 – an event that radically altered the course of Christendom – my hope (more modest!) is that the nine theological theses spelled out below – each of which underpins the overriding theme of the celebration of life – will have some effect in changing how we go about living Christianly in the world. In a metaphorical sense, I am nailing these nine theses to the doors of dualism. They represent an invitation to the church to consider afresh a number of important theological truths that breathe the joy of life and living, a joy that is God's gift to all people. Joy, declares Houston, 'is the capacity to accept, of saying 'yes' to a good world.'[273]

As a young monk Luther did not experience this joy. He struggled for many years over his spiritual condition as he desperately sought to please God. In order to distract him from his intense, even morbid, spiritual wrestling his superior, Johann von Staupitz, arranged for him to enter the academic world of theology, and eventually in 1512, after he was awarded his Doctor of Theology, Luther was appointed a professor of biblical studies at the University of Wittenberg. It was during his studies in the Bible that Luther came to realize the central gospel truths of justification by faith and the grace of forgiveness. The burden was lifted from his soul, and Luther began to teach his reformed doctrines at the university.

Wittenberg was only a backwater in Germany at the time, so Luther's teaching had little impact outside the university. But that all changed in 1517, when Luther, incensed by the Catholic Church's corrupt practice of selling indulgences, nailed his ninety-five theses to the door of the Castle Church in Wittenberg in protest. Typical of the events that catapulted Luther into action was the message of one of the Pope's commissioners for indulgences named Johann Tetzel, who was traveling throughout Germany and who is reputed to have declared that 'as soon as the coin in the coffer rings, the soul from purgatory springs.' Tetzel's mission was linked to the church's desperate need for money to renovate the basilica of St Peter's in Rome, and so indulgences were seen as a means of raising the required revenue. Luther was horrified by the way the promise of salvation was being tied to money, and his own newfound understanding of the gospel of grace set him on an irrevocable collision course with the established authorities. The rest, of course, is history, as the Lutheran Reformation, along with other reforming movements, led to the break with Rome and a lasting transformation of the religious and spiritual landscape.

It would, of course, be presumptuous to believe that the ideas presented in this book could similarly transform the contemporary Christian landscape. For a start, there is much that is good and gracious in congregational life today, and many Christians are gripped by the message of God's grace in their lives. And there are undoubtedly some very fine faith communities that are seeking to live out the ideas that are explored in this book. Furthermore, the themes that permeate the pages in each chapter are not new: many writers have exhorted the Christian church to move out of a paradigm of a narrow, exclusive holiness to one of holistic inclusiveness, engaging faithfully and redemptively in God's creation in rich, novel, and imaginative ways.

The more modest aims of this book have to do with helping those who are trapped in a narrow understanding of the Christian faith, one that has been shaped by dualistic thinking, to relocate out of a less-than-joyful Christian life into one that resonates with the dance of God in the world.

My nine theses are as follows:

(1) God is not a static deity, defined primarily by such adjectives as sovereign and holy – he is essentially a loving, dynamic and relational Trinity: Father, Son, and Spirit.

(2) God, in his triune glory, has opened up his life to all that he has created, human and nonhuman – he is immanently and intimately involved in all that he has created.

(3) The kingdom of God is a present reality that is not confined to the metaphysical domain – it is the dynamic rule of God that invades the material realm as well as the spiritual realm.

(4) The incarnation of Jesus Christ expresses the truth that God has chosen to make himself known as a human being in human culture and in the midst of the structures of society.

(5) Created in God's image, human beings are invited to participate in God's inner-Trinitarian life, dancing with him in the world that he ever seeks to reconcile to himself.

(6) Christians are likewise summoned to contextualize the gospel message – yet they necessarily call people beyond their personal and cultural horizons to participate in the culture of the kingdom of God.

(7) God is an inclusive God of grace, whose Spirit is at work throughout human life, and in mysterious ways throughout all creation, seeking to reconcile all things to himself.

(8) The gospel calls the church to be not just relevant, learning to speak the language of the surrounding culture, but prophetic in its redemptive presence and action in the world.

(9) Christians live in an eschatological tension between the 'now' and the 'not yet' of the kingdom of God – as they live in the world, they also look forward to the promised goal of the new creation.

The first three theses have to do with *the Trinity and creation,* the next three with *contextual incarnation,* and the last three with *the nature of redemptive grace.* The next three sections deal with each of these clusters, picking up in a number of places ideas that have already been introduced in earlier chapters, developing and summarizing them as appropriate.

The Trinity and creation

God is not a static deity, defined primarily by such adjectives as sovereign and holy – he is essentially a loving, dynamic, and relational Trinity: Father, Son, and Spirit.

God, in his triune glory, has opened up his life to all that he has created, human and nonhuman – he is immanently and intimately involved in all that he has created.

The kingdom of God is a present reality that is not confined to the metaphysical domain – it is the dynamic rule of God that invades the material realm as well as the spiritual realm.

In Chapter 2, I argued that the gospel is not so much about God giving us a new life, but of us being caught up into the very life of God himself, so that humanity and Trinity – and creation – are bound together forever. The first three theses expand this thought by outlining a theology of God who is relational and immanent, and whose kingdom is central to *all* of life, secular and sacred. So to divide the two is to misunderstand the very nature of God, for whom physicality is a profoundly spiritual reality. As we noted at the beginning of this book, much of Christendom has also labored under a false understanding of the nature of the gospel, and how we perceive the gospel has a lot to do with how we perceive God.

To say that God is Trinity is to underline one of the central affirmations of the Christian faith. God is actually God by virtue of the loving relationships that exist within the divine life: *it is the relations between the divine persons which constitute the unity of God*. Father, Son, and Spirit are united to such an extent that it is impossible to imagine any one person existing without the others. The being of each person of the Trinity lies in the fact that each exists for the other. In Chapter 5, we introduced the Greek word *perichoresis*, which refers to this intense mutual indwelling within the Trinity. It is an inclusive concept that directs us into the essential nature of God's inner being of community and dynamic relationality.[274]

However, for some of the early church fathers, and Augustine was a major influence in this regard, there was behind the Trinity the idea of something else that defines the mystery and reality – or essence – of God. This, of course, opened up the door for the notion that the ultimate truth about God was somehow *beyond the Trinity*, that behind relationship are concepts like sovereignty or holiness. So absolute statements about God are seen as greater than the relational reality that exists and defines the life of the triune God. Augustine's ideas owe much to the dualistic framework proposed by Plato. The result was, as we saw in Chapter 1, that his 'otherworldly' focus prioritized the spiritual over the physical, so contributing to the sacred–secular divide syndrome. But God is not to be summed up in the static language beloved by some classical evangelical theologians, who speak about the 'God of the omnis' – omniscient, omnipotent, omnipresent – at the expense of his inner relationality and his loving interaction with his creation. Clark Pinnock puts it well when he writes that 'God's fair beauty according to Scripture is his own relationality as triune community. It is God's gracious interactivity, not his hyper-transcendence and/or immobility, which makes him so glorious.'[275]

The movie *A Beautiful Mind*, in which Russell Crowe plays the part of John Nash, a brilliant mathematician afflicted with schizophrenia, gives us a helpful insight into the meaning of *perichoresis*. The movie concludes with Nash coming forward to receive the 1994 Nobel Prize for Economic Science at the prize-giving ceremony in Stockholm. In his (admittedly fictional) acceptance speech, Nash looks at his wife Alicia, who had supported him throughout much of his life, and speaks these words:

I've always believed in numbers and the equations and logics that lead to reason. But after a lifetime of such pursuits I ask: what truly is logic? Who decides reason? My quest has taken me through the physical, the metaphysical, the delusional, and back. And I have made the most important discovery of my career . . . the most important discovery of my life. It's only in the mysterious equations of love that any logic or reason can be found. I'm only here tonight because of you. You are the reason I am. You are all my reasons. Thank you.

There is no evidence that John Nash was referring – even obliquely – to any notion of divine love, though we might want to posit a direct correspondence between the love shown to him by his wife and his colleagues at Princeton and the love that resides in the heart of God. For Nash had experienced a quality of love that was quite remarkable. His wife learnt to entrust herself to him even as he realized the full extent of his condition. She gave herself to him, she made room, space in her life for him in such a way that she herself grew and was enlarged in the giving. The same might be said for his colleagues at Princeton later on in his life. Seeking a place to study, a place of refuge even, he approached an old university friend with whom he had studied earlier in his life, someone who was by then a professor at Princeton. The college offered him room, space to be. There he found a community of colleagues who learnt to accept him, love him, and give him purpose and possibility again for his life. In the life of John Nash, we see a man who was embraced by love, as his wife and his colleagues *made room* for him. In this love he experienced restoration, healing, and inner peace.

Note this: Nash's wife and colleagues *made room* for him. This is very close to what we mean by Trinitarian *perichoresis*. Each member of the Trinity so gives himself to the other two, each making room in himself for the others, that their very unity may be defined in terms of their relationships. Each exists for the others in utter self-giving love, united in a common purpose. Jürgen Moltmann suggests that the word

> grasps the circulatory character of the eternal divine life . . . The Father exists in the Son, the Son in the Father, and both of them in the Spirit, just as the Spirit exists in both the Father and the Son. By virtue of their eternal love they live in one another to such an extent, and dwell in one another to such an extent, that they are one. *It is a process of most perfect and intense empathy.*[276]

Perhaps we might suggest a more *energetic* dimension to *perichoresis*: we should not be talking so much about existence or mutual indwelling as *movement* within the divine life. And the wonder of Christian life is that we have been drawn into this life of divine energy and activity, this divine dance of love. We share in the perichoretic life of Father, Son, and Spirit that

Jesus spoke about in his high-priestly prayer to his Father in John 17: 20–23:

> I pray also for those who will believe in me through their message, that all of them may be one, Father, just as you are in me and I am in you. May they also be in us so that the world may believe that you have sent me. I have given them the glory that you gave me, that they may be one as we are one: I in them and you in me.

Perichoresis is a term which shifts us away from the static language of persons to the dynamic language of relationships. God's call to life for each one of us has its genesis in his gracious invitation not just to dwell in him, but to dance with him:

> Lovingly, gently, and with infinite patience, God teaches us the steps of the divine dance: when we stumble, he does not leave us helpless on the floor, nor does he point a disapproving finger at us. The Spirit who dwells within us, smiles over us as he reaches out a hand to pick us up and lead us on in the dance . . . When we *know* that God is smiling at us with joy we are encouraged to learn the steps of his dance, and then creatively to choreograph new steps, new sequences, which flow out of his life within us. They are still his steps, but we are the ones who are bringing them into being![277]

Our life in God, then, may be expressed in the language of dance, and it is of more than passing interest, as the English theologian Paul Fiddes points out, that although the word *perichoresis* does not technically have anything to do with dancing, there is another word, *perichoreuo*, which actually means to 'dance around.' The play on words is highly suggestive and, for Fiddes, illustrates well the dynamic sense of *koinonia*, of communion within the life of God.[278]

This 'Lord of the dance,' as Sydney Carter once described him in his famous hymn based on the tune of the American Shaker song 'Simple Gifts,' graciously invites us to share in his reconciling and saving work in all creation. As we argued in Chapter 2, entry into the life of the Trinity means entry into the life of a God who is immanently and intimately involved in every part of creation, a God who invites us to celebrate the joy of life and seek renewal in all the areas of brokenness around us. In that chapter, we explored the nature of God's relationship with his creation and, following Moltmann, suggested that we might adopt a view of God who, in his triune glory, creates space within himself, making room within himself for his creation. This leads us to the idea of a holistic, web-like 'creation-community' in which human beings are caught up with the whole of creation in the dynamic life of God.

Relationality, therefore, is at the heart of all created reality. This central dimension of Trinitarian theology – expressed in the doctrine of *perichoresis* – offers Christians a way of looking at God's good creation that is consistent with the insights of contemporary science, encouraging us to live *'in* the earth, and *for* the earth . . . understanding ourselves as excessively, superlatively concerned with nature and its well-being.'[279] The title of Sallie McFague's book, *Super, Natural Christians,* reflects her desire to place what she calls a 'subversive comma' between two words that might otherwise express a lop-sided view of the kingdom of God! We are, writes Ray Anderson, 'amphibious creatures'! Not in the sense that we are equally at home in water as on land, but because we have been created to inhabit both the spiritual and the material realms as an expression of our humanity. Kingdom living for Anderson has to do with *both* realms, with no polarity between them. Taking the Genesis creation narrative as his point of reference, he observes with characteristic insight that

> the story tells us of the realm in which the original humans, Adam and Eve, were taken from the dust of the ground, placed on earth, endowed with the image of the Creator by a divine inbreathing. They are placed there to till the ground, tend the animals and to be fruitful and multiply. These are tasks that occupied the first humans before the Fall. This was kingdom living![280]

So for us today. Caught up in the relational life of God, we are invited to value and rejoice in our humanity as an expression of the reality of the kingdom of God, whether that is in the enjoyment of God's creation, expressing ourselves in music and the arts, scientific exploration, fulfilling our vocation in politics or business, or in any of the many other dimensions of human living bestowed upon the human race. In every field of human endeavor we also find God involved, revealed, and glorified. There is no distinction in the kingdom of God between the chapel and the concert hall! The kingdom brooks no dualistic separation between sacred and secular. Of course, human beings may take God's myriad gifts and talents and distort or abuse them so that they no longer give glory to him. But that should not lead us to distance ourselves from them because they are capable of corruption. The missional task we have as Christians, as we have argued consistently throughout this book (and which we will summarize later in this chapter) essentially has to do with redemption, not denial. So we eschew any approach that *denies* our need to engage with culture, preferring one that recognizes the need to *redeem* what has been made unwholesome and ungodly. Redemption gets our hands dirty. Dualists, on the other hand, keep their hands clean because they are in the business of denial, not redemption.

Contextual incarnation

The incarnation of Jesus Christ expresses the truth that God has chosen to make himself known as a human being in human culture and in the midst of the structures of society.

Created in God's image, human beings are invited to participate in God's inner-Trinitarian life, dancing with him in the world that he ever seeks to reconcile to himself.

Christians are likewise summoned to contextualize the gospel message – yet they necessarily call people beyond their personal and cultural horizons to participate in the culture of the kingdom of God.

The incarnation of Christ lies at the very heart of the Christian gospel. 'The Word became flesh and lived for a while among us,' writes John in his gospel account, and this coming, this incarnation – or taking on human flesh – is God's *self*-interpretation, his *self*-communication. God's love for all that he has created governs his actions in history: he does what he does because he is who he is. It is precisely because of his love for all humanity that God, in his triune glory, elected to enter this world as a human being. But the incarnation is not first and foremost about God coming into our world, but about the possibility of our entering God's world! James Torrance points out that the prime purpose of the incarnation to 'lift us up into a life of communion, of participation in the very triune life of God.'[281] Indeed, the theology of the incarnation reminds us that all humanity has been caught up in Christ's ascended and glorified humanity, so making it possible for us to participate by the Spirit in the Son's perfect communion with his Father.

God's deepest desire in relation to humanity is to renew his image in us. In his treatise *De Incarnatione Verbi Dei* the early church father Athanasius taught that no one could do this save God alone: 'Therefore he assumed a human body, in order that in it death might once for all be destroyed, and that men might be renewed according to the Image.'[282] This is what Athanasius describes as 'the good pleasure of God,' so enabling us to participate in the gift of life in the Spirit, redeemed and made new by the grace of God, and free to share in the fullness of life and ministry within the community of the triune God. This means that we must now interpret all ministry from a new vantage point. As we discussed in Chapter 2, ministry does not depend upon human effort but originates in the heart of God, finding its source in our relationship with the triune God. It is within this interpretation of the theology of the incarnation that we understand the ministry of the church as redemptive presence in the world.

Jesus Christ came into our world at a particular time and in a particular place, and in a particular form of humanity. Necessarily his ministry among those whom he came to serve during his lifetime was contextually shaped. He came as a Jewish man, born in the land of Palestine, not as a Gentile woman in Africa or America. Throughout church history, reference has been made to this 'scandal of particularity,' How can this specific historical event have such astounding universal significance? Against those who would compromise the biblical witness in their clamour for a more contemporary and inclusive faith, Donald Bloesch insists that 'The object of our faith is not a universal Christ-consciousness or an all-encompassing Primal Matrix but the living, personal God who revealed himself only at one point in history and whose sacrifice is adequate to regenerate the entire human race'.[283]

In Christ, then, transcendence and immanence are held in exquisite tension: in the incarnation, we are reminded that God is 'not only the Infinitely Near but also the Wholly Other.'[284] As we rightly focus – especially throughout this book – on the contextual implications of the incarnation, we should not overlook the fact that God's transcendence has too often been bypassed by those whose ideological agendas demand a more politically correct deity. Bloesch cites the absurd efforts made by some translators to expurgate references to Jesus being seated at the right hand of God in order not to discriminate against left-handed people! While attempts to address cultural patri-archalism in the biblical narrative are more understandable, the central theological truth that is so often forgotten is that there is a vital distinction between God's exclusive self-revelation in the incarnation of Christ as Jesus of Nazareth and the *inclusiveness* of the promises enshrined in that revelation. In the man Jesus, *all peoples* are embraced and invited into the dance of the Trinity.

And that insight is precisely what the incarnation is all about. Thesis number four affirms that God has chosen to make himself known as a human being in human culture and in the midst of the structures of society. In this unique historical event we see God as he truly is, participating in the life of humanity, not in a vague, generalized way, but in the concreteness of human experience. As Eugene Peterson puts it so succinctly, 'theology divorced from geography gets us into nothing but trouble'![285] For him, all living is local, and this is reflected in the creation account in Genesis 2, which, after the cosmic framework of the first chapter, 'zooms in on earth, and then on one place in earth.'[286] Throughout the Old Testament God's dealings with human beings are localized in the unfolding drama of his relationship with his people Israel. And then in Jesus' life on earth, we see God involved in particular lives: celebrating with the happy couple at their wedding in Cana in

Galilee, healing the paralytic man at Capernaum, responding to the faith of the Syrian Phoenician woman whose daughter was possessed by an evil spirit, and lovingly welcoming those who were looked down upon by the religious authorities of his day. Jesus loved, laughed, played, wept, and cared, and in so doing he healed and transformed lives. He also challenged those who would put the gospel of grace into a straitjacket, exposing the hypocrisy and legalism of the religious teachers of his time.

This is the God in whose life we are summoned to participate. To be a Christian is to be involved with people as Jesus was, not with a general or abstract 'one-size-fits-all' approach, but with a deep awareness of specific realities: 'It is far too common in our fast-paced and technologically depersonalized society, impatient and zealous to get out the gospel message, to skip the Genesis context and slap together something improvisatory so that we can quickly get on with our urgent mission. More often than not these improvisations are dismissive of the intricacies and beauties of God's gifts of time and place.'[287]

Too often the urgent replaces the important, and we find ourselves looking for quick-fix solutions and pragmatic models of ministry at the expense of grounding ourselves in the life of the community, sensitive to its needs, and seeking to live graciously and unhurriedly among those who are our neighbors. This is Trinitarian life for the people of God, dancing with him in the specific contexts where he is at work by his Spirit, seeking to make a difference in the lives of the community. And in the process we may find ourselves learning lessons from those who may have nothing to do with the Christian faith. Tom Beaudoin is a young Catholic theologian who argues that popular culture, which has a negative image among many Christians, has served as a 'surrogate clergy' by which many 'Generation-Xers' have made sense of their lives: it has sharpened their religious awareness. Drawing on the notion of the *sensus infidelium* (wisdom of the unfaithful), he suggests that 'people (or forms of popular culture) who profess to know little or nothing about the religious may indeed form, or inform, or transform religious meaning for people of faith.'[288] Citing Beaudoin's work on culture and theology, Gordon Lynch notes that 'serious missiological engagement with the cultures of the

Celebrating Life

developing world led to the emergence of Third World theologies that have given new insights into the meaning of the Christian faith and tradition. In the same vein, he [Beaudoin] argues, Western Christianity could also be renewed and transformed if it listened seriously to the aspirations, concerns, and struggles expressed through contemporary Western popular culture'.[289]

This perspective – listening to contemporary culture, so that the traffic between gospel and culture is not one-way but two-way – runs all the way through this book. Incarnational presence has to do with an immersion into the particularities of people's lives in such a way that not only are people's lives transformed, but new insights are gained regarding the nature of the gospel. The current resurgence of concern for the state of planet Earth due to global warming and environmental degradation derives in part from the activities of such groups as Friends of the Earth and Greenpeace, who have galvanized Christians into a new awareness of the wider implications of the gospel. We noted in Chapters 3 and 4 that literature and movies have the capacity to 'enlarge our being,' and through the creative arts we may find ourselves encountering the 'real presence' of God. The examples given in those chapters indicate the way 'using popular culture as a medium for theological reflection can . . . provide an important means of exploring essential questions about our existence in ways that connect with the symbols, concepts, and concerns of contemporary culture.'[290]

If Christian ministry has to do with participation in the surrounding community, then what happens in the local neighborhood is, in a significant way, determinative of the life of the faith community. Christians do not live in the safe haven called 'church' – in a very real way they are called to partner with the community in the solution of its problems as well as in the celebration of its life. And these two dimensions – solution and celebration – often go together. In 2004, a Pentecostal church in suburban Adelaide, in South Australia, initiated a community project that stands as a lasting tribute to a fifteen-year-old boy who was tragically drowned earlier in the year. Danny Guglielmucci, the senior pastor of the church, Southside

Community Church, now renamed Edge Church International (or simply The Edge), wanted to 'put joy on the faces of kids by doing something positive,' and so the project was born to 'partner with the community' by completely renovating the local high school that the boy had attended. [291]

Hundreds of volunteers participated in a ten-hour makeover, in which the school was given a complete face-lift – classrooms were painted, carpets pulled up and replaced, handrails and beams repainted, windows cleaned, car park lines repainted, chairs cleaned and resprayed, trees planted, lawns laid, garden beds replanted. The school's radical overhaul attracted the attention of the news media, and the grateful school principal commented, with tears in her eyes: 'We are not only the best looking school – we are the most loved school.' Her response? With no way to pay back what had been so 'miraculously' provided, the school would 'pay it forward' by offering help and support to others in the local community. During his visit to the newly renovated school, John Howard, the Australian Prime Minister, commended the church for its 'practical Christianity' and its 'massive contribution to community life in Adelaide.'

The church has been engaged in other community assignments since then. In 2005, individual 'connect groups' in the church each received $100, and were encouraged to use the money in order to make a lasting difference in people's lives. A Sudanese couple who had been separated were reunited and their wedding arranged and paid for in full; a multiple sclerosis sufferer and his wife had their house and garden renovated; a woman whose husband had died in recent bushfires had treatment and air travel expenses covered for her young daughter who suffered from cerebral palsy; therapeutic units were provided for a dementia ward in a local hospital; boys of single mums were given a day out; a walker was purchased for a disabled man; and disadvantaged, poor, and migrant people were supported in a variety of ways. A total of $7,000 was turned into $110,000 for the benefit of the community, reminiscent of the parable of the talents, and over three thousand lives were directly affected. In 2006, the church embarked on perhaps its most ambitious project, mobilizing the support of churches all over Adelaide in a major community project over a two-week period, renovating the long-term accommodation block at the Women and Children's Hospital.

These initiatives are powerful examples of the church taking seriously its call to be 'salt and light' in the community. Solution and celebration – Christians have the opportunity to experience both in the communities in which they live, participating in God's reconciling work in the local context. And the 'pay it forward' response of the high school principal demonstrates the impact that these initiatives can have on those whose lives have been touched and transformed by this 'gospel of action.' The witness of those involved with the local community in compassionate and sacrificial service in these Adelaide initiatives testifies to a God who cares, a God who is not indifferent to the plight of the poor and the disadvantaged. And the more such initiatives are integrated into the life of the Christian church, the more likely will people be called beyond their own personal and cultural horizons to participate in the culture of the kingdom of God. Paul writes in 2 Corinthians 9:11 (*New Living Translation*): 'Yes, you will be enriched so that you can give even more generously. And when we take your gifts to those who need them, they will break out in thanksgiving to God.'

In Chapter 2, I argued that the church needs to take the incarnation seriously on the grounds not that we are different from other people, but precisely the opposite . . . because we are *no* different from them. Christians have no legitimate grounds for celebrating the good news of Jesus Christ in a world that is itself searching for answers if they proclaim a triumphalistic and truncated gospel – a *theologia gloriae* – that distances them from the world. But when they identify in radical solidarity with others in the misery and confusion of life – as well as in its more positive and hopeful expressions – the gospel is truly heard as *theologia crucis,* and the church becomes a prophetic voice. However, as Karl Barth rightly reminds us, the church's motto must be 'solidarity with the world, not conformity to it!'[292] An approach that substitutes conformity for solidarity trivializes the gospel – it is the danger of assimilation that we discussed in Chapter 1. We can only summon others to embrace the kingdom of God if we ourselves live under the shadow of the cross.

The nature of redemptive grace

God is an inclusive God of grace, whose Spirit is at work throughout human life, and in mysterious ways throughout all creation, seeking to reconcile all things to himself.

The gospel calls the church to be not just relevant, learning to speak the language of the surrounding culture, but prophetic in its redemptive presence and action in the world.

Christians live in an eschatological tension between the 'now' and the 'not yet' of the kingdom of God – as they live in the world, they also look forward to the promised goal of the new creation.

A minister once asked his congregation, What would Jesus do if he were in church today? And then, to the astonishment of everyone there, he walked out of the building! His point was powerfully made. Thesis number seven states that God is an inclusive God of grace, whose Spirit is at work throughout human life, and in mysterious ways throughout all creation, seeking to reconcile all things to himself. This is a theme that we have been reaffirming throughout this book. God is not a domesticated deity, confined within four walls, but active in reconciling love in every corner of his creation. The feminist theologian Elizabeth Johnson argues that the full range of the reality and activity of the Spirit at the very heart of the world has been lost in the Western theological tradition. She claims that the language we use to refer to the Spirit reflects this neglect: 'faceless, shadowy, anonymous, half-known, homeless, watered-down, the poor relation, Cinderella.'[293]

In contrast, the energizing presence of the Spirit who sustains all created things pervades the cosmos and is to be celebrated with thanksgiving and open response: 'the Spirit's renewing presence is always and everywhere partial to her beloved creatures suffering from socially constructed harm, working to liberate oppressed and oppressors from the distorted systems that destroy the humanity of them both. Like a baker-woman she keeps on kneading the leaven of kindness and truth, justice and peace into the thick dough of the world until the whole loaf rises (Mt 13:33).'[294]

Johnson's explicit eschatological orientation embraces a liberation that encompasses not only human life but all creation; as such, it shatters any dualistic notions we might have in which human beings are somehow 'caught up' by the Spirit, and transported out of this world and into some mystical, spiritual reality that has no bearing on the created order. For salvation has to do with living in the new creation – God is not in the business of abolishing creation, but *redeeming* it. And his longing is that no one should be left out. Hence the energizing life of the Spirit in creation, whose 'power makes all withered sticks and souls green again with the juice of life.'[295]

In Chapter 1, we noted that people tend to follow one of two options as they try and make sense of the relationship between God and the world: either they go down the dualist path, 'cutting the world in half,' or they try to put everything back together again, and become monists. Tom Wright, whose ideas on this we examined in that chapter, revisits these options in his recent book *Simply Christian*, suggesting that heaven and earth are overlapping, or interlocking, spheres that make sense only if you see them as belonging together. And God has committed himself to putting everything to rights again, not by demolishing physical creation, but by renewing it. In fact, physicality frames the biblical record of God's revelation in Scripture, and in the new creation of Revelation 21–22, heaven comes down to earth, not the reverse! The earth, 'turned into a place of God's absence by godless human beings, is to become once more the dwelling place of God.'[296] God's redeeming grace is at work throughout history bringing this future about, and one way in which we might understand this happening today has to do with what Wright calls four 'voices' that echo in the human subconscious: 'the longing for justice, the quest for spirituality, the hunger for relationships, and the delight in beauty.'[297]

Actually, argues Wright, these four voices point us towards God because they have their source in him: they are expressions of the one voice which alone can lead us out of the multiple alienations and frustrations of human existence into an authentic and specifically Christian way of life. When we respond to these echoes, however faint they may be, we are opening ourselves to the activity and energy of the Spirit of grace who knows no boundaries in reaching and restoring broken humanity. This is what grace means – it is the unmeasured and unmeasurable goodness of God who takes the initiative in putting everything right again. At the end of Chapter Two I suggested that the Spirit typically works in deep and hidden ways in order to restore people back to God. Taking an eschatological perspective, Wright suggests that these four 'voices', which have to do with justice, spirituality, relationships, and beauty, may actually help us to glimpse the glorious possibilities of the new creation opened up to us in Christ. Perhaps, then, we might interpret these voices as 'echoes of the Spirit', whose inclusive love for all people compels him to participate in every field of human endeavor precisely because they are 'highways into the centre of a reality which cannot be glimpsed, let alone grasped, any other way'[298]:

> Perhaps art can help us to look beyond the immediate beauty with all its puzzles, and to glimpse that new creation which makes sense not only of beauty but of the world as a whole, and ourselves within it. Perhaps.
>
> The artist can then join forces with those who work for justice and those who struggle for redemptive relationships, and together encourage and sustain those who are reaching out for a genuine, redemptive spirituality.[299]

This is our calling as Christians – to live redemptively *in* the world because we are looking forward to experiencing it in all its beauty and fullness in the new creation of God's promise. We have a new song to sing, the song of the redeemed, but we do not sing as those who have no part of the life of the world. 'Praying in the Spirit and interest in life drive one another on,'[300] writes Moltmann, and it is this ongoing tension between prayer and meditation, on the one hand, and solidarity with the imperfections and brokenness of this world, on the other, that marks our call to live life in the overlap between heaven and earth. This is how redemptive grace is played out in creation –

we are privileged to partner the triune God – Father, Son, and Spirit – as they sing their song in the world, always pointing forward to what is yet to come, yet always grounded in the concrete realities of human culture and society:

> The more Christians intervene for the life of the hungry, the human rights of the oppressed and the fellowship of the forsaken, the deeper they will be led into continual prayer. It sounds paradoxical, but *the more their actions are related to this world*, and the more passionately they love life, the more strongly they will believe, if they want to remain true to the hope which Jesus brought into the world.[301]

For Moltmann, there is no conflict between the 'vertical' dimension of faith and the 'horizontal' dimension of love: they are two sides of the Christian way of life. And, as we have seen throughout this book, they converge not only in the political struggle for justice, equality, and liberation, but also in the celebration of the myriad diverse expressions of cultural life that characterize human creativity, intellectual endeavor, and organizational behavior. For that is where God is pleased to reveal and glorify himself – and where he might be found for those who have ears to hear and eyes to see.

Many people ask the question, What on earth am I here for? Michael Wittmer relates an incident in the American TV series, *Everybody Loves Raymond*, in which Ally, Raymond's daughter, asks some questions about the origin of life. The typically inept Raymond thinks she is asking about how babies are made. Eventually he discovers that she is far more interested in why we exist at all. She asks, Why are we born? Why does God put us here? If we all go to heaven when we die, then why does God want us here first? Why are we here, Daddy? . . . Good questions! Poor Raymond fumbles around for a while until he blurts out a totally silly answer – God put us on earth to ease the heavenly congestion! It must be crowded up there, so God created this planet as a temporary measure until he could free up more space for everyone![302] The answer to the question, What on earth am I here for? is, in fact, as simple as it is profound: 'You are here to enjoy God on earth.' To live fully in God's image means to enjoy the experience of life in God, life with one another, and life in relationship to God's creation. Evangelical Christianity has given prominence (rightly) to the first, acknowledged the second, but in large part ignored the last of these three.

Earlier, I argued that the task of the church is not just about being relevant, learning to speak the language of the culture, but more critically about being prophetic in its redemptive presence in the world. The danger of identifying passionately with the political struggle for liberation or of immersing ourselves in the diverse cultural contexts that surround us is, as we saw in Chapter 1, that of assimilation. We become so like those around us that we cannot speak prophetically into their lives. When we see that beginning to happen, we need to take fresh stock of our lives and reorient ourselves within the creative tension of the 'now' and 'not yet' of the kingdom of God; we acknowledge that though there is much that is good and wholesome in the world – echoes of a voice, perhaps – there is also much that is corrupt and corrupting. The duality between light and darkness will not go away until that day when the old order of things has passed away, when 'every tear is wiped from our eyes,' and when there will be 'no more death or mourning or crying or pain' (Rev. 21:4). But until that day, we celebrate the truth that God has not deserted his world . . . and we celebrate with thanksgiving the many gifts of God's grace present throughout creation.

As we journey through life, we will inevitably find ourselves in danger of being lured away from our divine calling by the seductive singing of the sirens of cultural accommodation and socio-political activism, blunting our prophetic cutting edge. In reaction to this temptation, we may be persuaded to stuff our ears with beeswax and tie ourselves to the mast, after the fashion of Odysseus and his sailors when they encountered the nymph-like sirens of Greek mythology. Neither response is an acceptable Christian option. As God's kingdom people who are summoned to witness to God's redemptive grace we dare not succumb to the world's agenda, however attractive that may be. Nor can we just sail by until we reach the safe haven of church; that, quite simply, is idolatry. As Tom Wright reminds us so eloquently: 'We are called to be *part* of God's new creation, called to be *agents* of that new creation here and now. We are called to *model* and *display* that new creation in symphonies and family life, in restorative justice and poetry, in holiness and service to the poor, in politics and painting.'[303]

Anything less is a denial of our God-given humanity and a denial of what it means to be a Christian in today's world. To move from a sailing metaphor to the military imagery introduced at the beginning of this book, God has not given Christians the option of adopting a 'siege mentality,' hauling up the drawbridge in order to avoid contact with the world. Only the reverse can do justice to the divine purpose; so let us rejoice as we lower the drawbridge. Let us, with discernment and wisdom, participate with others in their enjoyment of life, partner with those who seek to liberate the oppressed, and celebrate all that is good in God's world.

Notes

1. What Has the Gospel To Do with Culture?

[1] See 1 Chr. 12:32, which refers to the men of Issachar, who 'understood the times and knew what Israel should do.'
[2] See, for example, Fox, *Coming of the Cosmic Christ*.
[3] Ryken, *Triumphs of the Imagination*: 14.
[4] Walsh and Middleton, *Transforming Vision*: 95.
[5] Wittmer, *Heaven is a Place on Earth*: 42.
[6] Frost and Hirsch, *Shaping of Things to Come*: 18–19.
[7] Wright, *Bringing the Church to the World*: 117.
[8] Watts, 'What Does It Mean To Be Saved?'
[9] Eliot, George, *Adam Bede*: 11–12.
[10] Quoted in Brown, *Spirituality and Liberation*: 13.
[11] See Brown, *Spirituality and Liberation*: 23–25.
[12] Brown, *Spirituality and Liberation*: 25–26.
[13] Fontaine, *Light and the Dark*, accessed on {http://home.wanadoo.nl/piet.fontaine/on_dualism.htm#definiti on}.
[14] Quote accessed on {http://home.wanadoo.nl/piet.fontaine/on_dualism.htm#definiti on}.
[15] Plato, *Republic*.
[16] Hare, *Plato*: 9; some of the insights in this chapter regarding the thought of Plato are drawn from Hare's brief but helpful text.
[17] Hare, *Plato*: 13.
[18] For a diagram representing the dividing line between the two orders of reality postulated by Plato, see Plato, *Republic*: 275.
[19] See Plato, *Republic*: 278–80.
[20] Bruce, *Plato's Theory of Forms*, accessed on {http://www.easy.com.au/igb/FormsEssay.html}.
[21] See Plato, *Republic*: 278–80.
[22] Sanders, John, 'Historical Considerations': 62.

23 Scott, *Dueling with Dualism*, accessed on {http://www.mckenziestudycenter.org/philosophy/articles/duali sm.html}.

24 Scott, *Dueling*, accessed on {http://www.mckenziestudycenter.org/philosophy/articles/duali sm.html}.

25 Brown, *Spirituality and Liberation*: 74.

26 See Sanders, John, 'Historical Considerations': 65–80.

27 McGrath, *Scientific Theology Volume 1: Nature*: 13.

28 Manicheism (started by Mani, AD 216–76) was a Christian form of gnostic religion that held to a radical dualism between good and evil. Gnostics believed that matter (the physical) was inferior to spiritual things and Manicheism taught that Jesus had come to release 'souls of light from the prison of their bodies.'

29 Augustine of Hippo, *The City of God* (London: Penguin Books, 1972): 22.24.

30 Walsh and Middleton, *Transforming Vision*: 114.

31 Walsh and Middleton, *Transforming Vision*: 115.

32 Wright, *Bringing the Church to the World*: 19.

33 Wright, *Bringing the Church to the World*: 19.

34 For a fuller account of these two representative positions, see Wright, *Bringing the Church to the World*: 116.

35 Wright, *Bringing the Church to the World*: 113, author's italics.

2. Connecting with Culture and Creation

36 Quoted in Kraft, *Christianity in Culture*: 46.

37 Walsh and Middleton, *Transforming Vision*: 18.

38 Clapp, *Peculiar People*: 140.

39 Isaiah 5:20–21.

40 On the concepts of faithfulness and relevance within the framework of contextualization in ministry, see Buxton, Graham, *Dancing in the Dark*: 79–83.

41 Published subsequently as a book: see Neibuhr, H. Richard, *Christ and Culture*.

42 Neibuhr, H. Richard, *Christ and Culture*: 4.

43 See, on this, Sweet et al., *Church in Emerging Culture*, especially Sweet's introductory chapter on pp. 13–50.

44 Sweet, *Church in Emerging Culture*: 115.

45 Sweet, *Church in Emerging Culture*: 144.

46 Sweet, *Church in Emerging Culture*: 195.

[47] See Drane, *Cultural Change and Biblical Faith*: 1–17.

[48] Drane, *Cultural Change*: 9.

[49] Drane, *Cultural Change*: 13.

[50] Hall, *Thinking the Faith*: 195.

[51] Kelly, 'Sacred Secular Divide': 36–38.

[52] Torrance, Thomas F., *Christian Doctrine of God*: 208, author's italics.

[53] Kidner, *Psalms 1–72*: 65–66.

[54] Moltmann, *God in Creation*; first presented as the 1984–5 Gifford Lectures at Edinburgh, and written in response to the contemporary environmental crisis.

[55] Moltmann, *God in Creation*: 156.

[56] Del Re, *Cosmic Dance*: 15.

[57] Moltmann, 'Perichoresis': 117.

[58] Chesterton, *Orthodoxy*: xvii.

[59] de Caussade, *Sacrament of the Present Moment*; de Caussade writes that 'to discover God in the smallest and most ordinary things, as well as in the greatest, is to possess a rare and sublime faith' (p. 84).

[60] From the first of four broadcast talks by the English mystic Evelyn Underhill, subsequently published under the title *The Spiritual Life*.

[61] Browning, *Aurora Leigh*, bk. 7, my italics.

[62] Gleick, *Faster*: 31.

[63] The phrase 'sea change' actually comes from a line in Shakespeare's *The Tempest*, where Ariel sings of the transformation of the body of Ferdinand's father: 'Full fathom five thy father lies: Of his bones are coral made: Those are pearls that were his eyes: Nothing of him that doth fade But doth suffer a sea-change Into something rich and strange.'

[64] Sine, *Wild Hope*: 271.

[65] Greene, 'The Great Divide': 51–54.

[66] See Banks, *Redeeming the Routines*.

[67] Brown, *Spirituality and Liberation*: 70.

[68] Ascribed to the theologian Joseph Kotva, and quoted in Clapp, *Peculiar People*: 155.

[69] John V. Taylor, *Go-Between God*: 36.

3. The Power of Literature To Enhance Our Humanity

[70] {http://www.peterweircave.com/dps/script.html}, accessed on 24 August 2005.

[71] Lewis, C. S., *An Experiment in Criticism*: 139.

[72] Guite, 'Christ and the Redemption of Language': 34. I am grateful for this article, which has been helpful in formulating some of the ideas presented in this section.

[73] The phrase 'ecclesial redemptive presence' is used by Farley in his essay, 'Theology and Practice Outside the Clerical Paradigm.'

[74] Orwell, 'Politics and the English Language': 150.

[75] See Truss, *Eats, Shoots and Leaves*.

[76] Eliot, T. S., 'East Coker': 23–32.

[77] Lewis, C. S., *Surprised by Joy*: 17.

[78] Veith, *Reading between the Lines*: 29.

[79] Worthing, *When Choice Matters*: 16.

[80] Ryken, *Liberated Imagination*: 199.

[81] Eliot, George, *Silas Marner*: 19.

[82] Lewis, C. S., 'The Language of Religion': 164–79.

[83] Buxton, Rachel, *Robert Frost and Northern Irish Poetry*: 88.

[84] Quoted in Edward Connery Lathem (ed.), *Interviews with Robert Frost* (London: Jonathan Cape, 1967):26, cited by Buxton, Rachel, *Robert Frost*: 87.

[85] Heaney, 'Digging.'

[86] Heaney, interview with Nick Gammage: 5.

[87] Ryken, *Words of Delight*: 187, my italics.

[88] Berlin, *Dynamics of Biblical Parallelism*: 99.

[89] Material in this section is drawn from Buxton, Graham, *Dancing in the Dark*: 226–9.

[90] Campbell, *Ruth*.

[91] Rauber, 'The Book of Ruth': 167.

[92] Childs, 'Ruth': 567.

[93] In the preface to Conrad, *The Nigger of the Narcissus*, author's italics.

[94] Spender, *The Making of a Poem*, 1962.

[95] Peterson, 'Pastors and Novels': 185–92.

[96] Peterson, 'Pastors and Novels': 186.

[97] Ryken, *Words of Delight*: 21–22.

[98] Sobosan, *Romancing the Universe*: 18.

[99] Veith, *Reading between the Lines*: 37.

[100] For one Christian perspective on the dangers of literature and 'vicarious sin,' see Veith, *Reading between the Lines*: 27–46.

[101] Pearce, *Tolkien: Man and Myth*: 58.

[102] See Lewis, C. S., 'Myth Became Fact,' in Hooper, *God in the Dock*.

[103] Martindale, *Beyond the Shadowlands*: 52.

[104] In a review in *Zadok Perspectives*, 74 (Autumn 2002): 22.

4. Seeing God in the Creative Arts

105 Chevalier, *Girl with a Pearl Earring*: 148–49.
106 Turner, *Imagine*: 16.
107 Turner, *Imagine*: 17.
108 Friesen, *Artists, Citizens, Philosophers*: 169.
109 L'Engle, *Walking on Water*: 155–56.
110 Other artistic media such as drama, dance, photography, graphic design, and fashion cannot be adequately treated in this chapter's brief survey.
111 Abrams, *Mirror and the Lamp*.
112 Friesen, *Artists, Citizens, Philosophers*: 207–9.
113 Potok, *Gift of Asher Lev*: 93; see also *My Name is Asher Lev*.
114 Friesen, *Artists, Citizens, Philosophers*: 195.
115 Deeks, *Pastoral Theology*: 44.
116 O'Connor, *Habit of Being*: 79.
117 Quoted in Kilcourse, *Flannery O'Connor's Religious Imagination*: 39.
118 Begbie, *Voicing Creation's Praise*: 212.
119 Ryken, *Liberated Imagination*: 131–48.
120 See Wolterstorff, *Art in Action*: 156 ff.
121 Source unknown.
122 Percy, 'Editorial':3.
123 Dark, *Everyday Apocalypse*: 13.
124 Dark, *Everyday Apocalypse*: 11–12.
125 Dark, *Everyday Apocalypse*: 44–45.
126 Dark, *Everyday Apocalypse*: 140.
127 In his foreword to Begbie, *Voicing Creation's Praise*: xi.
128 Grenz and Franke, *Beyond Foundationalism*: 162.
129 Quoted in Schomer, 'Barth on Mozart.' See also {http://www.religion-online.org/showarticle.asp?title=1382}, accessed on 8 December 2005.
130 I am grateful here for the insights of a good friend, Brad Bessell, who has been involved in the 'heavy metal' culture for over twenty years, and who continues to witness to Christ with his own Christian 'heavy metal' band.
131 See Walser, *Running with the Devil*: 142.
132 Wenstein, *Heavy Metal*: 220.
133 Wenstein, *Heavy Metal*: 171.
134 See {http://www.steiger.org/nlm.htm}, accessed 5 December 2005.
135 Barna, *Generation Next*: 115.
136 Stone, *Faith and Film*: 6.

137 Stone, *Faith and Film*: 4–5
138 'Spielberg Takes on Terror', *Time*, 49 (12 December 2005): 48–55.
139 Boorstin, *Making Movies Work*, cited in Frost and Banks, *Lessons from Reel Life*: 24–27.
140 Frost and Banks, *Lessons from Reel Life*: 25.
141 Worthing, *The Matrix Revealed*: 10.
142 Johnston, *Reel Spirituality*: 63–86.
143 Johnston, *Reel Spirituality*: 35.
144 Reviewed by Merrill Corney in *Zadok Perspectives*, 71 (Winter 2001): 27–28.
145 Frost, 'The Chocolate Remedy' 24–25.

5. Science: the Language of God?

146 The chapter title is taken from Collins, *The Language of God* (2006).
147 Cited from a speech that he gave for his induction into the American Academy of Arts and Sciences, and reproduced in part in *Time*, 45 (14 November 2005).
148 Sections of this chapter are drawn from an earlier book of mine, which examines the relationship between science and theology within a Trinitarian perspective; see Buxton, Graham, *Trinity, Creation and Pastoral Ministry*.
149 See Wilkinson, *God, Time and Stephen Hawking*: 16.
150 For a more positive assessment of the summons to 'play God' in the face of ethical dilemmas, see Dutney, *Playing God*.
151 See Barbour, *When Science Meets Religion*: 10–17; Haught, *Science and Religion*: 9–12.
152 Wertheim, 'The Odd Couple': 38–43.
153 Haught, *Science and Religion*: 203.
154 On Popper's understanding of verisimilitude, see Popper, *Conjectures and Refutations*.
155 See Sanders, E. P., *Paul and Palestinian Judaism*.
156 See, for example, Dawkins, *Selfish Gene*; and, most recently, *The God Delusion*.
157 Cited in McGrath, *Dawkins' God*: 84. See also McGrath, *The Dawkins Delusion*.
158 McGrath, *Dawkins' God*: 154.
159 Brooke, *Science and Religion*: 8, my italics.
160 Gould, *Rock of Ages*: 6.
161 Bacon, *The Advancement of Learning*: 8.
162 These words are taken from a message by John Paul II in Russell, Stoeger, and Coyne (eds.), *John Paul II on Science and Religion*: M13.

[163] Easterbrook, 'The New Convergence': 165–69.

[164] Haisch, 'Freeing the Scientific Imagination from Fundamentalist Scientism': 22.

[165] Haught, *Science and Religion*: 153.

[166] For a fine discussion of the compatibility of faith and science, see Collins, *Language of God*.

[167] Polkinghorne, *Science and Christian Belief*: 11.

[168] Davies, *The Mind of God*:16, author's italics.

[169] See Polkinghorne, *Serious Talk*: 34–59.

[170] Penrose, *Emperor's New Mind*: 95. For an introduction to Mandelbrot's background and groundbreaking work in fractal geometry, see Gleick, *Chaos*: 83–118.

[171] Del Re, *Cosmic Dance*: 19.

[172] Quoted in Gribbin, *Science*: xxii.

[173] For a compelling account of Lorenz's discovery, see Gleick, *Chaos*: 11–31.

[174] See Wilkinson, *God, the Big Bang and Stephen Hawkin*, for an introduction to the basic principles of quantum mechanics.

[175] Vanstone, *Love's Endeavour, Love's Expense*: 39–54.

[176] Allen, *Traces of God in a Frequently Hostile World*: 35.

[177] Edwards, *God of Evolution*: 50.

[178] Ward, *Divine Action*: 65.

[179] Rolston, 'Does Nature Need to be Redeemed?': 213.

[180] For a helpful nonscientific introduction to the concept of emergence, see Johnson, Steven, *Emergence*.

[181] Johnson, Steven, *Emergence*: 18.

[182] Fuller, *Atoms and Icons*: 32.

[183] From Donne, 'An Anatomie of the World': The First Anniversary: 172ff.

[184] Del Re, *Cosmic Dance*: x.

[185] See, especially, Buxton, Graham, *Trinity, Creation and Pastoral Ministry*: 97–142.

6. Actions Speak Louder than Words

[186] Downer, 'Australian Politics and the Christian Church.'

[187] Sunderland, *In a Glass Darkly*: 148.

[188] Neibuhr, Reinhold, *Moral Man and Immoral Society*: 4.

[189] Southam, 'Faith and Politics do Mix!': 47–51.

[190] Dorrien, *Soul in Society*: 93.

[191] Dorrien, *Soul in Society*: 161.

[192] These insights are taken from Timms, 'Christianity and Politics': 4–5.

[193] Timms, 'Christianity and Politics': 5.
[194] {http://www.stephentimmsmp.org.uk/cs.html}, accessed on 26 April 2006.
[195] {http://www.acton.org/publicat/books/freedom/christianity.html} accessed on 26 April 2006.
[196] Foster, *Money, Sex and Power*.
[197] Carter, *God's Name in Vain*.
[198] Lewis, Alan E., 'Unmasking Idolatries': 112.
[199] Especially evident in Hall, *Thinking the Faith*.
[200] Thielicke, *Theological Ethics*: 621.
[201] Thielicke, *Theological Ethics*: 642.
[202] Thielicke, *Theological Ethics*: 645, my italics.
[203] Thielicke, *Theological Ethics*: 646, author's italics.
[204] Yoder, *Politics of Jesus*: 157.
[205] Donnelly, 'Union Rhetoric Drives Parents from Public Schools.'.
[206] Wacker, 'The Christian Right.'
[207] Cromartie, 'The Evangelical Kaleidoscope': 27.
[208] Neibuhr, Reinhold, *Children of Light and the Children of Darkness*: 118.
[209] Mouw, *Uncommon Decency*: 11.
[210] Mouw, *Uncommon Decency*: 12.
[211] Wallis, *Agenda for Biblical People*: ix.
[212] See {http://www.calltorenewal.org/about_us/index.cfm/action/what_is_CTR.html}, accessed on 26 April 2006.
[213] Wallis, *Agenda for Biblical People*: 143.
[214] Pohl, *Making Room*:16.
[215] Gollings, 'Planting Covenant Communities of Faith in the City': 129.
[216] Battiscombe, *Shaftesbury*: 334.
[217] Stott, *Issues Facing Christians Today*: 11.
[218] Mouw, *Uncommon Decency*: 81–96.
[219] Anderson, *Shape of Practical Theology*: 280.

7. Is Capitalism a Dirty Word?

[220] Parts of this section first appeared in Buxton, Graham, *Dancing in the Dark*: 257–59.
[221] Soelle, *To Work and to Love*: 83.
[222] Simmons, 'Dorothy L Sayers' Theology of Work and Vocation in Everyday Life': 180.
[223] Soelle, *To Work and to Love*: 55.
[224] See McGregor, *Human Side of Enterprise*.

[225] McGregor, *Human Side of Enterprise*: 49, author's italics.

[226] Semler, *Maverick!*

[227] Sayles and Strauss, *Human Behaviour in Organizations*: 84, authors' italics.

[228] Semler, *The Seven-Day Weekend*: 275.

[229] Cited in Soelle, *To Work and to Love*: 100.

[230] Sunderland, *In a Glass Darkly*: 128.

[231] Newbigin, *Foolishness to the Greeks*: 114.

[232] This list is summarized from Chewning, Eby, and Roels, *Business Through the Eyes of Faith*: 9.

[233] Foster, *Money, Sex and Power*.

[234] Heslam, 'Checking the March of Capitalism.'

[235] Harper, 'The Ethics of Capitalism': 10.

[236] Cited in Higginson, 'Christian Response to Global Capitalism': 8–9.

[237] Newbigin, *Foolishness to the Greeks*: 110.

[238] Higginson, 'Christian Response to Global Capitalism': 10.

[239] Higginson, *Questions of Business Life*.

[240] A phrase borrowed from Peter Maurin (cited in Soelle, *To Work and to Love*: 87).

[241] Soelle, *To Work and to Love*: 104.

[242] Cited in Higginson, 'Christian Response to Global Capitalism': 10.

[243] Engstrom and Dayton, *Art of Management for Christian Leaders*: 38–39.

[244] Calvin, *Institutes of the Christian Religion*, 2.2.16: 236–37.

[245] Taylor, *Go-Between God*: 38.

[246] Taylor, *Go-Between God*: 40.

[247] Yergler, 'Management and Grace.'

[248] Greenleaf, *Servant as Leader*; and *Servant Leadership*.

[249] Yergler, 'Servant Leader,' author's italics.

[250] Yergler, 'Servant Leader,' author's italics.

[251] Newbigin, *Foolishness to the Greeks*: 122.

[252] Roddick, *Business as Unusual*.

[253] Substantial parts of the final three sections of this chapter first appeared in Buxton, Graham, *Dancing in the Dark*: 259–72.

[254] See, for example, McGavran, *Understanding Church Growth*; Wagner, *Your Church Can be Healthy*.

[255] Pinola, *Church Growth*: 261.

[256] Anderson, *Minding God's Business*: 48.

[257] Barna, *Power of Vision*: 28.

[258] Rush, *Management*: 32–47.

[259] See Callahan, *Twelve Keys to an Effective Church*.

[260] Anderson and Jones, *Management of Ministry*: 134.

[261] Cited in Anderson, *Minding God's Business*: 64.

[262] Watkins and Mohr, *Appreciative Inquiry*: 30.

[263] See Branson, *Memories, Hopes, and Conversations*.

[264] Branson, *Memories, Hopes, and Conversations*: 23.

[265] See the 'AI Commons' – a worldwide portal, serviced by Case Western Reserve University's Weatherhead School of Management in the United States, which is devoted to the sharing of academic resources and practical tools on Appreciative Inquiry – on {http://appreciativeinquiry.case.edu/}.

[266] Branson, *Memories, Hopes, and Conversations*: 34. For a fuller perspective on the contributions of quantum theory, complexity and chaos theory for management, see Wheatley, *Leadership and the New Science*.

[267] Branson, *Memories, Hopes, and Conversations*: 31.

8. Nine Theological Theses

[268] Lewis, C. S., 'Christian Reflections,' in Hooper, *God in the Dock*: 93.

[269] See Rudd, 'Faith in Politics': 22–30.

[270] Moltmann, *Spirit of Life*: 188, my italics.

[271] Houston, *I Believe in the Creator*: 207.

[272] Tournier, *Adventure of Living*: 5.

[273] Houston, *I Believe in the Creator*: 207.

[274] For a full discussion of *perichoresis* as a divine, human, and scientific concept, see Buxton, Graham, *Trinity, Creation and Pastoral Ministry*.

[275] Pinnock, *Most Moved Mover*: 5–6.

[276] Moltmann, *Trinity and the Kingdom of God*: 175.

[277] Buxton, Graham, *Dancing in the Dark*: 300–1, author's italics.

[278] See Fiddes, *Participating in God*: 71–81.

[279] McFague, *Super, Natural Christians*: 5–6.

[280] Anderson, *Emergent Theology for Emerging Churches*: 102.

[281] Torrance, James B., *Worship, Community and the Triune God of Grace*: 32.

[282] See *St. Athanasius on the Incarnation*: 41.

[283] Bloesch, *Jesus Christ*: 78.

[284] Bloesch, *Jesus Christ*: 78.

[285] Peterson, *Christ Plays in Ten Thousand Places*: 77.

[286] Peterson, *Christ Plays in Ten Thousand Places*: 72.

[287] Peterson, *Christ Plays in Ten Thousand Places*: 85.

[288] Beaudoin, *Virtual Faith*: 34; cited in Lynch, *Understanding Theology and Popular Culture*: 35).

[289] Lynch, *Understanding Theology and Popular Culture*: 35.

[290] Lynch, *Understanding Theology and Popular Culture*: 41.

[291] Material drawn from a DVD of the project, *Church and Community* (Southside Christian Church). See {http://www.edgechurch.com/webshop/ productdetail.asp?productid=82&productcategory1id=170}.

[292] Barth, *Church Dogmatics*: 773.

[293] Johnson, Elizabeth, *She Who Is*: 131.

[294] Johnson, Elizabeth, *She Who Is*: 137.

[295] Johnson, Elizabeth, *She Who Is*: 128.

[296] See Reid, 'Setting Aside the Ladder to Heaven': 232-245.

[297] Wright, *Simply Christian*: x.

[298] Wright, *Simply Christian*: 235.

[299] Wright, *Simply Christian*: 236.

[300] Moltmann, *Church in the Power of the Spirit*: 284.

[301] Moltmann, *Church in the Power of the Spirit*: 287, my italics.

[302] Wittmer, *Heaven is a Place on Earth*: 87–88.

[303] Wright, *Simply Christian*: 236, author's italics.

Bibliography

Abrams, Meyer H. *The Mirror and the Lamp: Romantic Theory and the Critical Tradition*. London: Oxford University Press, 1953.

'AI Commons.' Retrieved from {http://appreciativeinquiry. case.edu/}.

Allen, Diogenes. *The Traces of God in a Frequently Hostile World*. Cambridge MA: Cowley, 1981.

Anderson, James D., and Ezra E. Jones. *The Management of Ministry: Building Leadership in a Changing World*. San Francisco, CA: Harper & Row, 1978.

Anderson, Ray S. *An Emergent Theology for Emerging Churches*. Downers Grove, IL: IVP, 2006.

—, *Minding God's Business*. Grand Rapids, MI: Eerdmans, 1986.

—, *The Shape of Practical Theology: Empowering Ministry with Theological Praxis*. Wheaton, IL: IVP, 2001.

Augustine of Hippo. *The City of God*. London: Penguin Books, 1972.

Bacon, Francis. *The Advancement of Learning*. London: Dent, 1965.

Banks, Robert. *Redeeming the Routines: Bringing Theology to Life*. Wheaton IL: Bridgepoint, 1997.

Barbour, Ian G. *When Science Meets Religion: Enemies, Strangers or Partners?*, San Francisco, CA: HarperCollins, 2000.

Barna, George. *Generation Next*. Ventura, CA: Regal Books, 1995.

—, *The Power of Vision*. Ventura, CA: Regal Books, 1992.

Barth, Karl. *Church Dogmatics*. 13 vols., Vol. 4, *Doctrine of Reconciliation*, edited by G. W. Bromiley and T. F. Torrance. Edinburgh: T. & T. Clark, 1962.

Battiscombe, Georgina. *Shaftesbury: A Biography of the 7th Earl 1801–1885*. London: Constable, 1974.

Beaudoin, Tom. *Virtual Faith: The Irreverent Spiritual Quest of Generation X*. Chichester, NY: Jossey-Bass, 1998.

Begbie, Jeremy. *Voicing Creation's Praise: Towards a Theology of the Arts*. Edinburgh: T. & T. Clark, 1991.

Berlin, A. *The Dynamics of Biblical Parallelism*. Bloomington, IN: Indiana University Press, 1985.

Bloesch, Donald G. *Jesus Christ: Savior and Lord*. Downers Grove, IL: IVP, 1997.

Boorstin, Jon. *Making Movies Work: Thinking Like a Film-Maker*. Los Angeles, CA: Silman-James Press, 1995.

Branson, Mark Lau. *Memories, Hopes, and Conversations: Appreciative Inquiry and Congregational Change*. Herndon, VA: The Alban Institute, 2004.

Brooke, John Hedley. *Science and Religion: Some Historical Perspectives*. Cambridge: Cambridge University Press, 1991.

Brown, Robert McAfee. *Spirituality and Liberation: Overcoming the Great Fallacy*. London: Spire, 1988.

Browning, Elizabeth Barrett. *Aurora Leigh*. London: J. Miller, 1864.

Bruce, Ian. *Plato's Theory of Forms*. Retrieved from {http://www.easy.com.au/igb/FormsEssay.html}.

Buxton, Graham. *Dancing in the Dark: Participating in the Ministry of Christ*. Carlisle: Paternoster, 2001.

—, *The Trinity, Creation and Pastoral Ministry: Imaging the Perichoretic God*. Milton Keynes: Paternoster, 2005.

Buxton, Rachel. *Robert Frost and Northern Irish Poetry*. Oxford: Oxford University Press, 2004.

Callahan, Kennon L. *Twelve Keys to an Effective Church*. San Francisco, CA: Harper & Row, 1983.

Campbell, Edward F. *Ruth* (The Anchor Bible). New York, NY, Doubleday, 1975.

Calvin, John. *Institutes of the Christian Religion*. Translated by Henry Beveridge. Grand Rapids, MI: Eerdmans, 1989.

Carter, Stephen L. *God's Name in Vain: The Wrongs and Rights of Religion in Politics*. New York, NY: Basic Books, 2000.

Chesterton, G. K. *Orthodoxy*. New York, NY: Image Books/Doubleday, 2001.

Chewning, Richard C., John W. Eby, and Shirley J. Roels. *Business Through the Eyes of Faith*. Leicester: Apollos, 1990.

210   *Celebrating Life*

Chevalier, Tracy. *Girl with a Pearl Earring*. London: HarperCollins, 1999.

Childs, Brevard S. 'Ruth'. In *Introduction to the Old Testament as Scripture*. London: SCM Press, 1979.

Clapp, Rodney. *A Peculiar People: The Church as Culture in a Post-Christian Society*. Downers Grove, IL: IVP, 1996.

Collins, Francis S. *The Language of God: A Scientist Presents Evidence for Belief*. New York, NY: Simon & Schuster (Free Press), 2006.

Conrad, Joseph. *The Nigger of the 'Narcissus'*. Mineola, NY: Dover Publications, 1999.

Cromartie, Michael L. 'The Evangelical Kaleidoscope: A Survey of Recent Evangelical Political Engagement.' In *Christians and Politics Beyond the Culture Wars: An Agenda for Engagement*, edited by David P. Gushie. Grand Rapids, MI: Baker Books, 2000.

Dark, David. *Everyday Apocalypse: The Sacred Revealed in Radiohead, The Simpsons, and Other Pop Culture Icons*. Grand Rapids, MI: Brazos Press, 2002.

Davies, Paul. *The Mind of God: Science and the Search for Ultimate Meaning*. London: Penguin, 1993.

Dawkins, Richard. *The God Delusion*. Manhattan, NY: Random House (Bantam Books), 2006.

—, *The Selfish Gene*, 2nd ed., Oxford: Oxford University Press, 1989.

de Caussade, Jean-Pierre, S. J. *The Sacrament of the Present Moment*. Translated by Kitty Muggeridge. London: Collins Fount Paperbacks, 1981.

Dead Poets Society: Final Script. Retrieved from {http://www.peterweircave.com/dps/script.html}.

Deeks, David. *Pastoral Theology: An Enquiry*. London: Epworth Press, 1987.

Del Re, Giuseppe. *The Cosmic Dance: Science Discovers the Mysterious Harmony of the Universe*. Radnor PA: Templeton Foundation Press, 2000.

Donne, John. 'An Anatomie of the World' (The First Anniversary). In *The Works of John Donne*, Ware UK: Wordsworth Editions Ltd, 1999.

Donnelly, Kevin. 'Union Rhetoric Drives Parents from Public Schools.' *The Australian* (18 February 2006).

Dorrien, Gary. *Soul in Society: The Making and Renewal of Social Christianity*. Minneapolis, MN: Fortress Press, 1995.

Downer, Alexander. 'Australian Politics and the Christian Church'. Sir Thomas Playford Memorial Lecture, University of Adelaide, 27 August 2003.

Drane, John. *Cultural Change and Biblical Faith: The Future of the Church*. Carlisle: Paternoster, 2000.

Dutney, Andrew. *Playing God: Ethics and Faith*. East Melbourne: HarperCollins, 2001.

Easterbrook, Gregg. 'The New Convergence.' *Wired* 12 (2002).

Edwards, Denis. *The God of Evolution: A Trinitarian Theology*. New York/Mahwah NJ: Paulist Press, 1999.

Eliot, George. *Adam Bede*. London: J. M. Dent & Sons Ltd, 1906.

—, *Silas Marner: The Weaver of Raveloe*. New York: Harper & Row, 1965.

Eliot, T.S. *Four Quartets*. London: Faber & Faber, 1966.

Engstrom, Ted W., and Edward R. Dayton. *The Art of Management for Christian Leaders*. Waco: Word, 1976.

Farley, Edward. 'Theology and Practice outside the Clerical Paradigm.' In *Practical Theology*, edited by Don S. Browning. San Francisco: Harper & Row, 1983.

Fiddes, Paul S. *Participating in God: A Pastoral Doctrine of the Trinity*. London: Darton, Longman & Todd, 2000.

Fontaine, Petrus Maria. *The Light and the Dark: A Cultural History of Dualism*. Amsterdam: J C Gieben and Gopher Publishers, 1986–2002. Retrieved from {http://home.wanadoo.nl/ piet. fontaine/on_dualism.htm#definition}.

Foster, Richard. *Money, Sex and Power: The Challenge to the Disciplined Life*. London: Hodder & Stoughton, 1985.

Fox, Matthew. *The Coming of the Cosmic Christ: The Healing of Mother Earth and the Birth of a Global Renaissance*. San Francisco, CA: Harper & Row, 1980.

Friesen, Duane K. *Artists, Citizens, Philosophers: Seeking the Peace of the City*. Scottdale, PA: Herald Press, 2000.

Frost, Michael. 'The Chocolate Remedy.' *Alive* Magazine (August 2001).

Frost, Michael, and Robert Banks. *Lessons from Reel Life: Movies, Meaning and Myth-Making*. Adelaide: Openbook Publishers, 2001.

Frost, Michael, and Alan Hirsch. *The Shaping of Things to Come: Innovation and Mission for the 21st-Century Church*. Peabody, MA: Hendrickson, 2003.

Fuller, Michael. *Atoms and Icons: A Discussion of the Relationships between Science and Theology*. London: Mowbray, 1995.

Gammage, Nick. Interview with Seamus Heaney. *Thumbscrew* 19 (Autumn 2001).

Gleick, James. *Chaos: Making a New Science*. New York, NY: Penguin Books, 1987.

—, *Faster: The Acceleration of Just About Everything*. London: Abacus, 1999.

Gollings, Richard. 'Planting Covenant Communities of Faith in the City.' In *God So Loves the City: Seeking a Theology for Urban Mission*, edited by Charles van Engen and Jude Tiersma. Monrovia CA: MARC, 1994.

Gould, Stephen Jay. *Rock of Ages: Science and Religion and the Fullness of Life*. New York, NY: Ballantine, 1999.

Greene, Mark. 'The Great Divide'. *Christianity+Renewal* (June 2001).

Greenleaf, Robert. *The Servant as Leader*. Indianapolis, IN: The Robert K. Greenleaf Center, 1991.

—, *Servant Leadership: A Journey into the Nature of Legitimate Power and Greatness*. New York/Mahwah, NJ: Paulist Press, 2002.

Grenz, Stanley J., and John R. Franke. *Beyond Foundationalism: Shaping Theology in a Postmodern Context*. Louisville: Westminster John Knox Press, 2001.

Gribbin, John. *Science: A History 1543–2001*. London: Penguin, 2002.

Guite, Malcolm. 'Christ and the Redemption of Language.' In Jeremy Begbie. *Beholding the Glory: Incarnation Through the Arts*, London: Darton, Longman & Todd, 2000.

Haisch, Bernard. 'Freeing the Scientific Imagination from Fundamentalist Scientism.' *Research News and Opportunities* (January 2001).

Hall, John Douglas. *Thinking the Faith: Christian Theology in a North American Context*. Minneapolis, MN: Fortress Press, 1991.

Hare, R. M. *Plato*. Oxford: Oxford University Press, 1983.

Harper, Ian. 'The Ethics of Capitalism.' *Zadok Perspectives* 80 (Spring 2003).

Haught, John. *Science and Religion: From Conflict to Conversation.* New York, NY: Paulist, 1995.

Heaney, Seamus. *Death of a Naturalist.* London: Faber & Faber, 1966.

Heslam, Peter. 'Checking the March of Capitalism.' Retrieved from {http://www.licc.org.uk/articles/checking-the-march-of-capitalism}.

Higginson, Richard. 'A Christian Response to Global Capitalism'. *Zadok* paper S112 (Autumn 2001).

—, Questions of Business Life: Exploring Workplace Issues from a Christian Perspective. Milton Keynes: Paternoster Press, 2002.

Houston, James M. *I Believe in the Creator.* London: Hodder & Stoughton, 1979.

John Paul II on Science and Religion: Reflections on the New View from Rome, edited by Robert John Russell, William R. Stoeger, and George V. Coyne, S.J. Vatican: Vatican Observatory, 1990.

Johnson, Elizabeth. *She Who Is: The Mystery of God in Feminist Theological Discourse.* New York, NY: The Crossroad Publishing Company, 1992.

Johnson, Steven. *Emergence: The Connected Lives of Ants, Brains, Cities, and Software.* New York, NY: Scribner, 2001.

Johnston, Robert K. *Reel Spirituality: Theology and Film in Dialogue.* Grand Rapids, MI: Baker Academic, 2000.

Kelly, Gerard. 'Sacred Secular Divide'. *Christianity+Renewal* (December 2001).

Kidner, Derek. *Psalms 1–72: An Introduction and Commentary on Books I and II of the Psalms.* Leicester: Inter-Varsity Press, 1973.

Kilcourse, George A., Jr. *Flannery O'Connor's Religious Imagination: A World with Everything Off Balance.* New York, NY: Paulist Press, 2001.

Kraft, Charles H. *Christianity in Culture.* Maryknoll NY: Orbis, 1979.

L'Engle, Madeleine. *Walking on Water: Reflections on Faith and Art.* Colorado Springs, CO: WaterBrook Press, 2001.

Lewis, Alan E. 'Unmasking Idolatries: Vocation in the *Ecclesia Crucis.*' In *Incarnational Ministry: The Presence of Christ in Church, Society and Family,* edited by Christian D. Kettler and Todd H. Speidell. Colorado Springs, CO: Helmers and Howard, 1990.

Lewis, C. S. *An Experiment in Criticism.* Cambridge: Cambridge University Press, 1961.

—, 'Christian Reflections.' In Walter Hooper (ed.), *God in the Dock: Essays on Theology* (Grand Rapids: Eerdmans, 1970).

—, 'The Language of Religion.' In *Christian Reflections.* London: Collins Fount Paperbacks, 1981.

—, 'Myth Became Fact.' In Walter Hooper (ed.), *God in the Dock: Essays on Theology* (Grand Rapids: Eerdmans, 1970).

—, *Surprised by Joy: The Shape of My Early Life.* London: Geoffrey Bles, 1955.

Lord Acton. 'The History of Freedom in Christianity'. Retrieved from {http://www.acton.org/publicat/books/freedom/christianity.html}.

Lynch, Gordon. *Understanding Theology and Popular Culture.* Oxford: Blackwell Publishing, 2005.

Martindale, Wayne. *Beyond the Shadowlands: C. S. Lewis on Heaven and Hell.* Wheaton, IL: Crossway Books, 2005.

McFague, Sallie. *Super, Natural Christians: How We Should Love Nature.* Minneapolis, MN: Fortress Press, 1997.

McGavran, Donald A. *Understanding Church Growth.* Grand Rapids, MI: Eerdmans, 1980.

McGrath Alister. *Dawkins' God: Genes, Memes, and the Meaning of Life.* Oxford: Blackwell Publishing, 2005.

—, *A Scientific Theology.* 3 vols., Vol. 1: *Nature.* Edinburgh: T. & T. Clark, 2001.

—, The Dawkins Delusion? Atheist Fundamentalism and the Denial of the Divine. London: SPCK, 2007.

McGregor, Douglas. *The Human Side of Enterprise.* New York, NY: McGraw-Hill, 1960.

Moltmann, Jürgen. *The Church in the Power of the Spirit: A Contribution to Messianic Ecclesiology.* London: SCM Press, 1977.

—, *God in Creation: A New Theology of Creation and the Spirit of God.* San Francisco, CA: Harper & Row, 1985.

—, 'Perichoresis: An Old Magic Word for a New Trinitarian Theology.' In *Trinity, Community, and Power: Mapping Trajectories in Wesleyan Theology,* edited by M. Douglas Meeks. Nashville, TN: Abingdon Press, 2000.

—, *The Spirit of Life: A Universal Affirmation.* Minneapolis, MN: Fortress Press, 1992.

—, *The Trinity and the Kingdom of God: The Doctrine of God*. London: SCM Press, 1981.

Mouw, Richard. *Uncommon Decency: Christian Civility in an Uncivil World*. Downers Grove, IL: IVP, 1992.

Neibuhr, H. Richard. *Christ and Culture*. New York, NY: Harper & Row: 1951.

Neibuhr, Reinhold. *The Children of Light and the Children of Darkness*. New York, NY: Charles Scribner's Sons, 1944.

—, *Moral Man and Immoral Society: A Study in Ethics and Politics*. New York, NY: Charles Scribner's Sons, 1932.

Newbigin, Lesslie. *Foolishness to the Greeks: The Gospel and Western Culture*. Grand Rapids, MI: Eerdmans, 1986.

O'Connor, Flannery. *The Habit of Being*. New York, NY: Noonday Press, 1979.

Orwell, George. 'Politics and the English Language.' In *Nineteen Eighty-Four: Text, Sources, Criticism,* edited by Irving Howe. New York: Harcourt, Brace & World, 1963.

Pearce, Joseph. *Tolkien: Man and Myth*. London: HarperCollins, 1998.

Penrose, Roger. *The Emperor's New Mind: Concerning Computers, Minds and the Laws of Physics*. Oxford: Oxford University Press, 1989.

Percy, Martyn, 'Editorial: Liberal Theology in the Contemporary World.' *Modern Believing*, 42 (2001).

Peterson, Eugene H. *Christ Plays in Ten Thousand Places: A Conversation in Spiritual Theology*. London: Hodder & Stoughton, 2005.

—, 'Pastors and Novels.' In *Subversive Spirituality*, Grand Rapids, MI: Eerdmans, 1994.

Pinnock, Clark H. *Most Moved Mover: A Theology of God's Openness*. Carlisle: Paternoster Press, 2001.

Pinola, Sakari. *Church Growth: Principles and Praxis of Donald A. McGavran's Missiology*. Abo: Abo Akademi University Press, 1995.

Plato. *The Republic*. Translated by H. D. P. Lee. London: Penguin Books, 1955.

Pohl, Christine D. *Making Room: Recovering Hospitality as a Christian Tradition*. Grand Rapids, MI: Eerdmans, 1999.

Polkinghorne, John. *Science and Christian Belief: Theological Reflections of a Bottom-Up Thinker*. London: SPCK, 1994.

—, *Serious Talk: Science and Religion in Dialogue*. Harrisburg PA: Trinity Press International, 1995.

Popper, Karl. *Conjectures and Refutations*. London: Routledge and Kegan Paul, 1963.

Potok, Chaim. *The Gift of Asher Lev*. London: Heinemann, 1990.

—, *My Name is Asher Lev*. London: Heinemann, 1972.

Rauber, D.F. 'The Book of Ruth.' In *Literary Interpretations of Biblical Narratives*, edited by K. R. R. Gros Louis et al. Nashville, TN: Abingdon, 1974.

Reid, Duncan. 'Setting Aside the Ladder to Heaven: Revelation 22.1–22.5 from the Perspective of Earth.' In *The Earth Story in Genesis*, edited by Norman C. Habel and Shirley Wurst. Sheffield: Sheffield Academic Press, 2000.

Roddick, Anita. *Business as Unusual: My Entrepreneurial Journey – Profits with Principles*. London: HarperCollins, 2005.

Rolston, Holmes, III. 'Does Nature Need to be Redeemed?' *Zygon: Journal of Religion and Science* 29 (June 1994).

Rudd, Kevin. 'Faith in Politics.' *The Monthly* (October 2006).

Rush, Myron. *Management: A Biblical Approach*. Wheaton, IL: Victor Books, 1983.

Russell, Robert John, William R. Stoeger, and George V. Coyne, S.J. (eds.), *John Paul II on Science and Religion: Reflections on the New View from Rome*. Vatican: Vatican Observatory, 1990.

Ryken, Leland. *The Liberated Imagination: Thinking Christianly About the Arts*. Wheaton, IL: Harold Shaw Publishers, 1989.

—, *Triumphs of the Imagination: Literature in Christian Perspective*. Downers Grove, IL: IVP, 1979.

—, *Words of Delight: A Literary Introduction to the Bible*. Grand Rapids, MI: Baker Book House, 1992.

Sanders, E. P. *Paul and Palestinian Judaism*. London: SCM Press, 1977.

Sanders, John. 'Historical Considerations.' In C. H. Pinnock et al. *The Openness of God: A Biblical Challenge to the Traditional Understanding of God*. Downers Grove, IL: IVP, 1994.

Sayles, Leonard R., George Strauss. *Human Behaviour in Organizations*. Englewood Cliffs NJ: Prentice-Hall, 1960.

Schomer, Howard. 'Barth on Mozart.' *The Christian Century*, 18 July 1956 (also retrieved from {http://www.religion-online.org/showarticle.asp?title=1382).

Scott, Nancy. *Dueling with Dualism*. Retrieved from {http://www.mckenziestudycenter.org/philosophy/articles/dualism.html.

Semler, Ricardo. *Maverick!* Melbourne: Random House Australia, 1993.

—, *The Seven-Day Weekend: Finding the Work/Life Balance*. London: Century (Random House), 2003.

Simmons, Laura K. 'Dorothy L Sayers' Theology of Work and Vocation in Everyday Life.' In *The Bible and the Business of Life: Essays in Honour of Robert J Banks's Sixty-fifth Birthday*, edited by S. C. Holt and G. Preece. Adelaide: ATF Press, 2004.

Sine, Tom. *Wild Hope*. Tunbridge Wells: Monarch, 1991.

Sobosan, Jeffrey G. *Romancing the Universe: Theology, Science and Cosmology*. Grand Rapids, MI: Eerdmans, 1999.

Soelle, Dorothy (with Shirley A. Cloyes). *To Work and to Love: A Theology of Creation*. Philadelphia, PA: Fortress Press, 1984.

Sojourners/Call to Renewal. 'What is Call to Renewal?' Retrieved from {http://www.calltorenewal.org/about_us/index.cfm/action/what_is_CTR.html}.

Southam, Hazel. 'Faith and Politics do Mix!'. *Christianity+Renewal* (April 2001).

Southside Christian Church. *Church and Community* (DVD). Edge Church. Retrieved from {http://www.edgechurch.com/webshop/productdetail.asp?productid=82&productcategory1id=170}

Spender, Stephen. *The Making of a Poem*. New York, NY: W. W. Norton, 1962.

St. Athanasius on the Incarnation. Translated and edited by a religious of C.S.M.V. Crestwood, NY: St Vladimir's Orthodox Seminary, 1993.

Stone, Bryan P. *Faith and Film: Theological Themes at the Cinema*. St Louis, MO: Chalice Press, 2000.

Stott, John. *Issues Facing Christians Today*. London: Marshall Pickering, 1984.

Sunderland, Chris. *In a Glass Darkly: Seeking Vision for Public Life*. Carlisle: Paternoster, 2001.

Sweet, Leonard et al. *The Church in Emerging Culture: Five Perspectives*. Grand Rapids, MI: Zondervan, 2003.

Taylor, John V. *The Go-Between God: The Holy Spirit and the Christian Mission*. London: SCM Press, 1972.

Thielicke, Helmut. *Theological Ethics*. 3 vols., Vol. 2, *Politics*. Translated and edited by William H. Lazareth. Grand Rapids, MI: Eerdmans, 1979.

Timms, Stephen. 'Christianity and Politics.' *The Bible in Transmission* (Autumn 2001).

—, 'Christian Socialism'. Retrieved from {http://www.stephentimms.org.uk/ cs.html}.

Torrance, James B. *Worship, Community and the Triune God of Grace*. Downers Grove, IL: IVP, 1996.

Torrance, Thomas F. *The Christian Doctrine of God: One Being Three Persons*. Edinburgh: T. & T. Clark, 1996.

Tournier, Paul. *The Adventure of Living*. Crowborough, Highland Books, 1983.

Truss, Lynne. *Eats, Shoots and Leaves: The Zero Tolerance Approach to Punctuation*. London: Profile Books, 2003.

Turner, Steve. *Imagine: A Vision for Christians in the Arts*. Downers Grove, IL: IVP, 2001.

Underhill, Evelyn. *The Spiritual Life*. Harrisburg PA: Morehouse Publishing, 1997.

Vanstone, W. H. *Love's Endeavour, Love's Expense: The Response of Being to the Love of God*. London: Darton, Longman & Todd, 1977.

Veith, Gene Edward, Jr. *Reading Between the Lines: A Christian Guide to Literature*. Wheaton, IL: Crossway Books, 1990.

Wacker, Grant. 'The Christian Right.' Retrieved from {http://www.nhc.rtp.nc.us:8080/tserve/twenty/tkeyinfo/c hr_rght.htm}.

Wagner, C. Peter. *Your Church Can be Healthy*. Nashville, TN: Abingdon, 1979.

Wallis, Jim. *Agenda for Biblical People*. New York, NY: Harper & Row, 1976.

—, *God's Politics: Why the American Right Gets It Wrong and the left Doesn't Get It*. San Francisco CA: HarperSanFrancisco, 2005.

Walser, R. *Running with the Devil: Power, Gender and Madness in Heavy Metal Music*. New England, ME: University Press of New England, 1993.

Walsh, Brian J., and J. Richard Middleton, *The Transforming Vision: Shaping a Christian World View*. Downers Grove, IL: IVP, 1984.

Ward, Keith. *Divine Action*. London: Collins, 1990.

Watkins, Jane M., and Bernard J. Mohr. *Appreciative Inquiry: Change at the Speed of Imagination*. San Francisco, CA: Jossey-Bass/Pfeiffer, 2001.

Watts, Rikki. 'What Does It Mean To Be Saved?' *Working together* (4) 2002.

Wenstein, D. *Heavy Metal: The Music and its Culture*. Cambridge MA: The Perseus Book Group, 2000.

Wertheim, Margaret. 'The Odd Couple.' *The Sciences*, 39 (March/April 1999).

Wheatley, Margaret J. *Leadership and the New Science: Learning about Organization from an Orderly Universe*. San Francisco, CA: Berrett-Koehler Publishers, 1999.

Wilkinson, David. *God, the Big Bang and Stephen Hawking*. Tunbridge Wells: Monarch, 1993.

—, *God, Time and Stephen Hawking*. London: Monarch Books, 2001.

Wittmer, Michael E., *Heaven is a Place on Earth: Why Everything You Do Matters to God*. Grand Rapids, MI: Zondervan, 2004.

Wolterstorff, Nicholas. *Art in Action*. Grand Rapids, MI: Eerdmans, 1980.

Worthing, Mark W. *The Matrix Revealed: The Theology of the Matrix Trilogy*. Adelaide: Pantaenus Press, 2004.

—, Mark W. *When Choice Matters: An Introduction to Christian Ethics*. Adelaide: Pantaenus Press, 2004.

Wright, N.T. *Simply Christian: Why Christianity Makes Sense*. New York, NY: HarperCollins, 2006.

Wright, Tom. *Bringing the Church to the World: Renewing the Church to Confront the Paganism Entrenched in Western Culture*. Minneapolis, MN: Bethany, 1992.

Yergler, Jeffrey D. 'Management and Grace.' Retrieved from {http://www.refresher.com/!jdygrace.html}.

—, 'The Servant Leader and the Exercise of Forgiveness in the Context of the Organization.' Retrieved from {http://www.refresher.com/!jdyforgiveness1.html}.

Yoder, John Howard. *The Politics of Jesus*. Grand Rapids, MI: Eerdmans, 1972.

Series Titles Currently Available

Atonement for a 'Sinless' Society
Engaging with an emerging culture

Atonement for a 'Sinless' Society

Engaging with an Emerging Culture

Alan Mann

'Sin doesn't really exist as a serious idea in modern life,' wrote the journalist Bryan Appleyard. He is not alone in his views. 'Sin' has become just as tainted, polluted and defiled in the postmodern mind as the word itself indicates.

Atonement for a 'Sinless' Society is about an encounter between two stories: the story of the postmodern, post-industrialized, post-Christian 'sinless' self and the story of atonement played out in the Passion Narrative. Alan Mann charts a way through the apparent impasse between a story that supposedly relies on sin and guilt to become meaningful, and one that fails to recognize the plight of humanity as portrayed in this way. He shows how the biblical narrative needs to be reread in the light of this emerging story so that it can speak meaningfully and sufficiently to an increasingly 'sinless' society.

'Clear, creative, deep, compelling and inspiring' – **Brian D. McLaren**, author, speaker, networker

'Alan Mann's voice is needed and welcome . . . A penetrating analysis of the world we inhabit.' – **Joel B. Green**, Asbury Theological Seminary

'An insightful, timely and creative view of the atonement for our postmodern times.' – **Steve Chalk**, Oasis Trust

978-1-84227-355-5

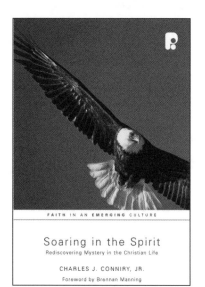

Soaring in the Spirit

Rediscovering Mystery in the Christian Life

Charles J. Conniry, Jr.

This is a book about experiencing the presence of Jesus Christ in the moment-by-moment 'nows' of daily life. James McClendon, Jr. observed that the first task of theology is to locate our place in the story. Like finding directions at a shopping mall with the brightly coloured words, 'you are here,' the author invites us into an encounter with the 'we-are-here' place in God's Great Story. The claim of this book is that the experience of Christ's presence in the 'right-here' of our daily walk – *Christian soaring* – is the birthright of every follower of Jesus Christ. This is a thoughtful, stirring, and ground-breaking book on the neglected topic of *Christian soaring through discerning discipleship*.

> 'This book is a *tour de force* . . . and can be read with profit by believers and unbelievers, philosophers and theologians, pastors and lay people, and anyone who longs to soar in the Spirit . . . It not only blessed me but drew me to prayer.' – **Brennan Manning**, author of *The Ragamuffin Gospel*.

Charles J. Conniry, Jr. is Associate Professor of Pastoral Ministry and Director of the Doctor of Ministry Program at George Fox Evangelical Seminary, Portland.

978-1-84227-508-5

Forthcoming Series Titles

Re:Mission

Biblical Mission for a Post-Biblical Church

Andrew Perriman

In this innovative and radical book postmodern mission and New Testament studies collide. Andrew Perriman examines the mission of the earliest church in its historical context and argues that our context is very different and *so our mission cannot simply be a matter of doing exactly what the earliest church did.* The key question at the heart of the book is, 'How do we shape a *biblical* theology of mission for a *post-biblical* church?'

> '*Re:Mission* distinguishes Perriman as a scholar who must be reckoned with in this time of rethinking and transition. A great piece of work!' – **Brian D. McLaren**, author (brianmclaren.net)

> 'Andrew Perriman has addressed one of the most challenging facets of New Testament teaching and he does so with remarkable insight and creativity. This fascinating book makes for urgent reading.' – **Craig A. Evans**, Payzant Distinguished Professor of New Testament, Acadia Divinity College, Canada

Andrew Perriman lives in Holland and works with Christian Associates seeking to develop open, creative communities of faith for the emerging culture in Europe. He is author of *Speaking of Women* about Paul's teaching on women, *Faith, Health and Prosperity*, and, *The Coming of the Son of Man: New Testament Eschatology for an Emerging Church.*

978-1-84227-545-0

Chrysalis

The Hidden Transformation in the Journey of Faith

Alan Jamieson

Increasing numbers of Christian people find their faith metamorphosing. Substantial and essential change seems to beckon them beyond the standard images and forms of Christian faith but questions about where this may lead remain. Is this the death of personal faith or the emergence of something new? Could it be a journey that is Spirit-led?

Chrysalis uses the life-cycle of butterflies as a metaphor for the faith journey that many contemporary people are experiencing. Drawing on the three main phases of a butterfly's life and the transformations between these, the book suggests subtle similarities with the zones of Christian faith that many encounter. For butterflies and Christians change between these *'phases'* or *'zones'* is substantial, life-changing and irreversible.

This book accompanies ordinary people in the midst of substantive faith change. It is an excellent resource for those who choose to support others through faith transformations. *Chrysalis* is primarily pastoral and practical drawing on the author's experience of accompanying people in the midst of difficult personal faith changes.

Alan Jamieson is a minister in New Zealand and a trained sociologist. His internationally acclaimed first book, *A Churchless Faith*, researched why people leave their churches to continue their walk of faith outside the church.

978-1-84227-544-3

Metavista

Bible, Church and Mission in an Age of Imagination

Colin Green and Martin Robinson

Metavista:
Bible, Church and Mission in an Age of Imagination

COLIN GREENE & MARTIN ROBINSON

The core narrative of the Christian faith, the book that conveys it (the Bible) and the institution of the church have all been marginalised by the development of modernity and post-modernity. Strangely, post-modernity has created an opportunity for religious thinking and experience to re-enter the lives of many. Yet, despite its astonishing assault on modernity, post-modernity is not itself an adequate framework for thinking about life. There is therefore a new opportunity for Christians to imagine what comes *after* post-modernity and to prepare the church, its book and its story for a new engagement of mission with western culture. The church on the margins, through a creative missionary imagination can audaciously re-define the centre of western cultural life. This book will attempt to sketch what such an approach might look like

> 'If you have a taste for the subversive, a passion for the church, a heart for biblical engagement, and an eye on the future; this book is a must-read.'
> – **Roy Searle**, Northumbria Community, former President of the Baptist Union of Great Britain

Colin Greene is Professor of Theological and Cultural Studies at Mars Hill Graduate School in Seattle. He is author of *Christology in Cultural Perspective*.
Martin Robinson is an international speaker, a writer, and Director of 'Together in Mission'.

978-1-84227-506-1